Dr. Banov's book is a comprehensive source of information for patients suffering from depression, as well as their families and friends. It addresses the intricacies of neuroscience of depression without intimidating the reader. This book is a compass in the stormy seas of antidepressant information: it helps the patients navigate throughout the treatment process, from the selection of their physician and diagnosis, to the challenging balance between the risks and benefits of the medications. An indispensable read for those interested in depression and its treatment.

Vladimir Maletic, M.D.
Clinical Professor of Neuropsychiatry and Behavioral Sciences
USC, School of Medicine

Dr. Banov's book is an excellent resource for consumers and family members who live with mood disorders. This guide is written in a friendly and easy-to-read format. Case studies provide a personal approach to explaining and understanding the alternatives and challenges associated with the treatments of mood disorders. This practical guide is an objective tool to help make informed choices. It truly supports person-centered care.

Allen S. Daniels, Ed.D.
Director of Scientific Affairs
Depression and Bipolar Support Alliance (DBSA)
www.dbsalliance.org

Dr. Banov's book is an incredible resource for patients – a must read for anyone taking or considering taking antidepressants. The appendices are a practical and usable collection of information, tools, and scales and screeners for consumers. By reading Dr. Banov's book, patients are empowered to take a proactive stance when it comes to their treatment. This book should be on every clinician's desk and in every patient's hands.

Saundra Jain, PsyD, MBA, LPC
Executive Director
Mental Health Educational Initiative (MHEI)

In his book, *Taking Antidepressants,* Dr. Banov provides a thoughtful and comprehensive look at the many questions and concerns facing individuals who are considering taking antidepressants. He also discusses the issues patients may face once they begin antidepressant medication and the things they should consider when they are ready to discontinue this medication. While Dr. Banov presents a fair and balanced view of the pros and cons of the most current antidepressants on the market, he also gives the reader information about a number of alternative therapies, including psychotherapy, dietary supplements, and others. This is a well-written and informative book, which is an excellent source of knowledge for patients considering antidepressants. It can also serve as a great reference for a wide variety of mental health professionals as they counsel their patients who may benefit from taking antidepressant medications.

Warren Kaplan, PhD
Private Practice Psychotherapist
Woodstock, Georgia

Taking Antidepressants

Your Comprehensive Guide to Starting, Staying On, and Safely Quitting

Michael D. Banov, MD
Medical Director, Northwest Behavioral Medicine

Sunrise River Press
39966 Grand Avenue
North Branch, MN 55056
Phone: 651-277-1400 or 800-895-4585
Fax: 651-277-1203
www.sunriseriverpress.com

Edit by Karin Craig
Layout by Monica Seiberlich

ISBN 978-1-934716-06-9
Item No. SRP606

Library of Congress Cataloging-in-Publication Data

Banov, Michael D.
   Taking antidepressants : your comprehensive guide to starting, staying on, and safely quitting / by Michael Banov.
      p. cm.
   Includes index.
   ISBN 978-1-934716-06-9
   1. Antidepressants—Popular works. I. Title.
   RM332.B36 2010
   615'.78—dc22

                              2010007669

Printed in USA
10 9 8 7 6 5 4 3 2 1

Contents

Dedication

To my patients—who taught me everything I know about medicine

Acknowledgments

I would like to thank all the staff at Northwest Behavioral Medicine and Research Center in Marietta and Alpharetta, Georgia, for their support and time dedicated to me and our patients that really made collecting the information for this book possible. My experienced and reliable clinical nurse specialists Cathie Preston and Karen Greenhood for their input and manuscript review. Lisa Tener for her editorial comments and general guidance making this information consumer-friendly. Regina Brooks of Serendipity Literary Agency and Karin Craig at Sunrise River Press for believing in this topic and my ability to communicate this information. Christopher Hilton and Emily Siegel for their assistance in research. Dr. Warren Kaplan for manuscript suggestions. Charles and Nancy Banov for their ongoing love and encouragement for this project. Yadin Kaufmann for sharing his publishing pearls. Elizabeth Johnsboen for contributing to the cover design. Michael Swain for illustrations. And, most importantly, my wife Lisa Banov and sons, Zachary and Jacob Banov, for tolerating—and encouraging—my late-night "kerplunking."

About the Author

Michael Banov, MD, completed his psychiatry training at McLean Hospital, Harvard Medical School, and is medical director of Northwest Behavioral Medicine and Research Center in Atlanta, Georgia. He has been a principal investigator in hundreds of psychiatry studies and has published dozens of articles and research papers on the treatment of mental-health problems. He is the founder and director of psychsource.org, a non-profit organization dedicated to helping people find appropriate mental-health resources in their area. When not practicing medicine, he is traveling, writing, playing guitar, and practicing martial arts.

Dr. Banov has served on advisory, consulting, and speaking boards for the following pharmaceutical companies: Astra-Zeneca, Eli Lilly, Pfizer, Wyeth, Forest, Bristol Myers Squibb, and GlaxoSmithkline. He has conducted clinical research studies for Astra-Zeneca, Eli Lilly, Pfizer, Janssen, Wyeth, Forest, Bristol Myers Squib, Otsuka, Shire, Novartis, Sanofi Adventis, GlaxoSmithkline, and Solvay. He has no major financial holdings in any pharmaceutical or medical device company. More information is available at www.psychatlanta.com.

References for studies are available at www.takingantidepressants.com.

Introduction

Depression is a common condition, and more people are being diagnosed and treated than ever before. Nearly one in four women and one in ten men will suffer from depression at some point in their lives. The impact depression has on your life and the lives of those who care about you can be profound. The World Health Organization reports that depression is the second leading cause of disability worldwide and, by 2020, is estimated to be the leading cause of disability. The good news is that recent advances in treatments have given doctors better tools to identify depression than even just a few years ago, and more effective treatments are now available.

Your challenge is finding the right treatment for you. There are many ways to successfully overcome depression, yet each has limitations and liabilities. Antidepressant treatment has become one of the more popular treatments over the last several decades. In fact, antidepressants are the most commonly prescribed class of medications in many of the developed nations of the world. Despite 50 years of antidepressant experience and millions of people having been successfully treated with these medicines—190 million prescriptions were written each year in the United States alone since 2005—their use still raises many questions and concerns. These include:

- How do I know when I need an antidepressant?
- How do I know which antidepressant to take and how do I start it?
- How do antidepressants work?
- Are antidepressants safe?
- Are antidepressants effective?
- Are antidepressants habit forming?
- What if the antidepressant does not work?
- When and how do I stop an antidepressant?

Taking Antidepressants answers these and many other questions about antidepressant treatment.

Surprisingly, there are few reliable resources that educate consumers about depression and its treatments in a fair and balanced fashion. Most books about antidepressants on the market today have a strong bias regarding their use. Some are decidedly against antidepressants and paint them as overused and dangerous drugs. In a few cases, authors do not accept that depression and other mental-health problems are even true medical conditions. Other authors are too biologically focused; they see pharmacological intervention as the only reliable means to overcome depression. I wrote *Taking Antidepressants* as a research psychiatrist who also spends most of his professional time treating real-world patients and looks at depression and antidepressant use from a practical, clinical perspective. This book educates you about current depression research and its limitations. You will learn what most doctors do to help their patients get better and, if possible, eventually get off medication.

Taking Antidepressants walks you through *all* phases of antidepressant therapy and gives you a personalized process to make the best choices about:

- Starting antidepressants.
- Staying on antidepressants.
- How and when to safely stop taking your antidepressant.

You will learn about different kinds of depression and how mood disorders can impact your brain and body. *Taking Antidepressants* offers tips and tools for helping you identify whether you really have depression and whether you should consider antidepressant treatment. There are suggestions for helping you decide with your doctor which antidepressant to take and what to expect when first starting the medicine. Non-medication depression therapies to be used alone or with antidepressants are reviewed as well.

If you are already taking antidepressants, you'll find a section dedicated to issues that often arise during treatment. This includes information on managing side effects and concerns about long-term safety. You will discover interventions that can help you if your medicine is only partially effective or stops working. There are suggestions for dealing with unexpected problems that can occur, such as pregnancy, traveling out of the country, or being unable to afford your medication. Finally, the last part of this book addresses how to decide when you may be able to safely stop your antidepressant treatment. You will learn how to work with your doctor to develop a dosage taper schedule to increase your likelihood of success in coming off the medicine, as well as tools to help you stay well after coming off antidepressants.

If you, or someone you know, struggle with depression, you know how difficult an experience it can be. All the misinformation out there about depression may confuse you, as can sorting through the many different ways to treat the condition. The road to recovery from depression can take many twists and turns, but, fortunately for most, has a rewarding destination. *Taking Antidepressants* is your partner through this journey. After finishing this book, you will be educated enough about depression to take a more active role in your treatment and know how to interpret new information as it becomes available in the future. The more you know, the more you are empowered to change the course of your condition. Congratulations on taking the first step on the road to your recovery.

Chapter One

Deciding Whether to Start an Antidepressant

In the following chapters, we will follow the story of four people each suffering from some type of depression, but whose attitudes and concerns about treatment widely differ. You will see how depression has affected each of their lives and the obstacles they had to overcome. Through their stories, you will be brought up to date on what we do know about depression and antidepressants. You will be able to make more informed treatment decisions and better identify your own personal roadblocks to recovery. You will also find plenty of other reliable resources included to help answer any other questions not fully addressed in *Taking Antidepressants*. By reading this book, you are taking an important step in becoming an informed consumer and active participant in your healthcare.

Jane's Story

Jane, a 28-year-old woman, is currently working as an assistant professor of physics at a local college. Her parents were also teachers and always valued reading, education, and family. Her childhood had very few events that created stress or tension between her, her siblings, or parents. Although her mother suffered a brief depression when Jane was very young, she could not recall any time that anyone lost their cool or seemed overwhelmed. This did not strike her as odd until she was in graduate school, when she began to experience trouble balancing school, work, and a relationship for the first time in her life.

The first problem she noticed was difficulty sleeping at night and feeling exhausted during the day. After a few months, she was unable to concentrate enough to complete the deadlines for her doctoral thesis. This caused such anxiety that she would have periods of extreme heart racing, shortness of breath, and feeling like she was going to have a heart attack. They would usually occur at the worst times, such as right before class or while student teaching. She started feeling sad a great deal of the time and withdrew from her friends and fiancé.

Convinced something was physically wrong, she went to a local primary care doctor for a physical exam to see if he could figure out what was causing her symptoms. She had a few medical textbooks on hand and did an extensive Internet search. She came to her doctor with a list of possible conditions including heart arrhythmias, thyroid abnormalities, and anemia. Even a few psychiatric diagnoses made it to the list such as panic disorder, attention deficit disorder, and depression.

An extensive interview and medical workup showed no clear physical cause for her symptoms. When her physician suggested that the most likely culprit was depression, Jane asked, "Should I start taking an antidepressant?"

"Should I start taking an antidepressant?"

Depression is a mental-health condition that affects nearly 19 million people over the age of 18 every year in the United States alone. Being sad or feeling down is a normal emotion experienced under stressful and difficult conditions. Depression occurs when these feelings persist for several weeks and are accompanied by other symptoms including changes in your sleep, appetite, energy, concentration, and motivation that impair your ability to function normally. Antidepressants are the most common class of medications prescribed of all medicines on the market today. It is estimated that one quarter of the population will suffer from depression at some point in their life. Even though antidepressant use is a medically accepted form of treatment for depression, the decision to start such medicines often elicits a wide range of emotions from anger and denial to confusion and concern. No one wants to *have* to take any medicine for a medical problem, but people are more reluctant to take antidepressants than other medicines. They also have more questions about them. Are they safe? Are they addictive? Will they change my personality? Do I really need to take them?

Despite advances in our understanding of depression and greater acceptance of mood disorders as real medical conditions, there is still a stigma associated with antidepressants. There are many conflicting opinions about what depression is and what the role of medicine should be, even among professionals in the mental-health community. This is confusing to someone suffering with depressive symptoms and trying to figure out how to get better.

This book's intent is to bring you up to speed on what we know about depression and its treatment by taking you on a journey that includes stops inside the human brain and body, doctors' offices, research laboratories, and the homes and workplaces of those suffering from its symptoms. This journey is designed to help you, or someone you care about, make the safest, healthiest, and most responsible choices to become depression free. Many common questions will be addressed, such as:

- Is depression really an illness or just a feeling?
- How do I know I have depression?
- Who do I see to get help?
- Why do I need medicine to get better?
- Are there ways to get better other than medicine?
- What if I don't do anything to treat depression?
- How do I know if I need medicine?
- What will medicine do to me?
- How do medicines work?
- What side effects can I expect?
- Are medicines dangerous?
- If I start them, can I stop them?
- How long do I have to take medicine?
- Once treated, will depression come back?

If you do not know all the answers to these questions, you are in good company. Even those in the mental-health field struggle with these questions. There is still so much we do not understand about depression despite tremendous advances in our understanding of human behavior, emotions, and the brain. However, this is true in every area of medicine—there are huge gaps in our knowledge about many diseases and their treatments. Aspirin was commonly used for more than 100 years for pain relief before scientists finally figured out how it worked in the mid 1970s. But people seem more concerned about taking medicines used to treat mental-health problems than they are about medicines used to treat other medical illnesses that are just as poorly understood.

Frank delivers baked goods every morning at 5:00 am and has done so for the 30 years of his working career. He has never minded getting up so early and has always enjoyed the quiet of the few hours before sunrise. He has also been able to get home by the time his four children arrive from school. His wife, Candace, has never put pressure on him to make more money, but finances are getting tighter as their oldest son is approaching college age and the other kids are becoming more involved in sports and other extracurricular activities.

His wife commented last year that he was becoming more irritable with her and the children. He also seemed to withdraw more, watching TV for hours after he got home instead of spending time with the family or even his favorite hobby, gardening. His wife recalled that he had a spell like this for a few weeks in the past when his hours at work were cut, but things got better when he was back working full time. This time was different, though, because it was lasting so long and the irritability was more severe.

His family doctor, whom Frank had known since childhood, had recently retired, and Frank was reluctant to see his replacement. Candace, suspecting Frank may be experiencing some depression, pushed him to make an appointment with the new doctor for his yearly physical. She came with him to make sure he discussed the changes in his behavior she had noticed.

"My wife wanted to make sure I mention that I am cranky lately. What woman married to the same guy for 25 years doesn't think her husband is cranky? Right, doc?"

Candace added, "It's not just that, and it's not just me. He has been having trouble sleeping for months. He stays up for hours at night thinking about work. He has been afraid of losing his job after snapping at several of his customers when they complained about some deliveries. His boss and two co-workers told me he isn't himself."

Frank knows he is irritable, but he also knows why. They demand too much from him at work. When he gets home, his wife gives him a list of things to do. He is tired and would rather lie on the couch than deal with it all. If he could just get a nice long vacation everything would be fine.

When Dr. Gregory mentioned depression and possible antidepressants, Frank flipped his lid. "Who said I'm depressed?" To Frank, someone with depression cries all the time or wants to die. And he definitely doesn't want to die.

"I just need some time away from everyone and everything," he said. People always try to manage their problems through a pill, he thought to himself. Not me. He had a flashback to several years ago when his mother was put on "some nerve pill" and never got out of bed.

"No way," he said. "I don't believe in that stuff."

"Who said I'm depressed?"

Deciding whether to take an antidepressant begins with recognizing that there is a problem that requires some type of intervention. That is not as easy as it sounds for many people. If you have struggled with depression yourself in the past or know someone who has, you are more likely to recognize the symptoms and seek help. You would be less reluctant to reject the diagnosis and more willing to consider different treatment suggestions. You would probably be less resistant to take medication, particularly if you are knowledgeable about antidepressants from past personal use or from knowing someone who has been on them.

However, if you are not very familiar with depression, as in Frank's case, you might be aware that you are not feeling or behaving like your usual self, but may not believe it is because you are depressed. Or, you may be one of those people who is not even aware that they have a problem. You may have been told by a friend, family member, or co-worker that they have seen a change in you and that you should get help. You may react to these suggestions with appreciation for their concern, resentment for meddling into your personal affairs, or complete bewilderment at what they are talking about.

A healthcare professional, including a medical doctor treating your physical health or a mental-health counselor you are seeing for an emotional or relationship problem, could bring up the possibility that you have depression. They may have mentioned it because of something you said to them or something they observed. There are many physical signs that point to possible mood problems. For example, your physician, seeing you for a routine physical or treating you for another health problem, notices you have newly onset elevated blood pressure or stomach pains. Your dentist sees signs of you grinding your teeth or clenching your jaw. A chiropractor treating you for back pain finds more knots up and down your back and shoulders, causing worsening pain.

Usually when someone else tells you they think you are depressed or should take medication, they have good intentions (there are exceptions addressed in Chapter 4, including expectations others may have when you start an antidepressant). While they may be looking out for your best interest, they may not always bring up their concerns in a supportive or comforting manner. When someone says you could be depressed, it can feel belittling, accusatory, or critical, even if it is not meant that way. But, hopefully, you can look beyond that and make the decision that is best for you and your health.

Lucy's Story

Lucy became visibly uncomfortable when Elaine, her psychotherapist, brought up antidepressants again in their session. Lucy had been in therapy for more than five years. She started in counseling to deal with some difficult childhood issues but has found it helpful in better managing her day-to-day stressors as well. In addition to her weekly therapy sessions, she takes yoga twice a week and practices meditation.

When Lucy shared that she has put on more weight over the last three months because of worsening midnight food binges and 12- to 14-hour sleeping marathons, the therapist commented, "Overeating and oversleeping can be signs of clinical depression. I think you should reconsider medicine. I don't think it is the whole solution, but it may help break the cycle." Lucy has noticed that her therapist brings up the possibility of medicine every few months but never really pushes the issue.

"You know how much I hate the idea of taking unnatural substances to change my feelings," Lucy said. "I am still taking St. John's Wort and the vitamins I got from my homeopathic doctor. I think they are helping."

"But you have taken those for over a year now and are still having symptoms," Elaine pointed out.

The therapist was not surprised when Lucy responded, "I know I have some depression. I am open to antidepressants but would rather not take them. I think they are okay for some people, just not for me. There are a few other things I have read about that I'd like to try first to see if it helps."

"I know I have some depression. I am open to antidepressants but would rather not take them. I think they are okay for some people, just not for me."

It is helpful to know your "depression and antidepressant attitude"—open, closed, or blindsided—when considering treatment for mood or behavior changes. Identifying your attitude early on can help you and your doctor address your particular questions at the onset and develop a treatment strategy that you find more agreeable. Accepting a diagnosis of depression and starting an antidepressant is a decision that you must make by yourself for yourself. While it is important to listen to feedback from others on why they think getting help for depression may be a good idea, any treatment, including medicine, is usually not as helpful if you feel coerced or threatened into it. Antidepressants are usually just one part of a successful treatment strategy and often not sufficient for a complete recovery without lifestyle changes, counseling, or other interventions. If you do not feel anything is wrong and disagree with the diagnosis of depression, you are unlikely to engage in those other necessary components of treatment even if you do take the medicine.

If you accept that you have depression but are reluctant to take medicine, you are more likely to stop them prematurely or be inconsistent in taking them. You may be hesitant to follow up with the doctor who prescribed you the medicine or share information about your progress that would help ensure you are on the right medicine or dose. Antidepressants are more effective when someone has a positive attitude about taking them and wants to see a change in themselves. You can identify your attitude by answering the following questions: *"Do you think you may have depression? Are you open to the possibility? Would you be willing to take antidepressants?"*

When you are "open" to a depression diagnosis, you acknowledge something is wrong and are willing to consider that you may have a mental-health problem. If you are "closed" to the diagnosis, you do not believe you have depression, despite whatever changes you have experienced or others have observed. Being "blindsided" means you do not believe that there is anything wrong with how you are feeling or behaving. An open attitude about taking antidepressants means that you are willing to take them if needed. A closed attitude means that you are unlikely or unwilling to do so. Each of these attitudes has its pluses and minuses. Which description best fits you?

If you have experienced depression in the past, known someone who has dealt with depression, or are knowledgeable about mental-health problems, you are more likely to have an open attitude. You are less likely to let things get too bad before you get help. The downside is that you could be too quick to diagnose yourself when there could be another problem causing your symptoms. A misdiagnosis could lead to the wrong treatment. Although feelings of sadness or changes in sleep, appetite, and energy can all be typical signs of depression, they can also result from other medical or psychiatric problems. Even if you have had depression in the past with similar symptoms, you cannot assume that depression is the reason for how you are feeling now.

A closed attitude means you acknowledge that you are having some mood or behavior changes, but you believe there is a more probable cause for your symptoms. You may feel any problems you are having are normal reactions to stressful events at home and work or caused by a physical illness like thyroid problems, chronic fatigue, a virus, or other medical problem. You may not associate physical complaints (stomach aches, muscle and joint pain, or headaches), getting angry more easily, or excessive alcohol consumption as possible signs of depression. A closed attitude can stem from not believing that depression is a real health condition or believing that it is real but does not apply to your circumstance.

If your attitude is "blindsided," you are surprised at the suggestion of depression because you do not recognize that anything is wrong. It may be hard to fathom how anyone could experience the dramatic changes associated with depression and not recognize it. Of course, there is always the possibility that nothing is wrong. Just because people may tell you they think you are depressed doesn't necessarily mean that you are. Maybe a family member, friend, or co-worker misinterpreted something you said or did. You could be having problems at home that cause you to be more irritable or withdrawn around your co-workers. Someone at work may see these changes as a sign of depression rather than simply a reaction to a situation at home that they know nothing about. If a couple is having a fight, one spouse may blame the other's irritability and anger on depression rather than on something he or she is doing to anger them. They may want to believe that their marriage problems are due to the spouse's depression, thereby relieving themselves of any responsibility for the couple's difficulties.

When someone overidentifies depression in others, it may be because they have successfully overcome their own depression and want to share their positive life changes with others. Even some counselors, psychiatrists, and medical doctors can fall victim to overdiagnosing depression. (Unfortunately, there are also some who are too slow to diagnose.) A counselor—or the counselor's client—may believe there is not enough progress being made in therapy and hope that a depression diagnosis and medication will facilitate greater change. Physicians may get frustrated with patients who have a series of unexplained physical complaints and hope that diagnosing them with depression will better explain their patient's symptoms and that antidepressants will manage those complaints.

Others with a blindsided attitude may have something wrong, but simply do not see it in themselves. It may be hard for those who have felt the devastating effects of this illness to imagine that you could not be aware of the symptoms of depression. The mind has an incredible capacity to mask our awareness when things are too emotionally difficult to deal with. Depression can be one of those difficult things to accept. Once you become more open minded and learn more about the condition, you will be better able to identify and manage those changes other people see in you.

The upside to an open attitude about taking antidepressants is that you are less likely to delay treatment. This improves your chances of recovery. An open attitude means you will probably work closely with your doctor to make sure that the medicine is helpful and be more willing to work through any side effects or other difficulties you may experience. The downside to an open attitude about taking antidepressants is that you may be too quick to take a pill to treat depression. Medicine may not be the best or only treatment for you. Although some dread the idea of taking medicine for their mood, others see it as an easy solution to their problems. They may want to take a pill rather than confront the life stressors that are possibly causing or worsening their depression. Even if you took medicine successfully before, you may not need it now. Keep in mind that, while the benefits of antidepressants usually far outweigh the risks, there are, as with all medicines, risks. There may be healthier and safer alternatives.

A closed attitude about taking antidepressants could prevent you from getting the help you need. Delaying antidepressant treatment can be very problematic. There are research findings demonstrating that the longer depression goes untreated, the harder it is to respond to therapy. Untreated depression can cause physical changes in the brain and body that can impact your mental and physical health (examples are described in Chapter Three). Untreated depression can have consequences on your home and work life. If you lose your job because of your inability to perform to your expected level, you could suffer more distress with loss of income, health insurance, and self esteem. When marriages, family, and social relationships are affected by depression, the resulting social isolation and loneliness can make you feel even worse.

The upside is that you are more likely to make sure that medicine is truly necessary before taking it and will likely look into other possible treatment options as well. Some skepticism about taking antidepressants is appropriate. You want to make sure that the medicine recommended is safe, proven to be effective, and that it is the best choice for you. Whoever is prescribing the medicine should be able to convince you why you need it. Understand the consequences of not taking antidepressants before you refuse them, and make sure you know what your alternatives are.

Chris' Story

Chris, age 45, has never married and lives alone. He has struggled with depression off and on much of his life. His symptoms include a general malaise and lack of enthusiasm for anything. He gets tired during the day and really has to push himself to do basic chores. He has not worked for many years because of his condition, but his savings are running out and his family is becoming less willing to help financially. He started seeing counselors and doctors as a teenager but never took antidepressants until 10 years ago. He was amazed at how good he felt, at least for a few years. All his symptoms improved so much that he was productive again and even started having a social life. Slowly, however, the medicine's positive effects seemed to wear off, and his previous symptoms returned. Since then he has seen dozens of psychopharmacologists (experts in psychiatric medications), seeking medication suggestions that could help him get back to feeling like he did his first time on antidepressants.

His previous psychiatrist described Chris as the "most compliant patient I ever had." He followed all of his recommendations to the letter. He takes his medicines exactly as prescribed. During his doctor's appointment, he brings in a list of detailed questions and keeps precise records on how he is feeling on a daily basis.

Chris found a new psychiatrist recently who just moved into town from a prestigious academic institution, and he was hopeful he would have some new ideas to better manage his depression.

During his initial visit, Chris said, "I am realistic about treatment. I know it will take time to get better, and I am ready to do what it takes to get there. Tell me what I should and shouldn't do to overcome this depression. What do you need to know about me and my history to help you help me?"

"Tell me what I should and shouldn't do..."

There are several things you should and should not do when considering whether to start an antidepressant. These apply no matter what your baseline depression and antidepressant attitude may be, and they include the following:

- See your own healthcare professional who is experienced in mental healthcare.
- Ask questions and challenge your doctor on the diagnosis and treatment recommendations.
- Get second and third opinions if you are not convinced you are getting the right care.
- Educate yourself and be open minded.

- Get a good medical examination.
- Don't diagnose yourself.
- Don't treat yourself.
- Don't believe everything you hear or read about depression.

See your own healthcare professional who is experienced in mental healthcare.

To get a true, objective assessment, you must see your own healthcare professional. If you are in couple's therapy, family counseling, or have a spouse or other family member in treatment, the therapist may have suggested you could be depressed based on what she hears from others. Perhaps a friend or someone you know socially with a medical or mental-health background could have mentioned the possibility of depression. These kinds of suggestions can feel intrusive unless you specifically asked for their opinion. While their judgment could be clouded by a lack of objectivity since they are not seeing you in a professional setting, they still may have something helpful to tell you and could be worth listening to. If someone close to you wants to share information with your healthcare professional, make sure you agree in advance on what you are and are not comfortable with them mentioning.

When you decide to see a professional for an evaluation, make sure he or she has a strong background in diagnosing mental-health disorders. There is long list of different types of healthcare professionals who treat depression. Each has a different skill set. Psychiatrists are medical doctors who can prescribe medication and have training in providing psychotherapy and other types of counseling. Some psychiatrists identify themselves as psychopharmacologists, meaning they have expertise specifically in medication therapies. Medical doctors (MD and Doctor of Osteopathic Medicine), master's-level advanced practice nurses such as nurse practitioners and clinical nurse specialists, and physicians assistants (PAs) can prescribe medicine. While any of them can legally write a prescription, they may not necessarily have special training in treating mental-health problems.

There are some family doctors, gynecologists, internists, and other non-psychiatric physicians who are very skilled at recognizing and managing depression. They have years of experience, attend conferences, and stay up to date on the latest developments. Make sure you are seeing someone who takes a special interest in this area and can suggest non-medication treatment options. Some physicians mistakenly see all antidepressants as interchangeable and tend to use the ones they are most

Healthcare Professionals Treating Depression

There are many types of healthcare professionals who diagnose and treat depression. They have varying degrees of training, expertise, and tools they can use. The following list includes the different healthcare professionals you may see for depression.

Healthcare Providers Who Can Diagnose and Treat Depression as well as Prescribe Medicine

Training and licensing requirements vary from state to state and country to country. Each licensing organization has a Web site that describes their requirements in detail.

I. **Medical Doctor (MD)**
    Doctor of Osteopathic Medicine (DO)
    Bachelor of Medicine, Bachelor of Surgery (MBBS)

Primary Care Doctor: Internal medicine, family physicians, and pediatricians. Some obstetricians and gynecologists are considered primary care physicians. Primary care doctors see and treat many cases of depression since they manage the overall health of their patients. As a whole, they prescribe more antidepressants than any other field of medicine. They are trained to identify depression and use medication. They are also good at making sure there are no medical issues causing or worsening depression symptoms. Some are more comfortable than others in treating depression and some make a special effort to stay up to date on mental-health disorders. Others are uncomfortable and refer to specialists such as psychiatrists. More complicated cases should see a mental-health specialist.

Psychiatrist: They are medical doctors who also attend medical school but have specialized training in diagnosing mental-health problems. They can also assess whether there are medical illnesses contributing to how someone feels. Some psychiatrists only diagnose and treat with medication, while others are therapists as well. Psychiatrists are also good at knowing what other treatments, such as counseling, would help someone and can make the right referrals to the right therapist. Some people are uncomfortable seeing a psychiatrist because of the stigma in our society, or they think you have to be "really mentally ill." Fortunately this has changed as more people see depression as a real medical illness and, going to a psychiatrist has become more accepted.

Other Medical Specialists: These are medical doctors who specialize in treating other medical problems. These would include neurologists (specializing in diseases of the nervous system), rheumatologists (specializing in autoimmune diseases), orthopedic surgeons (specializing in diseases of the bones), anesthesiologists (they put people to sleep in surgery and many do pain management), physiatrists (specializing in diseases of muscles), cardiologists (specializing in diseases of the heart and vascular system), and surgeons (they cut things out of or repair abnormalities inside the body). There are many others. Some of these specialists take a special interest in depression and may see a great deal of it in their practice. For example, oncologists who treat those with cancer are more likely to see depression since their patients are dealing with such serious diseases. Many specialists will try to get their patients to see someone with more expertise in depression, but some are comfortable with straightforward cases.

II.   Physicians Assistant (PA)
Nurse Practioner (NP)
Clinical Nurse Specialist (CNS)

These are healthcare practitioners who can also prescribe medicine and usually work under the supervision of a delegating physician. A physician's assistant (PA) has two to three years of training (unlike four years of medical school) and is not required to have a post-graduate residency (though some do if they want to specialize). Nurse practitioners and clinical nurse specialists (also called an advanced practice nurse) are nurses with master's degrees. They usually work under a delegating physician, but, in some states, can practice independently. PAs and NPs are trained in a broad range of medical services, whereas a CNS specializes in one therapeutic area. PAs and NPs, not involved in primary care, find themselves eventually specializing in one area.

Like physicians, they are trained to assess medical problems that could cause or worsen depression. They may start depression treatment, but refer your case to another provider if they are not comfortable treating mental-health conditions or if there are other complicating factors. Some patients would rather see "the doctor" and not a nurse or assistant, while other patients prefer a PA, NP, or CNS. They find them willing to spend more time and, in some cases, may be more empathic and caring. Depending on their experience and education, they can treat many diseases as comfortably as a physician, but, most importantly, they are specially trained to know when to have a physician become more involved. There are CNSs who choose psychiatry as their specialty and have unique training and expertise in mental-health disorders.

III.   Clinical Pharmacist

These providers have a doctorate in pharmacy and usually one or more years of post-graduate training. They have a unique understanding of medications and usually provide recommendations to patients and healthcare professionals. In some states they can write prescriptions. Some take a special interest in psychiatric medications, particularly in patients who take multiple medicines that can have problematic interactions.

Healthcare Providers Who can Diagnose and Treat Depression but *Cannot* Prescribe Medicine

While the following healthcare professionals cannot prescribe medication, they are often able to determine when someone should consider medication therapy. They are often required to receive continuing education about psychiatric medication updates and can often identify when there are problems with medicine. They may be able to answer questions about side effects. Some have enough training or clinical experience to make recommendations about medicine to the patient's physician.

I.   Licensed Psychologist (PhD, PsyD, EdD)

These providers have all completed a four- to seven-year doctoral program in psychology. A PsyD is a doctor of psychology, PhD is a doctor of philosophy trained in psychology, and an EdD is a doctor of education. Both PhD and PsyD can identify, diagnose, and treat most health conditions but can't prescribe medications. In addition to clinical training, some PhD programs also offer a research and teaching component for those interested in that area. An EdD goes to a similar doctoral program as a PsyD and PhD, with an emphasis on teaching, administrative, research, and clinical services in the field of education. They can focus on providing mental-health counseling services.

II.   Master's-Level Therapist

Social Worker: There are several types of social workers with different areas of interests. They all attend a social work master's program that lasts about two years. There are doctorate programs as well. They all receive extensive education about mental-health disorders. Licensed Clinical Social Workers (LCSW) and Licensed Independent Clinical Social Worker (LICSW) have additional supervised clinical experience in providing different types of counseling services to those with mental-health issues. Like psychologists, they cannot prescribe medicine but are trained to recognize when medicine can be helpful and may even be able to make some specific recommendations to the patient's doctor.

Licensed Counselor: These mental-health professionals attend a master's program lasting two to three years, or longer if attending a doctorate program. They also have additional supervised clinical experience required before getting licensed. They identify, diagnose, and treat a variety of mental-health illnesses but do not prescribe medication. Similar to psychologists and social workers, they can determine when medicine may be helpful and provide some guidance to their patients. There are Licensed Marriage and Family Therapists (LMFT), Licensed Mental Health Counselors (LMHC), and Licensed Professional Counselors (LPC). Some of these titles are determined by the requirements of the state in which the therapists are licensed.

III.　Others

Certified Addiction Counselor (CAC): There are different training requirements to become a CAC, which is a discipline that focuses on psychological problems associated with alcohol or drug abuse. They are required have some amount of education in this area as well as clinical experience depending on the regulating state. There is a certification examination as well. Some take a special interest in learning more about mental-health problems that often come along with substance abuse problems.

Pastoral Counseling: These are spiritual leaders such as ministers, rabbis, or priests who provide counseling with a religious component. There are usually not regulating agencies for these providers but many do attend continuing education training to become more familiar with mental-health issues. Some people with depression feel the added spiritual component to their treatment is helpful and more meaningful.

Life Coach: These individuals are not licensed or regulated by the state and provide a wide range of support and encouragement to those wishing to make changes in their life. People going to them may seek help related to career problems, organizational difficulties, or motivational concerns. Life coaches usually do not have any specific training in mental-health problems, though some mental healthcare professionals provide life coaching as an additional service.

comfortable with. Look for a physician who is familiar with a variety of medications and understands their subtle but important differences.

Non-physicians, including psychologists (PhD and PsyD) and master's-level therapists, have training in recognizing depression and provide non-medication treatments, including many types of counseling services. They often suggest you have a thorough medical assessment by your physician and may encourage medication if they believe it is necessary. Others may be reluctant to suggest antidepressants because they know little about them and are unable to prescribe them. Make sure your therapist is familiar with a variety of treatment modalities and does not suggest the same type of therapy for all their clients. No one type of counseling is suitable for all people or all conditions. The more options you are given, the greater likelihood of finding the right treatment for you.

Ask questions and challenge your doctor on the diagnosis and treatment recommendations.

One of the most frustrating aspects of getting mental-health treatment is that there is no conclusive medical test like there is for diagnosising many other diseases. A blood test, head scan, or even the doctor putting a stethoscope on your chest usually makes you feel more confident about a diagnosis for a medical problem. Just talking with someone may not seem like a very scientific or reliable way to determine that you have depression. When the doctor decides you should take an antidepressant or see a counselor, you might think she gives the same recommendations to everyone she thinks has depression. A skilled doctor or therapist can explain why she is making these suggestions. You need to put her to the task of convincing you before you follow her advice. You can help your doctor by educating yourself as much as possible about depression and its treatments. Reading Chapters Two and Three is a great place to start.

Get second and third opinions if you are not convinced you are getting the right care.

Since diagnosis and treatment of mental-health problems is generally based on symptoms rather than objective tests or physical findings, you may want to get one or more other opinions if you are uncertain about their recommendations.

Some people worry that they may offend their healthcare provider if they get a second opinion, but keep in mind this is commonly done and accepted in the medical community. If your provider takes offense at this, then you may be dealing with someone whose ego is too inflated to serve you well. You should be upfront with your doctor or therapist if you are considering a second opinion. He might even be able to recommend another local expert in the area to consult with who could provide both of you with valuable ideas.

Make sure the clinician giving the second opinion is also well trained and not biased for or against any particular type of medically accepted treatment options. Also, check to see whether that person is comfortable with seeing you only for a second opinion. Not all healthcare providers are willing to do so.

Educate yourself and be open minded.

You should always be a proactive and an informed consumer when it comes to your health. Many patients no longer unconditionally follow the advice of their doctor without educating themselves about their condition. There are countless ways to get up-to-date information about any medical illness from books and the Internet to health fairs and support groups. The challenge is finding reliable information and making sense of it all. Before accepting a mental-health diagnosis and any type of treatment, you should be able to engage in an educated dialogue with your healthcare provider. You have choices in your treatment, but you may not have been told what they all are. You will find recommendations for reliable Web sites, books, and support groups in the Resources Section (on page 295) and at www.takingantidepressants.com.

Get a good medical work up.

Common medical conditions can mimic depression. Anyone diagnosed with depression should have a thorough physical examination if they have not had one recently to make sure there are no other medical problems that could be causing or worsening their symptoms. If you are otherwise healthy, you may not have seen a physician in a long time. Or, even if you are under regular medical care, do not assume your physician is routinely checking for conditions that could cause symptoms similar to depression. For example, there are people on blood thinners who get a blood test every few weeks to check how well their medicine is working, but they may not have had a simple thyroid or blood sugar test in years.

If you do find you have a medical problem such as a thyroid condition, do not assume that this explains your depression symptoms. It may be unrelated or just making the depression worse and more difficult to treat. Your doctor should also review any prescription medicines, over-the-counter drugs, or herbal products you are taking, since some of these can have depression-like side effects.

Do not diagnose yourself.

While some people resist the idea that they have depression, others may be too willing to accept the diagnosis. That can be problematic if you assume that explains any problems you are having when, in fact, there could be another cause. Information about depression is all over the media, from antidepressant commercials on television and in magazines to reality television and talk shows profiling the emotional struggles of famous people. With all this exposure, you may be a tempted to self-diagnose, particularly if you have been diagnosed with depression in the past.

Identifying and treating depression early and aggressively is wise, but don't do it without professional help. You cannot be objective about your own health, and particularly, not your mental health. It is well known that

Some Health Conditions That Can Mimic or Worsen Depression

This is a partial list of some medical conditions that may present as depression or may make an underlying depression harder to treat. Before you start to worry that you or someone you care about may have one or several of these illnesses, keep in mind that there are usually many other symptoms that would go along with it. It would be very rare to only have depression-like symptoms. Most of these are easily diagnosed with a basic physical exam, blood test, or imaging scan such as an MRI or CT.

Consult your doctor if you are concerned that you may be affected by one of the following:

Thyroid problems: Disorders of the thyroid gland in the body that produces a hormone regulating metabolism.

Parathyroid problems: Disorders of the parathyroid, a small gland next to the thyroid that regulates calcium and phosphate, two necessary chemicals that play a role in bodily functions.

Diabetes: A disease characterized by fluctuations in blood sugar caused by the inability of the body to produce insulin or use the insulin it does make effectively.

Infections: These can include many viral or bacterial infections such as Lyme disease, hepatitis, mononucleosis, and sexually transmitted diseases such as herpes, HIV, or syphilis.

Seizures: Certain types of epilepsy may cause emotional and behavioral changes without the physical symptoms seen with typical glandular seizures.

Autoimmune diseases: Various conditions in which the body starts to attack itself, such as lupus, multiple sclerosis, and rheumatoid arthritis.

Stroke: Depression can occur with even minor strokes that people may not be aware they had.

Head injury: People who were in accidents or had serious falls in which they hit their head. Often seen with soldiers coming back from battle.

Blood disease: Examples include low iron and porphyria.

Vitamin deficiencies: Examples include low folate, low vitamin B12, and vitamin D.

Heart disease: Poor heart function or irregular heart rhythm can mimic depression, making some easily tired and amotivated.

Low hormone levels: Low testosterone, estrogen, or high and low cortisol production (Cushing's and Addison's disease), to name a few.

Chronic Fatigue Syndrome and Fibromyalgia: While difficult to diagnose and not accepted by the whole medical community, there is more research to suggest these conditions are real and may look similar to depression.

Parkinson's disease: A disease affecting motor movements but may have depression associated with it as well.

Certain cancers: Pancreatic, lung and blood cancers such as leukemia are examples.

doctors are the worst at correctly diagnosing themselves and close family members with medical conditions that they would rarely mistake if it were one of their patients. The reason for this is lack of objectivity.

Do not treat yourself.

If you do believe you suffer from depression, do not be tempted to treat it yourself. Many people are reluctant to see a doctor because of the time, expense, and privacy concerns that it will go into their medical record. Some feel embarrassed discussing emotional problems with their medical doctor with whom they may have a personal relationship. But the consequences of not getting help or trying to determine your own course of therapy, including medication, could lead to far more expensive, embarrassing, and dangerous problems.

In some countries, and through some Internet pharmacies, people can have access to medication without seeing a doctor. There are plenty of true horror stories about patients getting the wrong drug or fake medicines that have been life-threatening or even fatal. People have started themselves on medicine they received from a friend or family member. They may even have leftover medicine from a previous episode. What might have been the right medicine for someone else may not be the right one for you. What might have been an appropriate antidepressant for you at one time may not be the right one for you now. Depending on your physical health, new medicines you may be taking for other conditions, or different symptoms you may be experiencing, could make a medicine given to you in the past ineffective or even dangerous now.

Another self-treatment trend to avoid is asking your doctor for a specific medicine. You may have heard from someone how helpful a certain antidepressant has been for them. Perhaps you saw one of those seductive television advertisements telling you about a "new treatment to ask your doctor about." Some doctors with little experience in managing depression may give you what you want and not consider whether it is truly the right therapy for you. Let your doctor tell you what he would choose, challenge him as to why, and then ask about other treatment options. Your doctor should be able to justify his decision.

Do not believe everything you hear or read about depression.

This is probably one of the more important pieces of advice in the book. People have a tendency to access resources that validate their preconceived ideas about a subject. Political conservatives like to read conservative news sources, while liberals stick to those with their bias. This is true with our health as well. If you are skeptical about depression and antidepressants, you will likely gravitate toward information sources with that bias. There are plenty of places to find an anti-mental-health-treatment viewpoint as well as those that strongly advocate one or another type of treatment. Pharmaceutical Web sites are singularly focused on pushing their specific medication despite attempts by the Food and Drug Administration (FDA) to force them to be fair and balanced. You will hear all kinds of conflicting messages such as "depression doesn't exist" to "25 percent of adults will suffer from depression in their lifetime" or "antidepressants are safe and effective" to "antidepressants are dangerous and addictive." There is truth somewhere in between all those messages, and you have to educate yourself enough to figure out what is right for you.

There is a great deal we know about depression and much we do not know. Our scientific research has limitations, and just because a specific study gives us a certain answer to a question does not make it necessarily true. Neither does one person's experience. Even mental-healthcare professionals will have certain theories about depression and treatment that may be biased. While they could justify their practices through observations in their practice, research they have conducted, or, management of their own mental-health problems, they can be affected by other motives such as monetary gain or notoriety. In recent years, the medical community has come under fire for being too closely affiliated with pharmaceutical companies that have rewarded some physicians with lucrative speaking contracts and consulting fees, as well as fancy pens, notepads, and other trinkets for their offices. Most of these small gifts have been eliminated through a voluntary program initiated by a consortium of drug companies called the Pharmaceutical Research and Manufacturers of America (PhRMA). One wonders whether a physician is unconsciously, or even consciously, predisposed to prescribe certain medicines because of these rewards. Some argue that these gifts were too insignificant to change prescribing habits and that most physicians ultimately choose what is best for their patients. Others are not completely convinced that they have no effect. However, even non-prescribers, such as psychologists and other therapists, could be biased toward choosing to use certain tests or treatments that could generate more revenue for them.

Because of these concerns, people often turn to other patients' experiences for suggestions on how to best handle their problems. With all the Internet healthcare sites, blogs, and social network sites, there are plenty of places to turn. There is potential bias here as well, and what works for one person may not work for you. They may have a completely different condition and not be aware of it, such as an anxiety disorder or bipolar illness. Some people are angry about having a mental-health problem and blame the medical community for their difficulties ("I never had such problems before seeing that therapist or taking that medicine."). The Church of Scientology is one of the more outspoken groups against psychiatry and the mental-health treatment community. It disseminates a great deal of misinformation about mental illness, often without identifying itself as the source.

There is nothing wrong with having some healthy skepticism about something you hear or read, including the information in this book. While this book attempts to provide a mainstream medical approach to managing depression, the most important lessons taught here are how to understand new information you may learn and the limits of what science has taught us.

Tips for Choosing a Well-Qualified Mental-Healthcare Provider

Get several recommendations from people you know and trust. The best resources are those who have seen a certain doctor or therapist themselves for a similar problem or other healthcare professionals familiar with those working in your community. You may also ask someone who works in medically related fields such as medical front-office staff, nurses, medical assistants, and pharmaceutical representatives. They often hear about good providers or can ask around.

- Avoid referrals directly from insurance companies unless you speak to an experienced, hands-on case manager who has worked closely with that provider. Many insurance company representatives live in a different part of the country and just read off a list on their computer. Doctors or therapists often fill out a questionnaire about their specialties when they apply to be on an insurance panel. These specialties are sometimes not verified. Some insurance companies reimburse so little for doctors' or therapists' services that some of the better and busier providers in the community refuse to be on their panel.
- Do not make cost your only consideration. If there are no good providers included in your insurance plan, you should pay out of pocket at least for the first few visits. Once you feel better, you can always switch to someone covered by your insurance for maintenance care. Mental healthcare, unlike surgery or other medical procedures, is not prohibitively expensive. Also, many providers are willing to negotiate their fees for those who have trouble affording their services.
- Check with the state licensing board whether the provider you are considering going to has any license violations on their record. Any licensed professional is responsible to a credentialing board in their state. You can look up a physician on the state medical board, a psychologist on the state psychologist licensing board, etc. There are professional associations such as American Psychiatric Association, American Psychological Association, American Medical Association, American Nurses Association, American Board of Internal Medicine, etc. Most healthcare professionals

belong to some professional group. Those groups often have information about providers if there are concerns about their background. There are also numerous healthcare sites that run background checks for a fee, such as www.healthgrades.com.

- If you're seeing a medical doctor, find out how often he treats depression. Is that an area of interest for him? What are the areas of mental-health treatment he is uncomfortable with treating? Does he receive regular education updates or attend continuing medical education conferences on depression? Are these conferences fair and balanced, or are they supported by a drug company that's pushing certain medicines?

- If you're seeing a mental-health therapist, find out how she receives educational updates. Ask her about her areas of interest and specialties before you tell her your problem. What is she most and least comfortable treating? Does she use a variety of therapeutic techniques, or does she stick with one or two treatment modalities? How does she decide which techniques to use?

"What do you need to know about me and my history to help you help me?"

Your doctor (or other prescriber) is responsible for taking a good medical and psychiatric history and asking the right questions to determine whether you would benefit from taking an antidepressant. Based on what she learns from you, a competent prescriber should be able to give you some reasonable antidepressant options to choose from. Your responsibility is to be prepared and bring as much information as possible to the visit. The relationship with your doctor should be a partnership in which you both are involved in the data gathering and in the decision making.

There are some simple steps you can take to help your doctor. Listed below is a series of questions your doctor may ask you. It is helpful to try to answer as many of these as you can before your visit:

- When did you first have symptoms, and what were they?
- Did they ever go away and then come back?
- Did you ever get help before? Medicine, counseling, or both?
  - If counseling, with whom? What kind of counseling? How frequently and how long did you go? Why did you stop?
  - If medicine, what medicine did you take and what was it for?

When and how long did you take if for? What doses and why did you stop? Any side effects or problems?

- How long have your current symptoms been going on?
- Did anything significant happen in your personal life at the time your symptoms started or worsened?
- Do you have any blood relatives with depression or other psychiatric problems? If they were treated, what was it with? How did that work for them?
- What are all the prescription medicines or over-the-counter pills or supplements you take now? Were you on any different medicines, herbal/nutritional supplements, or birth control pills when the symptoms started?
- Do you use any alcohol or illicit drugs now or when your symptoms started?
- Do you have any medical problems?
- When you were growing up, did you have any medical problems requiring medicine or surgery? Were there any problems when your mother was pregnant with you, or did you have any developmental problems such as not walking or talking on time, etc.? Did you ever have to repeat a grade in school or take special classes?

Some other important items you could bring in on your visit:

- A list of all your current medicines, doses, and which doctor is giving them to you.
- A list of all your current doctors.
- A summary of your past psychiatric medicines and your experiences with them. See Appendix A, "Past Medication History Form," for a sample form you can use to help summarize this. Also, there is an easy-to-use Web site, www.pastmeds.com, that helps you organize all that information and summarizes it for your doctor. It is free and you do not have to give any personal or identifying information.
- Any psychological testing you have had in the past.
- Names and addresses of any healthcare professional (or hospital) who has treated you for psychiatric problems.
- A summary of current symptoms (You can use one of the self-rated tests in the Appendix.)

This all may sound like a good deal of work. If you can't do any or all of it, don't worry or let it delay you from getting help. Doctors are used

Don't Do What Your Doctor Says? You are in Good Company!

Did you know that 25 percent of people who are prescribed antidepressants either do not fill the prescription or stop taking them after two weeks? Approximately 35 percent of those taking antidepressants stop after two months.

If you are not going to take your medicine, or if you choose to stop taking it shortly after starting, let your doctor know why. If you have unanswered questions, she may be able to address those. She can also let you know her concerns if you do not take them and maybe even be able to give you some alternatives.

to patients having little or no information when they come into their offices. They will not be disappointed, and it will not drastically affect your care. But they can do their job better if you come prepared.

I have set the stage for accepting a diagnosis of depression and deciding whether to start medication. You have met Jane, Frank, Lucy, and Chris and may be able to relate to some or many of their struggles with depression and taking medication.

By determining your own depression and antidepressant attitude, you know which issues may be affecting your decision-making process. You have reviewed what you should and should not do before starting medicine, and you know where and how to get the right diagnosis and treatment recommendations.

The next step is to figure out whether you really have depression. Chapter Two explores whether depression is a real physical condition or a normal reaction to difficult and stressful life events. I also describe different types of depression and you can determine if any of these describes you or someone you care about. This is important because not all depressions are treated in the same way. The first leg of our journey is underway.

Do I Really Have a Mood Disorder?

Diagnosing Depression and Depression Type

Chris' Story Continues

Chris is looking forward to a fresh approach with his new psychiatrist. Dr. Jackson admittedly felt overwhelmed by Chris' extensive medication history and desperate plea for help. She wondered whether he was putting too much faith in medicine and whether he would be open to some other treatment strategies. But for now she let him do the talking.

"Since the medicines do not seem to work, I wonder if I have been properly diagnosed," Chris said. "How do these doctors know I have depression, and how do I know I'm getting the right help? There must be a medicine or other treatment out there that will make me feel like I did 10 years ago!"

Understandably, after years of frustration with his re-emergence of depressive symptoms, Chris wants to make sure that he has been correctly diagnosed and is getting the right treatment.

Most medical doctors listen to your symptoms, perform a physical examination, run diagnostic tests, and then give you a diagnosis. They usually show you an abnormality on a blood test, x-ray, or other laboratory report that convinces you that your diagnosis is a real condition.

You may assume that once the doctor knows what is wrong, she will be able to recommend the appropriate treatment. Unfortunately, it does not always work that way in psychiatric medicine. There are no telltale findings on a physical exam, blood tests, or high-tech imaging scans to determine whether you definitely have a mood problem or what type it may be.

This chapter gives you an overview of what depression is and how it is diagnosed. It also explains the different depression types so you can understand how each may require a different approach to treatment. Topics covered are:

- Whether depression is a real condition or normal emotional reaction to stress.
- How our understanding of depression has changed over time.
- How depression is diagnosed.
- The different depression types and how to tell which one you may have.
- What to expect with your depression type.
- How each type may be treated differently.

The chapter includes a listing of different symptoms that you can use to help you determine your most likely depression type. These are not given to be used to diagnose yourself or someone else. Only a trained professional can do that.

Frank's Story Continues

Frank regretfully remembers telling his family doctor about his stress at work and trouble sleeping. Dr. Gregory was a bright, young doctor just out of training who started asking a whole lot of personal questions. Some of these were downright insulting, like whether he ever thought of ending his life.

"What is depression anyway?" asked Frank. "Isn't it normal to feel this way sometimes? I don't think I'm depressed. I don't want to die or anything. I just don't want to do anything. I think if I could get a good night's sleep, I wouldn't feel so bad in the day. If you were about to lose your job and had the problems I have at home, wouldn't you feel this bad?"

"What is depression anyway?
Isn't it normal to feel that way sometimes?"

Doctors and counselors treating reluctant patients often hear these types of comments. Frank is not unusual, as there are many opinions about depression and a great deal of misunderstanding. Some people think of depression as a condition in which you are sad all the time or have suicidal thoughts. Some think depression means you are "crazy." There are those who believe that any mood change, such as feeling grumpy or being withdrawn, is a sign of clinical depression. Others question whether it is a real problem or just an excuse for not taking responsibility for one's circumstances. There are those who are convinced that depression is caused by chemicals in the brain that can only be remedied by finding the right mix of medications, while others refuse to accept that depression is a medical illness at all and deny that any medical intervention is necessary, especially medication.

Where do these diverse opinions come from? Throughout time, people have been fearful of and ignorant about mental illness. Countless stories tell how those with a mental illness suffered throughout history: being ostracized, ridiculed, or even labeled as possessed by demons. One of the challenges in accepting depression and other mental-health disorders as real illnesses is that, at least until recently, you could not see it in the brain or body. Another obstacle has been that having a sad mood can be a normal emotional reaction to stress or loss. The line between justifiable sadness and depression is not always clearly drawn.

We all suffer challenges throughout our lives that make us feel sad. The upside of sadness is that it demonstrates the significance of those things one feels sad about. Sadness also fuels us to grow and make changes in our lives. If we never felt sad in a bad job or relationship, we would not be motivated to work to make them better. Since we have all experienced periods of sadness and defeat and have pushed ourselves through it, you may wonder why people with depression cannot do the same. The *emotion* of depression is different from the *illness* of depression.

Conventional medicine teaches that depression is an illness affecting normal functions of the brain and body. Sadness or grief may feel similar to depression, but not cause the same physical changes or impairment in ability to function day to day. It may be hard to accept that depression is real because it is diagnosed by checking off whether you have certain symptoms, not by some test or exam that identifies those physical changes. Imagine going to a medical clinic and complaining of headaches. You might not accept your doctor's diagnosis of high blood pressure if he based that only on your symptoms without also checking your blood pressure.

Some argue that depression is an invention of a modern world in which people are reluctant to take responsibility for their actions or feelings. They may believe that our society is labeling laziness or lack of self-control as a disease, which only fosters more of such behavior. There are those who are convinced that depression is a result of one's spiritual deficiency. Some people believe that psychiatrists, and other mental-health professionals, foster and promote mental-health disorders for monetary gain. They see pharmaceutical companies as agents that encourage this to expand their market for expensive, new medications.

For those healthcare professionals who treat depression and those who suffer from the condition, this lack of understanding is frustrating and demoralizing. While there may be people who need to take more responsibility for their actions or may need some spiritual energizing, that does not mean that others do not suffer from a real medical illness. No one tells someone with a kidney stone or diabetes that, with a little effort or positive attitude, they can manage the condition without help.

Certainly there are behavioral changes that can help people with depression improve. In fact, these details are reviewed in Chapter Five. Yet, by its very nature, depression impacts your ability to do the things you need to do to feel better. It may even cause feelings of hopelessness or helplessness, making you think nothing you do will help. Some skepticism about whether depression is truly a medical condition is good. This puts a burden on the medical community to "prove" that depression is an abnormal functioning of the human body. This also holds the medical community accountable for good scientific research on determining ways to reliably and accurately diagnose depression. Chapter Three explores some of this research on the physical changes in the body that occur with depression.

Jane's Story Continues

Jane is more comfortable reading a research study on depression than hearing someone's opinion or own experience with the condition. She believes that depression is a real phenomenon, but she is troubled by the lack of hard science behind the diagnosis and treatment. She gets frustrated with the guesswork she has experienced in getting help.

"I still don't understand how you can tell someone they have depression just because they feel this way or that way," said Jane. "It doesn't make any sense! How do you know I really have depression? There must be some test that says I do or don't have depression. I read all the time about changes in the brain in people with depression. I read that depression can be caused by a chemical imbalance. Why can't we do a brain scan or blood test and see if those changes are there?"

"How do you know I really have depression?"

With all the advances in our understanding of how the brain works, you would think that we would have better tools to diagnose depression. The standard of care is still an interview with a trained healthcare professional who asks a series of relevant questions, gathers information about past symptoms and family history, and assesses interpersonal interactions. While that may not seem very scientific, it is actually more reliable than you might expect. These symptoms were derived from years of scientific observation and research.

Professionals who are trained in diagnosing depression usually base their decision on an ever-changing consensus guidebook called the Diagnostic and Statistical Manuel (DSM). The DSM specifies which certain symptoms you must experience over a certain period of time in order to be diagnosed with depression. These symptoms cannot have any other cause, such as medical problems, alcohol or illicit drug use, or the use of prescription medicines, and they must have a significant impact on the person's life. Many healthcare professionals deviate from the DSM and use what they know about the person and their clinical experience over the years. While the DSM is still the gold standard diagnostic reference, most doctors and counselors agree that some people with depression experience fewer or different symptoms than the DSM includes.

The DSM was created in the 1950s to standardize identification of mental-health problems. More than 100 years earlier, doctors attempted to first classify psychiatric disorders in order to obtain statistics on how many people suffered from these conditions. Over the years, the DSM was revised as the number of different classifications expanded from one (idiocy/insanity) to well over a hundred. Despite the scientific rigor undergone to validate these classifications, the guide is still highly criticized by the public and medical community. Some object to how certain disorders are defined

Depression Types According to DSM-IV-R

- Major Depressive Disorder
- Dysthymic Disorder
- Depression Not Otherwise Specified
- Bipolar I Disorder
- Bipolar II Disorder
- Cylcothymic Disorder
- Bipolar Disorder Not Otherwise Specified
- Mood Disorder Due to a General Medical Condition
- Substance-Induced Mood Disorder
- Mood Disorder Not Otherwise Specified

Source: American Psychiatric Association. *Diagnostic and Statistical Manual of Mental Disorders. Text Revision.* 4th ed. Washington, D.C.: American Psychiatric Association; 2000;352,356.

or express concern that certain disorders are included and others omitted. The DSM has undergone five revisions with a sixth version (DSM V) due out by 2013. Since the approval of new medications is based on DSM diagnosis, the current committee developing the DSM V is responding to public concerns about drug company influence by minimizing involvement of researchers who have strong ties to the pharmaceutical industry.

The current DSM says you are having a "depressive episode" when you have at least five of the following nine symptoms for most days, nearly every day, for at least two weeks (including one or both of the first two):

- Feeling sad or down.
- Loss of interest in most or all usual activities.
- Changes in usual weight or appetite.
- Changes in usual sleep patterns.
- Changes in usual motor activity, i.e., being restless or slowed down.
- Feeling worthless or excessive guilt.
- Loss of energy.
- Difficulty with concentrating.
- Frequent thoughts of death or suicide.

Just checking off whether you are experiencing enough of the above symptoms is not sufficient. Only a trained professional can determine whether there are other potential causes and whether the severity justifies the diagnosis. Recall from Chapter One the list of possible medical causes for depressive symptoms. Also, as discussed next, not everyone with depression experiences those exact symptoms in the same way.

"There must be some test that says I do or don't have depression."

While researchers can identify changes in certain body chemicals and brain structures that happen in depression, there is great variation in these changes. This makes it hard to reliably say what is normal for any given individual. You can take large groups of people, with and without depression, and calculate average levels of certain hormone levels or neurotransmitters in each group and find differences. You can measure brain waves (electric activity) and the sizes of certain brain structures in groups with and without depression and also find differences. But you cannot yet measure these physical changes in any one person and determine if those findings are normal or abnormal. These bodily changes are useful in proving that there are physical changes with depression but are not useful in diagnosing depression in any one person at this time.

In the mid 1970s there was a great deal of excitement over the use of a simple diagnostic blood test called the Dexamethasone Suppression Test (DST). Cortisol, a hormone produced in the body, is elevated in depression and other stressful conditions. If you give an artificial variation of that hormone, called dexamethasone, to someone without depression, the body produces less cortisol. In someone with depression, cortisol levels do not change when given dexamethsone. Despite a promising debut, later research showed the results were unpredictable because other conditions made it falsely positive or negative. There was also a test to look at abnormal production of thyroid hormone in depression (the thyrotropin-releasing hormone stimulation test or TRH), but it also turned out to be unreliable. Doctors and hospitals still occasionally use these tests when researching new treatments or in situations that are difficult to diagnose or treat.

An electroencephalogram (EEG) measures brain electrical activity. Small wires are attached to the head and detect electrical signals from different parts of the brain. There are some characteristic patterns in people with depression. While these findings are not reliable, there are also characteristic patterns on EEG after someone starts a new medication that may predict whether they will respond to that medication. Given the time, expense, and unpredictability of the test, it is not commonly used.

We know that chemicals in the brain that regulate moods—such as serotonin, norepinephrine, and dopamine—are affected in depression. The levels of these chemicals can be measured in the blood, brain, and urine, but the normal ranges are so diverse that these tests are not useful either. The same is true when measuring the volume of certain brain structures impacted by depression. The findings are inconsistent, and normal ranges are hard to accurately determine.

Since we still do not have a reliable objective test, we have to depend on a trained healthcare professional's opinion based on experience, observation, and interview for now. But scientists are making progress, and a test to help with an evaluation is sure to come in the near future.

Frank's Story Continues

Frank, already skeptical about the depression diagnosis, did a little reading and found the DSM criteria for depression. He took the checklist to his doctor to show him that he only had three of the symptoms. "I told you Doc. I don't have depression, because you have to have at least five of these," he said, pointing to the list." I don't have those other symptoms, so I must not be depressed, right?"

"I don't have those other symptoms, so I must not be depressed, right?"

Maybe, but maybe not. Medical practitioners have long observed that there is great variation in how each person's body functions. When doctors study human anatomy in their first year of medical school by dissecting cadavers, they often find malformed structures or extra organs that baffle the professor. Many diseases present in a variety of ways and respond differently to treatments in different people. We all hear stories about the occasional miraculous survival from a certain fatal illness or successful response to an unusual therapy. Depression is probably more varied than most health problems in how it affects people as well as in its recovery and response to treatment.

Despite all the brain power that has gone into developing the DSM, many patients fall outside these diagnostic categories. Some of the commonly seen signs of depression that are not listed in the DSM include:

• Anger.
• Obsessive rumination.
• Anxiety or phobias.
• Irritability.
• Crying spells.
• Physical pain or preoccupation with physical health.

Does that mean that someone who does not have five or more of nine symptoms but only experiences anger, irritability, and daily thoughts of suicide is not suffering from depression? Healthcare providers frequently diagnose depression even though the person does not exactly meet the DSM definition.

Lucy's Story Continues

Lucy shared with a friend her experience at the therapist's office when the issue of medication came up. She was open with others about her battle with mood symptoms and difficulty with the idea of depression.

"Our society is out of whack," she said. "I think depression is a new disease resulting from the conditions of modern life. Most of us have little balance in our lives. Many of us cannot make ends meet. We work all the time. We don't take care of our bodies or our souls. That's when my depression hit me. I was in college and I remember juggling my work in student government and different volunteer groups while still expecting to keep a 4.0 average. I drove myself into this."

"I think depression is a new disease resulting from the conditions of modern life."

Modern life is difficult as we struggle with rapid changes in technology and the fast-paced demands of work and home. There are concerns about family and communities becoming fragmented as well as fears of global problems such as terrorism or weapons of mass destruction. But is life really more challenging than when there were rampant diseases and plagues and no effective ways to control them? What about life without modern conveniences of refrigeration, grocery stores, and washing machines? It is hard to compare historical levels of stress since every generation has its own challenges.

Depression is not a modern-day invention, nor, as some may claim, is it a result of the medical community labeling every human condition as a disease. The earliest of civilizations have recorded states of profound sadness that affected people's ability to function—even before the arrival of $500-per-hour New York psychoanalysts and the big business of pharmaceuticals. Over time, our understanding of the causes and different forms of depression has changed. Fortunately, some of the more bizarre theories about depression have disappeared, opening the door to a more enlightened view.

Historically, depression was often lumped together with other mental illnesses as though they were all one phenomenon. There was also a pervasive belief that mental illness originated from some negative outside force, such as demons or other evil spirits. These ideas may have planted the seed for later prejudice against those with mental illness. This began to change at the time of Hippocrates, a physician in ancient Greece who lived around 400 BC. He is often described as the "father of medicine." Some of his accomplishments include developing ideas about disease based on scientific observation, encouraging healthy lifestyle choices, and teaching that feelings, thoughts, and emotions come from the brain, not the heart. You may have heard of the famous oath he created that physicians must take after graduating medical school.

Hippocrates taught that the human body was balanced by four humors (or fluids): blood, phlegm, yellow bile, and black bile. Depression was described in his day as "melancholia" and was characterized by mood changes, sleep and appetite problems, and restlessness. The idea that melancholia originates from black bile in the body suggests that even early physicians thought of depression as having a biological cause. Greek and Roman medical practitioners also supported the notion that life stressors and bad lifestyle choices, such as excessive consumption of wine and poor sleep habits, could cause depression.

Other descriptions and possible causes are found in medieval Arabic medical texts and those of sixteenth- to eighteenth-century Europe. The preeminent physicians of those times postulated theories including inflammation of the brain or poor circulation. Throughout this time there were also strong religious forces that suggested depression was a result of a spiritual disconnect. By the ninteenth century, the common term melancholia was replaced by the term depression because of the work of German psychiatrist Emil Kreaplin. He is considered by some to be the father of modern psychiatry because he created the foundation for the current classification system of mental-health syndromes. He was also a strong advocate for the biological and genetic basis of mood disorders.

Most people are more familiar with Sigmund Freud, who first described the concept of the unconscious. He developed many theories on how the mind processes information, and how the unconscious impacts one's thoughts, behaviors, and feelings. These ideas became the basis for internal psychological conflict as a trigger for depression and anxiety and the beginning of psychoanalysis and modern-day psychotherapy. Proving his theories has been challenging because they are based on his observations while working with a handful of patients and were not tested in a way that is considered scientifically reliable.

We now have far more sophisticated techniques of evaluating the role of psychological, environmental, and biological factors in depression. Some believe that nowadays there is too much emphasis on the physical nature of depression and too many research dollars going into developing medication therapies. We may have gone from a historical state of ignorance to an overemphasis on the biological origins, losing sight of other factors that may play a role in depression and its treatment.

Jane's Story Continues

&& I remember asking my psychology professor in college 'What are my odds of getting depression?'" said Jane. "I knew it must be high since my mother had depression, her mother had it, and I am sure whatever gene in our family causes depression has been kindly left to me to pass on to future generations." Jane shared this with her doctor when asked whether she wants children.

"And I am in no rush to have kids. I have heard some scary statistics about how depression is passed down in families. Why would I want to pass this on to anyone? What is the risk of depression if it runs in your family? I am sure it must be high. Do you think they can test me for a depression gene?"

"What are my odds of getting depression?"

It seems that more and more people are being diagnosed with depression and prescribed antidepressants. Is the number of people with depression truly growing, or are we just hearing more about it? Celebrities, politicians, and other high-profile individuals have become more public about their struggles with depression. What was once an illness associated with shame and blame has now become a topic of conversation from television talk shows to dinner parties.

No one knows how many people may have suffered from depression in earlier generations and whether those numbers are truly increasing over time. Even figuring out today's depression rates is difficult. Insurance companies know how many of their insured are being treated for depression, but there are many more people with depression who do not get help, or they don't use insurance if they do. Even if they are on antidepressants, they could be taking them for other problems since these medicines have other uses as well. So, how do we calculate your chances of getting depression?

There is no way researchers can factor in all the variables that put one at risk for depression. If the risk of depression for a male adult in the United States is 10 percent, how would that change if you were a non–English-speaking immigrant from Nigeria with a traumatic childhood, an alcoholic mother, and long family history of mental illness? These statistics help give us ideas about the general risk but are not as useful in calculating *your* specific risk.

The percentage of people who currently experience depression and the number predicted to have had it in their lifetime are called current and lifetime prevalence rates. The most comprehensive studies performed in the last 25 years showed current rates of depression in the United States ranging from 3 to 9 percent (average 6 percent) and lifetime rates from 5 to 16 percent (average 13 percent).

These rates are impressive and do support depression as a major public health problem. As a matter of fact, the World Health Organization (WHO) published a report in 2007 on the impact of depression worldwide, showing global rates of depression at about 3 percent. Depression was also shown to have a worse impact on one's overall health than the four most common chronic diseases: angina (heart disease), arthritis, asthma, and diabetes. It is a leading cause of disability and the fourth leading contributor to global burden of disease.

All that said, figuring out your individual risk is more complicated. You may have at least a 13 percent risk of having depression in your lifetime, but many factors could raise or lower that number. Your lifestyle, history of traumatic life events, stress level, social supports, social and economic status, genetic predisposition, and ethnicity all play a role. No matter what your risk, you can significantly improve your chances of staying well by 1.) being proactive in lifestyle choices that reduce your chances, and 2.) getting help if you start to notice problems.

"What is the risk of depression if it runs in your family?"

Depression can run in families. If you have a parent who is depressed, you have a three times greater risk than someone who does not have a depressed parent. Is that because growing up around a depressed family member is in itself depressing or teaches children poor coping skills? Could it be that families are exposed to similar stressful life events? While these could be factors that contribute to mood problems, there is other evidence that there may be some shared genes that can put you at additional risk. The good news is that an increase in genetic risk does not mean you will definitely get depression, but simply that you are more vulnerable.

Genes are the instructions the body uses to manufacture life-sustaining proteins. Normal variations of genes determine something as innocuous as brown hair or blue eyes. Other genetic variations can be life threatening. If you are tested and have the genetic abnormality for Huntington's disease, for example, you have a 50 percent chance of the neurological disorder occurring, while having the extra gene associated with Down's syndrome gives you near certainty of being born with the condition. Unlike those diseases associated with one gene alteration, a hereditary risk of depression is related to many different genes. That means it is harder to accurately predict your risk since we still do not understand how all those depression related genes work together.

Evidence for genes playing a role in developing depression in families is the observation that an identical twin (sharing 100 percent of genes) of a person with depression is at much greater risk of also becoming depressed (70 to 75 percent) than is a fraternal twin (sharing 50 percent of genes) of a person with depression (20 to 25 percent). If it were only environmental, both types of twins would have a similar risk. Scientists have also isolated possible depression genes. One gene tells the body to make a protein that regulates serotonin, a chemical that impacts mood and anxiety (more on that in Chapter Three). If that gene is altered, you are more likely to get depressed than someone with a normal version of the gene if both are under a high level of stress.

Researchers have followed children who were adopted but had biological parents with depression. They were small studies, but the results support an increased risk of depression in those children. Also, an adopted child with depression is more likely to have depression among their biological relatives than their adoptive relatives. It appears that depression is likely "nature and nurture"; i.e., genetic and environmental.

"Do you think they can test me for a depression gene?"

Not yet. A 13-year project called the Human Genome Project began in 1990 with the goal of identifying all 20,000 to 25,000 genes in human DNA. While the project has been completed, it will take years for the full analysis to be finished. Despite all that scientists learned, they still cannot identify all the depression genes or how they interact with one another. However, they can already better identify risk of illnesses like Crohn's Disease, Parkinson Disease, diabetes, prostate and breast cancer, and rheumatoid arthritis.

Even if you do carry genes that increase your risk for depression, you may need certain environmental conditions to trigger it. Someone with genes that increase their risk for breast cancer or diabetes may only develop the diseases with poor diet or lack of exercise. The same may be true for depression. A genetic predisposition combined with stress, traumatic life events, unsupportive home environment, alcohol or illicit drugs, and poor coping skills can be just the right recipe for a depressive episode. A high genetic risk may require fewer environmental triggers, while a low risk may mean many environmental triggers are needed to set off an episode.

Whether genetically predisposed to depression or not, you should take good care of yourself by eating right, reducing stress, and taking good care of your body. A family history of depression in your family should be a warning to take extra care of yourself and to watch for signs of depression, should the symptoms occur in yourself or someone close to you.

Chris' Story Continues

Chris came into his psychiatrist's office with reams of paper in hand printed off the Internet.

"I have been doing a lot of research. All you ever told me was that I have depression, but there are many different kinds. What are the different types of depression? What is my depression type? My friend Carol told me that her doctor diagnosed her with a condition called dysthymia. When I looked it up online, it sure sounded like me. I also took a test from an Internet site that said I had more anxiety than depression. It even said I could be bipolar! Isn't that manic–depression? I know someone like that and I don't think that's me. I am moody at times. Do you think I could be bipolar? What about melancholic depression? What is that? If you know my depression type, will it change my treatment? How can I get tested for these types of depressions?"

"What are the different types of depression?"

Not everyone with depression has the same symptoms or is affected in the same way. While one person may get up every day, go to work and seem normal in their functioning, another may struggle to simply to get out of bed and take care of their basic needs like eating or bathing. Some overcome depression with a brief course of counseling or a small dose of the first antidepressant they try. Others may find no help in medicine after medicine, need years of regular psychotherapy, or even require such aggressive treatments as hospitalization or electroshock therapy. How do we account for these differences? There are many different kinds of depression, and you may hear a variety of different terms used to describe depression such as:

- Unipolar depression.
- Major depression.
- Endogenous depression.
- Manic-depression.

Healthcare professionals use some terms differently from the non-medical public. For instance, melancholia may mean sad to most people but, to medical professionals, melancholia describes a specific depression type. People often use the term bipolar to describe feeling moody. The terms nervous breakdown, and clinical or chemical depression, are commonly used but have no scientific meaning.

Giving someone a diagnosis of depression is as non-specific as a diagnosis of cancer. Cancer can mean a life-threatening brain tumor or a benign, easily removed skin cancer. Similarly, a mild, chronic depression may prevent someone from fully enjoying life and impact their success at work or relationships, while a severe, major depressive episode can stop one from eating, getting out of bed, and in the worst of circumstances, can lead to suicide.

To get the right treatment, your doctor must know what type of depression you have since different depressions can require very different interventions. Asking your doctor for a medicine to treat depression is like asking for a medicine to treat chest pain. Chest pain from a heart attack is treated very differently from that caused by a pulled muscle or lung infection, such as pneumonia. Even if your chest pain is from pneumonia, many different infectious agents can cause similar symptoms such as trouble breathing, fever, and weakness. An antibiotic that is effective with one infection may do little good, or even be harmful, with a different type of infection, so it is important to identify the correct type of pneumonia.

Depression types can share some, or many, symptoms, but may not respond equally to treatment with the same antidepressant. Someone with atypical depression may have a better chance of responding to a certain family of antidepressants than would someone with melancholic depression. Antidepressants can actually worsen bipolar depression in some cases. Other depressions may not even need, or respond to, medicine and require a different treatment altogether, such as psychotherapy or cognitive-behavioral counseling. Certain depressions are more likely to affect people at an earlier age, respond better to treatment, or come back more frequently than others. Some may require medication therapy for a short period of time, while others need medicine indefinitely. If you know your depression type, you will have a better idea of what to expect and a better chance of getting the right help.

There are nine different mood disorders described in the most recent DSM (DSM-IV-R). Depressive episodes are most commonly associated with having major depression, but they can be seen in the other mood disorders as well. Each of these mood disorders has features that distinguish them from one another even though the depressive episode (described earlier as having at least five of nine possible symptoms) can look very similar. The list of current mood disorders is bound to change over time as our knowledge about depression evolves and our method of classification changes.

The "major" in major depression does not mean it is the most serious of depressions. Any of the mood disorders can be more or less serious, or more or less difficult to treat than another. Major depression has four different subtypes (melancholic, atypical, catatonic, and post-partum) that have a unique set of symptoms and a number of additional qualifiers to help doctors determine the right course of treatment. These include:

- Whether the person has had depression before.
- The severity of symptoms.
- Whether the depression is of a long or short duration.
- Whether it is psychotic or non-psychotic.
- Whether there is a seasonal or non-seasonal pattern.
- Whether there has been full recovery between episodes.

Keeping all these subtypes and qualifiers straight can get overwhelming, and may not even be all that useful, unless you make a living studying and researching depression. Your doctor may tell you that "you have depression," but your technical diagnosis may be, "major depression, recurrent, severe, without psychotic symptoms, with full interepisode recovery." A doctor, or other mental-healthcare specialist, would rarely use that official DSM terminology to describe the type of depression to a patient, but such language may be found on a comprehensive psychological testing result or other report. Here is a quick breakdown of the different subtypes of major depression:

Melancholic: Melancholic depression, or melancholia, refers to a particular type of depression that affects around 10 percent of people with major depression. There are signs that this depression type may have more of a biological basis than psychological and may respond better to medical treatments than psychotherapy. You must meet criteria for major depression but also have one or both of the following:

- Little or no pleasure in nearly all activities.
- Mood does not improve even if something very good happens.

And also at least three of the following:

- Mood feels very different than when someone you are close with dies.
- Mood is worse in the morning.
- Wake up two or more hours earlier than normal.

- Feel either really slowed down or agitated.
- Little to no appetite or a lot of weight loss.
- Feel very guilty about things you shouldn't or more guilt than others would about the same situation.

Atypical: This may be the most common subtype of depression, affecting an estimated 25 to 40 percent of people with depression. This affects women more than men (70 versus 30 percent) and is more likely to cause disability, suicidal thoughts, or have other psychiatric problems. With atypical depression, your mood can still brighten up when something good happens and you must have at least two of the following:

- Increased appetite or weight gain.
- Sleeping too much.
- Feeling like your arms and legs are heavy or weighed down.
- Very sensitive to feeling rejected by others, affecting your ability to work or relate well to other people, even when not feeling depressed.

Post-partum: Many women feel sad, overwhelmed, or moody after giving birth to a child. This can result from hormone changes, sleep disturbances, and new lifestyle demands. Post-partum depression is an abnormal extreme of the more common "post-partum blues" and can become very serious if not identified and treated early. It is estimated that between 50 and 75 percent of women get "baby blues" and up to 13 percent of woman develop post-partum depression (as compared to 7 to 10 percent risk of depression in the general population).

Post-partum depression has symptoms that are similar to other types of depression but is diagnosed when it occurs within four weeks of giving birth. A woman is at higher risk of developing post-partum depression if she has any of the following:

- Past history of depression or depression associated with menstrual cycle (premenstrual dysphoric disorder, or PMDD).
- Younger age during pregnancy.
- Depression while pregnant.
- Marriage problems, single parenthood, or limited social supports.
- Family history of depression or past-partum depression.

Also, the more children a woman has, the higher her risk.

The biggest concern with post-partum depression is the rare, but

DSM IV-R Criteria for Hypomania and Mania

Bipolar disorder, also known as manic-depression, is characterized by episodes of mania or hypomania and usually (though not always) depression.

A **hypomanic episode** is characterized by the following:
1. A distinct period of persistently elevated, expansive, or irritable mood, lasting throughout at least four days, that is clearly different from the usual nondepressed mood.
2. During the period of mood disturbance, three (or more) of the following symptoms have persisted (four if the mood is only irritable) and have been present to a significant degree:
   - Inflated self-esteem or grandiosity.
   - Less need for sleep (i.e., feels rested after only three hours).
   - More talkative than usual or pressure to keep talking.
   - Flight of ideas or subjective experience that thoughts are racing.
   - Distractibility (i.e., attention too easily drawn to unimportant or irrelevant external stimuli).
   - Increase in goal-directed activity (at work, at school, or sexually) or psychomotor agitation.
   - Excessive involvement in pleasurable activities that have a high potential for painful consequences (i.e., engaging in unrestrained buying sprees, sexual indiscretions, or foolish business investments).

Note: The mood disturbance is not severe enough to cause marked impairment in social or occupational functioning, or to necessitate hospitalization, and there are no psychotic features.

A **manic episode** is characterized by the same criteria as in hypomania with two exceptions:
1. The duration of the mood problems is at least one week or is severe enough to require hospitalization.
2. Unlike hypomania, the mood disturbance is sufficiently severe to cause marked impairment in occupational functioning or in usual social activities or relationships with others, or to necessitate hospitalization to prevent harm to self or others, or there are psychotic features.

Source: American Psychiatric Association. *Diagnostic and Statisti-*

cal *Manual of Mental Disorders. Text Revision.* 4th ed. Washington, DC: American Psychiatric Association; 2000;352,356.

serious, risk of post-partum psychosis. This can have serious consequences and may represent a very severe form of depression or possible underlying bipolar disorder. A woman can become agitated, confused, and even experience paranoia or hallucinations. When you hear tragic stories in the news about a new mother doing something terrible to her child, it is often a result of post-partum psychosis. The good news is that it is uncommon and, if recognized and treated early, these women, and their children, do very well.

Catatonic: This is a rare type of depression that causes changes in motor movements. In extreme cases, someone can look frozen with their arms or legs locked in one place or exhibit strange, purposeless movements. While the description may seem frightening, keep in mind that most mental-health professionals see only one or two of these cases in their whole career.

Other types of depression include:

Dysthymia: This is a more chronic, low-grade depression, but it can still have a significant impact on one's ability to fully enjoy and participate in life. Those with dysthymia are at high risk for developing major depression as well (called double depression). You must have a depressed mood most days for at least two years and have two or more of the following:

- Poor appetite or overeating.
- Insomnia or hypersomnia.
- Low energy or fatigue.
- Low self esteem.
- Poor concentration.
- Feelings of hopelessness.

Depression Not Otherwise Specified (NOS): This category captures those who are clearly suffering from some type of depressive disorder but do not meet any specific criteria. Some examples include women with depressed symptoms around their menstrual cycles or depression that lasts two weeks but does not have five of the nine symptoms for major depression.

Bipolar Disorder I, II, Cyclothymia, Bipolar NOS: These mood disorders are typically thought of as different types of manic-depression or bipolar disorder. A diagnosis of bipolar I is given if someone has had at least one manic episode or mixed episode (features of a manic and depressive episode at the same time). A diagnosis of bipolar I does not require a depressive episode, but most experience some depression if their condition is not well controlled. A hypomanic episode differs from a manic episode in that you only need to have the symptoms for four days and the severity is far less. If you have never had a full manic episode, only hypomania, then you are diagnosed with bipolar II. Depressive episodes are common in bipolar II but not required for the condition. Cylothymia is similar to dysthymia in that it is low-grade mood disorder (lasting at least two years or more) with hypomania and mild depression but does not meet the full criteria for a depressive episode. Bipolar Not Otherwise Specified (NOS) is another catch-all category for those with symptoms highly suggestive of bipolar disorder but which does not meet the full criteria for any other category.

More people reporting mostly problems with depression are being diagnosed with bipolar disorder than in years past. Medical doctors such as family physicians who treat depression but do not specialize in treating mental-health problems are learning more about bipolar disorder and are getting better about asking the right questions to identify it. They have not always aggressively explored bipolar symptoms with their patients, who are not often aware of them, do not feel they are important to share with their doctor, or are too embarrassed to mention them. Antidepressants can trigger manic or hypomanic episodes. As more people are exposed to antidepressants, more cases of bipolar depression are being uncovered. Also, new medications coming to market to treat bipolar disorder have increased awareness of the condition. One sign of possible bipolar disorder, if there is no obvious history of hypomanic or manic symptoms, is if someone does not respond to multiple antidepressants or is intolerant of them.

Mood Disorder Due to a Medical Condition, Substance-Induced Mood Disorder, and Mood Disorder Not Otherwise Specified (NOS): These three mood disorders are lumped together because they fit outside the typical area of what we commonly think of when someone is depressed. Mood disorder due to a general medical condition is exactly that—a medical condition causes depression that resolves when the condition is treated. Some examples include hypothyroidism (low thyroid hormone), multiple sclerosis, or stroke. At times, depression can be caused by taking certain prescription medicines, using illicit drugs, or consuming excessive amounts of alcohol. Usually, stopping the casual agent is sufficient for treatment. Mood disorder NOS is for those who clearly have some mood impairment but there are so many other factors or uncharacteristic symptoms that make a clear diagnosis impossible.

"If you know my depression type, will it change my treatment?"

Research demonstrates that different depressive types may do better with certain medicine (and non-medicine) treatments. This research is also more evidence that categorizing depression into different types is legitimate, otherwise treatments would not differ among them. Unfortunately, correctly identifying your depression type does not ensure you will respond to that treatment, but it can improve the odds.

Melancholic: This seems to respond better to the older family of medicines called the tricyclic antidepressants, which typically affect more chemicals or neurotransmitters in the brain than the more commonly used newer medicines. The different families of antidepressants are reviewed in more detail in Chapter Three. Tricyclic antidepressants usually tie, or beat, newer medicines in effectiveness. Of the newer medicines, those that work on two or more neurotransmitters do better in melancholic depression than those that work on only one neurotransmitter. A downside of tricyclic antidepressants is that they cause more side effects and can pose more safety concerns, so your doctor may still try you on a newer medicine in hopes that you will respond with far fewer risks and side effects. Electroshock therapy (ECT), which is considered one of the strongest therapies, is also very helpful.

Melancholic depression is less responsive to placebos and certain types of non-medicine therapy, such as cognitive therapy or interpersonal psychotherapy. This is evidence that melancholic depression has more of a biological basis than non-melancholic depression.

Non-melancholic: Non-melancholic depression includes all forms of major depression that do not meet criteria for melancholic, atypical, catatonic, or post-partum depression. The newer antidepressants (SSRIs, or selective serotonin reuptake inhibitors) that work on the neurotransmitter and serotonin (Prozac, Zoloft, etc.) are just as effective in non-melancholic depression as the more potent tricyclics. SSRIs are easier to start and have fewer side effects or safety concerns than tricylics. Some of the non-medicine therapies, like cognitive therapy or interpersonal psychotherapy, are also quite effective. This suggests that there may be less of a biological basis and less aggressive medicine treatment is required for this type of depression.

Catatonic and psychotic: These two depression types represent a more serious form of depression that often requires more than just antidepressant treatment. They must be treated early and aggressively, usually requiring a mood stabilizer or antipsychotic medicine as well—at least for a short time. Some believe that, in certain cases, these depressions may be forms of bipolar illness or other psychiatric disorders. Occasionally if someone's health is in danger, electroconvulsive therapy (ECT) is used because it works fast.

Psychosis can occur in many types of depression and simply means there is a distortion in one's ability to perceive what is real and what is not. Although the term has a strong negative connotation in the non-medical community, it is not always as bad as it sounds. Severe cases of psychosis can mean paranoid thoughts or hearing voices in your head or seeing things that are not real. If you believe these are real, it may cause you to do things that are harmful to yourself or others. Often though, psychosis in depression can mean trouble getting your thoughts together, being easily confused, or feeling disconnected or out of place. Psychotic depression only responds to antidepressants 20 percent of the time, but this goes up to 60 to 70 percent if an antipsychotic is taken simultaneously.

Post-partum: As in non-melancholic depression, tricylic antidepressants and the SSRIs seem to be equally effective in treating post-partum depression. The main reason for using SSRIs in post-partum depression are the better side-effect profile and less weight-gain risk. Also, many of the SSRIs have been studied in breastfeeding women and seem to be safe for both mother and baby. If there are signs of post-partum psychosis, then an antipsychotic or mood stabilizer is usually required.

Can Men Get Post-Partum Depression?

About 10 percent of men who become fathers have symptoms of moderate to major depression following the birth of their child. This is compared to 5 to 7 percent of the general male population.

Bipolar: This can be a complicated area when it comes to treatment, and there are many different opinions on the subject. Generally, antidepressants should be avoided in bipolar depression, since there is little evidence that they help and may even worsen symptoms in some cases. Despite the research against their use, many doctors still use them with caution at times, because their experience shows they help in certain situations. The best medication treatment is the use of mood stabilizers.

Atypical: Another older class of antidepressants called the monoamine oxidase inhibitors (MAOIs) have been shown to work better in this depression type than the tricyclic antidepressants. MAOIs are not commonly used because they require you to avoid certain foods, medicines, and alcohols. They can cause uncomfortable, and even dangerous, side effects (listed in Chapter Three). But they are also highly effective and safe medicines when taken responsibly.

Frank's Story Continues

Frank conceded that maybe something more than just stress was going on as he answered the doctor's questions about how he was doing. But he still refused to see a psychiatrist or counselor to confirm his doctor's diagnosis.

"Isn't there some quick and easy test to see if I might really have depression?" he asked. "I saw some questionnaires in your waiting room."

"Isn't there some quick and easy test to see if I might really have depression?"

There are many screening tools and rating scales available in print and on the Internet that will tell whether you may have depression and its possible severity. While some of these must be completed by a professional who is trained to administer the test, you can do some yourself. These tests are helpful in clinical research studies to monitor specific symptom improvement with a certain treatment. They can help a doctor or counselor with questions they may not have asked. In addition, if someone scores high on a self-administered test, it may prompt them to seek professional help. However, these tests are not meant to be used alone to make a diagnosis.

Two of the more common scales used in clinical trials are the Hamilton Rating Scale for Depression (HAM-D) and Montgomery Asberg Depression Rating Scale (MADRS). Each must be administered by someone trained to use it, though there are also self-reported versions. Most doctors find these scales too lengthy to use on a routine basis and prefer to tailor their own questions for diagnosis and measuring improvement. Several self-reported scales include Beck Depression Inventory of depression, Quick Inventory of Depressive Symptomotology Self Report (QIDS), and Zung depression rating scale. These can be found easily on the Internet. There are many others, but each has its limitations. Two of the easiest to use to self-assess depression and possible bipolar disorder are the PHQ-9 and MDQ, respectively (see Appendix B "Mood Disorders Questionnaire" and Appendix C "Patient Health Questionnaire").

Now that you know more about depression and the depression types, I explore some of the exciting new discoveries about how depression impacts the brain as well as some of our current understanding of how antidepressants work. This information has practical applications for choosing whether to go on an antidepressant, which antidepressant to take, and when to stop.

Chapter Three

Changing the Depressed Brain

How Antidepressants Work

D r. Gregory listened intently to everything Frank and his wife had shared about the changes in Frank's mood and behavior over the last year. He also heard loud and clear that Frank was not open to a diagnosis of depression or taking another medicine to help with his problems.

Frank's wife pointed out that he'd been through more difficult times in his life, but had handled things better than now. Wasn't he feeling worse than the situation warranted? Would he consider that the doctor might be right?

Frank replied, "I already take too many pills. I have two for my heart, one for my leg pain, three for my breathing, and now you want me to take one for my brain. Why do I have to take a medicine to feel normal? Can you explain to me in a way I can understand what's going on in my head making me feel depressed?"

One of the more convincing arguments for taking an antidepressant is that depression is a medical condition that affects the normal functioning of the human body. In order to prove that, there must be some evidence that real physical change takes place in the body and medication can reverse those changes. This has been difficult to demonstrate until scientists developed the technology to be able to look inside the brain and observe what happens when someone suffers from depression. The last 50 years has brought an explosion of information in this area.

How Many Nerve Cells Are in the Brain?

The brain is made up of about 100 billion neurons, which, if stretched end to end, would extend about 4 million miles (about the distance of all the roads and streets in the United States *put together*).

But, like a complex jigsaw puzzle, we have many small pieces of data but do not quite know how they all fit together.

This chapter focuses on possible biological causes and effects of depression. There are also many plausible psychological theories explaining mood disorders but these are reviewed in Chapter Five.

The brain is made up of intricate connections of billions of nerve cells. These nerve cells continuously maintain vital bodily functions, monitor everything we sense in our environment, and regulate our emotional reactions to events going on around us. The brain constantly multitasks.

Imagine yourself dining at a nice restaurant. Your brain must juggle the manual dexterity to consume that spicy pasta primavera while simultaneously coordinating your enjoyment of the delicious taste of your meal, engaging in intellectually stimulating conversation with your dining partner, keeping your body temperature at precisely 98.7 degrees, and maintaining your heart rate at an even 72 beats per minute. Of course, these are only a few of the many functions going on at any given time in your body. Nerve cells, or neurons, communicate with one another to carry out these complex tasks through a combination of chemical and electrical activities. With new technologies, we can now measure these activities. Researchers can compare their observations of those with, and without, depression, as well as before and after medication treatment.

Anyone deciding whether or not to take medication should understand how depression affects their brain and body. Even if you still choose an alternative to taking an antidepressant, you will see how important it is to get some type of help. Some people who are not scientifically inclined feel intimidated when trying to muddle through complex information about brain anatomy and neurochemistry. Once you learn the language scientists use to describe certain areas and functions of the brain, you can grasp most anything you read on the subject. This chapter will help by covering:

- What physical changes occur in the brain with depression.
- How depression affects your body and physical health.
- How antidepressants work.
- How antidepressants differ from one another.
- The risk to your brain and body if you do not get treatment.

Some of this material includes new terminology and gets very detailed. If you have a passion for science and are interested in more specifics, additional information as well as a glossary of terms is included in the side bars. You will capture the essence of the material even if you pass on the sections that seem a bit too technical for your liking. Remember, there is no test at the end of the chapter so you don't have to worry about anything you choose to skip.

"Can you explain to me in a way I can understand what's going on in my head making me feel depressed?"

If you look at the human body from an evolutionary perspective, mechanisms have developed to keep you safe from dangers in your environment. Some of these defenses include learning and remembering what is potentially harmful—such as poisonous snakes or dark alleys late at night—and developing quick reactions for protection. One of those reactions is the "flight or fight" response, a preprogrammed response that happens when you feel threatened. Your heart beats quickly, breathing gets heavier, and blood vessels constrict allowing you to flee from the danger or fight. These serve as automatic responses to learned information about what may be dangerous. If you have to take much time deciding whether something is safe, or thinking too long about how to respond, it will probably be too late to do so.

To facilitate this, the brain is organized in such a way that the parts that control our five senses form and keep memories (particularly ones with strong emotional associations), regulate our vital functions such as heart rate and breathing, generate emotions, and impact our behavioral responses all tie together. This whole system talks to itself through various hormones and a group of proteins called neurotransmitters (NT).

Another protective mechanism is through the body's immune system that helps you fight off foreign objects that get inside your body such as bacteria or viruses. An inflammatory response is the redness, swelling, and pain that occur when an irritant enters your body such as a bee sting or poison ivy. This causes a release of chemicals called inflammation. Inflammation is one way the body protects and heals you when you are injured.

There is evidence that some or all of these normal defense mechanisms are not working properly in someone with depression. Either parts of the brain, or the chemicals that regulate brain function and inflammation, malfunction because of genetic abnormalities or as a result of being overworked due to chronic stress or trauma. New scientific research tools demonstrate changes in the size and physical functioning of many brain areas as well as alterations in neurotransmitters and hormones. When the system no longer functions properly, you begin to experience the signs and symptoms of depression. What is not certain is whether depression is the result of these changes or whether depression itself causes these changes to occur.

Chris' Story Continues

Chris brought out several pamphlets about depression from the waiting room. He pointed out to the doctor several complicated illustrations of what happens to the brain when someone has depression, pictures of sections of the brain that looked like they should be on a movie marquee of a bad horror film, and cartoon drawings of complex shapes that were supposed to illustrate nerve cells in the brain. Dozens of little round balls scattered about the drawing represented brain chemicals tossed about from neuron to neuron.

Chris expressed his frustration: "I'm not a science guy, and I can't understand all these diagrams and drawings. I know depression is a brain disease, but I can't understand what is happening in all the different areas. Can you explain the different parts of the brain and how it all works? I have heard depression is a chemical imbalance in the brain. What are these chemicals they mention—serotonin, norepinephrine, and dopamine? How are they related to depression?"

**"Can you explain the different parts
of the brain and how it all works?"**

If you want to know where and how depression impacts the brain, you need to understand its basic structure and functioning. The brain is the control center for the human nervous system and has many complex, interconnected parts. Some parts of the human brain resemble those found in the nervous system of primitive organisms such as fish and reptiles. Other areas are similar to those seen in more evolved animals such as dogs and monkeys. The less evolved areas regulate essential body functions like eating, drinking, breathing, and avoiding danger. The more evolved parts play a role in controlling one's thoughts, feelings, and impulses as well as coordinating the use of language and conscious thought. The brain is divided into the brainstem, cerebellum, cerebrum, and limbic system, each managing different bodily functions.

The brainstem is located at the base of the brain and connects with the spinal cord. It regulates basic critical activities such as breathing, heart rate, and blood pressure. The brainstem also helps keep you awake, alert, and conscious. The cerebellum is located in the lower backside of the brain and controls coordination and motor movements. The cerebrum is the top part of the brain. It is the largest and most evolved area. This is what you see when you look at most pictures of the brain (see

The Limbic System

The hypothalamus receives sensory information from all the parts of the brain and acts like the body's thermostat. It adjusts your temperature if you are hot or cold; tells you if you are hungry or thirsty; controls your autonomic nervous system, including heart rate, blood pressure, breathing; determines levels of pleasure and pain, and adjusts your emotional responses. It sends signals to other parts of the brain to release certain hormones and NTs that control your body's response to stress. The hippocampus helps you convert your thoughts into longer-term memories, and the amygdale helps generate emotional and behavioral responses when you are threatened. If the hippocampus does not work properly, you have trouble forming new memories. When the amygdale is damaged, people become passive and less emotionally reactive to stress. The cingulate gyrus also affects emotions, learning, and memory formation. The prefrontal cortex takes information from the other areas of the limbic system and helps with planning complex tasks, making decisions, and determining what is a good and bad choice based on the possible outcome of our actions.

Figure 1). It has two halves, the right and left hemisphere, and is composed of four lobes that carry out different tasks. Memory, learning, motor control, language, communication, thoughts, and processing information from our senses are just a few of the vital functions performed by the cerebrum. The limbic system is composed of several connected and interrelated structures that play an important role in moods, emotions, memory, and behavior. Some of the limbic structures include the hippocampus, amygdale, cingulated gyrus, hypothalamus, and thalamus. All these different parts of the brain communicate with each other through an exchange of chemicals.

A normally functioning limbic system receives input from areas of the brain that pick up information from one or more of the five senses, such as a sound of footsteps behind you when walking in the park. The amygdala or hippocampus maintain a "rolodex" of emotions and memories and help determine if the sound is familiar and if it is likely from something friendly or dangerous. If you had an experience in the past with being chased in the woods or you heard others have been attacked recently in the park, these limbic structures will send alarm bells to the hypothalamus and other areas. This generates a release of neurotransmitters and hormones that help put you in a "fight or flight" mode.

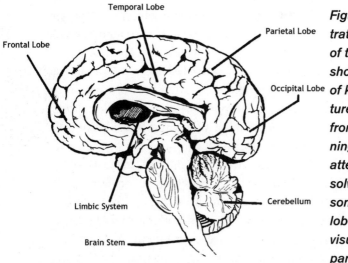

Figure 1. This illustrated cross-section of the human brain shows the location of key brain structures, including frontal lobe (planning, organizing, attention, problem solving, and personality), occipital lobe (understanding visual images), parietal lobe (reading, writing, language, math, and identifying sensory input), temporal lobe (memory, sensory input, learning, and language), limbic system (emotion, behavior, and memory), brain stem (connecting brain to spinal cord, and regulating breathing and blood pressure), and cerebellum (balance, posture, coordination, and emotion).

When your prefrontal cortex receives this information, it does its job of planning and organizing, telling you to reach for your cell phone and call 911. It may also warn you not to take a swing at whatever is behind you without looking in case it is an innocent bystander. Messages are also sent to other areas of the brain, including your brainstem (which helps keep your alertness, heart rate, blood pressure, and breathing up), cerebellum (which helps coordinate the fine movement in your arms and legs, making you run better), and the cerebral cortex (which helps you recall the little dog following you the whole time that you forgot about). You realize that sound of footsteps was the dog and you feel safe enough to shout at the little critter for scaring you so much (see Figure 2). That is a simplified version of how the different parts of the brain work together to keep you alive and safe.

"I have heard depression is a chemical imbalance in the brain. What are these chemicals and what do they do?"

Many different chemicals are involved in normal brain functioning, and they each play an important role in how the brain talks to itself. If something goes wrong with this method of communication, the system cannot work properly.

The brain is made up of a variety of cells, including nerves (or neurons) and other cells that support the neurons so they can perform their

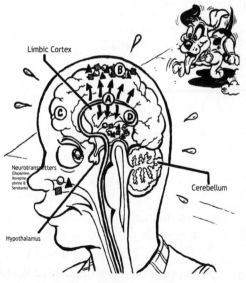

Figure 2. This is an illustration of how the brain regions work together to respond to stress. For example, a man is walking in the park and hears the sounds of something following closely behind him. Parts of the limbic system that control memory signal the brain that danger could be close at hand. Neurotransmitters are released in the areas of the brain that control heart rate, breathing, and movement to take defensive action, such as running away. When the senses pick up the signs that it's just a friendly dog in pursuit, the system turns off the stress response.

Limbic Cortex

Neurotransmitters
(Dopamine,
Norepine
phrine &
Serotonin)

Hypothalamus

Cerebellum

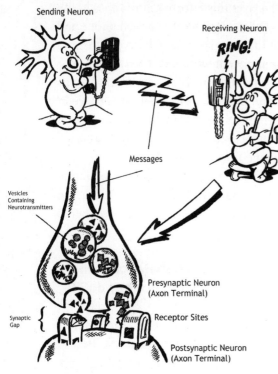

Sending Neuron

Receiving Neuron

RING!

Messages

Vesicles Containing Neurotransmitters

Presynaptic Neuron (Axon Terminal)

Synaptic Gap

Receptor Sites

Postsynaptic Neuron (Axon Terminal)

Figure 3. This illustration is a visual representation of how two neurons talk to one another. The sending or presynaptic neuron sends chemicals (neurotransmitters, or NTs) across the synapse to the receiving or postsynaptic neuron to relate a specific message. Each receptor on the receiving neuron is designed to receive a certain type of neurotransmitter, such as serotonin, norepinephrine, or dopamine.

job. The neurons communicate to one another through a complex system of chemical and electrical impulses that occur in milliseconds. Neurons do not directly touch each other, but instead have a small space between them called the synapse. Neurotransmitters, chemicals manufactured in the neuron, are packaged, stored, and released out into the synapse from one neuron and used to send a message to an adjacent neuron. The neuron that manufactures and releases the NT is called the presynaptic neuron and the neuron that receives the NT is called the postsynaptic neuron (see Figure 3).

Another important player in this communication process is the receptor. Receptors are made up of amino acids: molecules that share certain characteristics and come together to form life-sustaining proteins. Receptors are located on the outer protective covering of the neuron called the cell membrane. When the amino acids making up the receptor come together, they form a unique three-dimensional shape that is specially designed to fit a certain NT. The receptor is often described as being a lock and the NT a key. When the NT fits into the receptor, a message is generated chemically or electrically into the post-synaptic neuron (see Figure 4).

When scientists observed many years ago that several medicines used to treat a variety of health problems had an unintended effect on mood, they proposed that chemical imbalances might be at play. One such medicine was a high blood pressure medicine, reserpine (no longer on the market), that was found to make people depressed. It worked by lowering levels of the NT norepinephrine (NE), a clue that maybe NTs also played a role in regulating emotions. Scientists soon discovered other medicines that increased chemicals in the brain called serotonin (5-HT) and dopamine (DA). NE, 5-HT, and DA are all related and are classified in a group called monoamines. The medicines that affected monamine levels also seemed to affect moods. This led to the "monoamine hypothesis" that implicated one or more of these NTs as the cause of depression.

Parts of a Neuron

The neuron has three main parts that are relevant for learning how depression affects the brain and for understanding how antidepressants work.

- **Dendrites:** long, branching arms of the neuron that mainly receive messages from surrounding neurons and transmit the information to the cell body.
- **Cell Body:** the control center of the neuron that contains the genetic material to manufacture NT and other life sustaining proteins.
- **Axon:** a long projection from the cell body that mainly sends out NT and other messengers to other neurons.

A neuron has dendrites that receive messages from other neurons and transmit that message to the cell body. The cell body contains the genetic material for making neurotransmitters and other proteins in response to the received message. The axon projects out from the cell body and sends messages to other adjacent neurons.

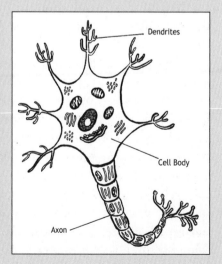

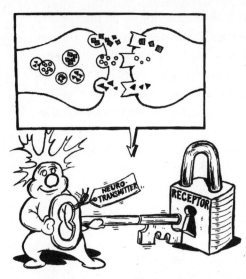

Figure 4. When neurons communicate, they use chemicals called neurotransmitters, or NTs (i.e., serotonin, norepinephrine, dopamine), that signal a receptor on the adjacent neuron. The receptor is a protein that has a three-dimensional structure that fits with that particular NT. Researchers describe the relationship of the NT to the receptor like a key to a lock.

Proving the Monoamine Hypothesis

Researchers began to look for more evidence to support the "monoamine hypothesis." They discovered reduced levels of byproducts of certain NTs in the spinal fluid and urine in depressed patients that suggested those people had low levels of the NTs. A more recent study took one group that responded to antidepressants that increased serotonin levels and one group that responded to antidepressants that increased norepinephrine levels. By restricting their intake of certain essential amino acids needed to generate these two NTs, they caused a sudden drop in their serotonin or norepinephrine levels.

The patients who had responded to serotonin-enhancing medicines experienced a return of their depression when their serotonin levels were dropped, but not when their norepinephrine levels were lowered. The norepinephrine medicine responders had the opposite effect. Decreasing their norepinephrine levels caused a depression relapse, but lowering serotonin did nothing. Not only did this further support the neurotransmitter theory, but it also suggested that for some people one NT may be more of a factor than another. One other interesting finding from the study was that normal volunteers did not get depressed when either NT was decreased meaning something else must be contributing to depression as well as NT levels.

What Do the Different Receptors Do?

Receptors are found in many other areas of the body as well and can be affected by a variety of hormones and proteins. Some medicines work by turning on a receptor (agonist) and others turn off a receptor (an antagonist). A receptor can sit on a neuron that sends out a message (presynaptic receptor), or it can sit on the neuron that receives a message (postsynaptic receptor). Some presynaptic receptors are autoreceptors, which means they regulate NTs by measuring their levels in their immediate environment and then tell the neuron to increase or decrease their production and release. Each of these important components of neuron functioning can be affected by depression and impacted by antidepressants.

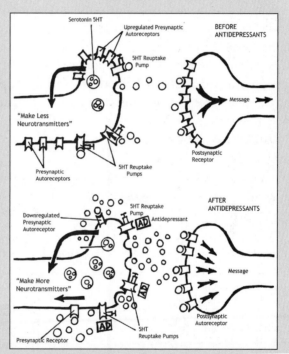

Autoreceptors tell the neuron to make less neurotransmitters (NT). Before antidepressants, depressed neurons have an overproduction of "presynaptic autoreceptors" (called up-regulation), which means more signals to shut off NT production. Antidepressants block the reuptake pumps making more NT available. This leads to a reduction in the autoreceptors (down regulation), which means the neuron is no longer told to make less NT. The result? Even more NT.

A group of proteins called neurotrophic factors may also play a role in depression. They function like brain fertilizer helping neurons grow and flourish. One of the best studied is called brain-derived neurotrophic factor, or BDNF. Depression, stress, and pain all reduce BDNF levels, which can be measured in the brain or the blood. When BDNF levels are lower than normal, certain structures in the brain controlling mood, thoughts, and behaviors appear smaller and less active than those without depression. Neurons begin to wither with fewer dendrites and axons reaching out to their surrounding environment. This could affect signaling between the different brain structures. There may even be a connection between the monoamines and neurotrophic factors. The monoamines may be one of the ways the body regulates BDNF levels. Low monoamines levels could translate to low BDNF or other neurotrophic factors. Restoring monamine levels to normal could normalize BDNF (see Figure 5).

One study demonstrated the importance of BDNF and other neurotrophic factors as well as their possible relationship to the monoamines in treating depression. Scientists are able to simulate depression in rats

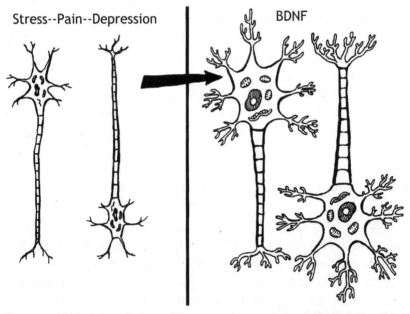

Figure 5. Under stressful conditions, such as pain and depression, there is a decrease in the brain-nourishing chemical brain-derived neurotrophic factor (BDNF). This can cause neurons to wither and atrophy. With antidepressant treatment (as well as exercise, pain relief, and mental stimulation), BDNF levels rise and neurons begin to flourish again.

by putting them into seemingly hopeless situations. They start to experience characteristic behavior changes as well as physical alterations in their brains, such as reduced number and size of neurons. Scientists gave the rats the antidepressant Prozac (fluoxetine), which increased their serotonin levels. Their physical and behavior changes returned to normal. They repeated the experiment, but this time they exposed them to radiation, which prevented neurotrophic factors from repairing the neurons and triggering nerve growth. Their depression did not improve. This suggests that increasing serotonin helped reduce depression when neurotrophic factors were able to work properly as well.

"...serotonin, norepinephrine, and dopamine? How are they related to depression?"

The three monoamines—serotonin, norepinephrine, and dopamine—play an important role in regulating people's moods and responses to emotional situations. All three are distributed throughout the body and serve a variety of other functions as well. Serotonin goes by the chemical name 5-hydroxytryptamine, or 5-HT, and plays a role in managing mood, body temperature, pain, anxiety, aggression, appetite, and sexual functioning. Medications that work on serotonin can help many health problems, including schizophrenia, migraine headaches, depression, anxiety disorders, drug abuse, and heart disease.

Norepinephrine helps with attention, arousal, and memory, which may explain why medicines that increase NE help with attention deficit disorder (ADHD) as well. NE comes primarily from an area of the brain

Not All Serotonin Receptors Are Created Equal

There are seven known families of serotonin receptors, labeled 5-HT1, 5-HT2, etc. Within those families are different subtypes, such as 5-HT1A, 5-HT2A, etc. Some functions of the different serotonin receptors have been identified, but much remains unknown, particularly how they interact with one another. We know that side effects of some antidepressants that target serotonin can be explained by how the medicines work on specific receptors. For example, 5-HT2A receptor impacts sexual functioning while 5-HT3 can cause appetite, nausea, and other stomach problems.

called the locus coeruleus, which is activated when you sense stress or danger. The release of NE helps you become more alert and attentive in those situations. Our perception of pain is affected by NE in the spinal cord. Medicines that work on both 5-HT and NE have been shown to help with chronic pain.

Dopamine controls motor movements in the brain and also helps with learning, motivation, and memory. Its role in depression is less clear. Medicines that only increase dopamine in the brain have helped people have more energy and motivation but are not consistently good antidepressants. Some describe it as a "feel-good" neurotransmitter since an increase in DA in certain brain areas makes you feel somewhat euphoric. This can be a problem with drugs that drastically increase dopamine levels like cocaine or methamphetamine. Addictive behaviors have been linked to dopamine. Drug abuse, alcoholism, gambling, sky diving, and other thrill-seeking activities elevate dopamine levels which may explain why people get "hooked" on certain activities even when they know it can be dangerous. Changes in dopamine levels and their receptors may also play a role in some psychotic disorders such as schizophrenia. Medicines that block dopamine in some brain areas may improve symptoms associated with psychosis.

Jane's Story Continues

Jane accepted the diagnosis of depression but could not understand how this would explain all of her physical symptoms. Depression is a problem with emotions. How would that turn into trouble with concentration, a racing heart, or shortness of breath? Anyway, she knew people who had health problems, and of course they became depressed when their health deteriorated.

"I understand that depression can affect my mood, energy, and motivation," she said. "But I don't understand why I would have trouble with my memory and concentration. What is depression doing to my brain? And why do I feel so bad physically? Maybe I have depression and another problem? How can depression affect my physical health?"

Could there be a Problem with the Neurotransmitter Receptor that Causes Depression?

When NT levels are low, there are usually changes that occur in the post-synaptic receptors, too. Neurons compensate for abnormal NT levels by increasing the number of post-synaptic receptors. This phenomenon is called *up regulation*. Scientists have looked at brains of people who have committed suicide and found that they have more post-synaptic receptors than those without depression. This up regulation may somehow prevent the receptors from doing their job properly, thereby affecting normal brain functioning.

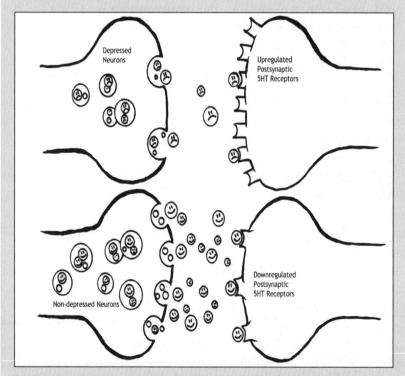

Depressed Neurons

Upregulated Postsynaptic 5HT Receptors

Non-depressed Neurons

Downregulated Postsynaptic 5HT Receptors

In depression, neurons respond by generating more receptors on the receiving (postsynaptic) neuron. This is called up regulation, which researchers believe may be responsible for some depression symptoms. With antidepressants, more neurotransmitters become available, and the receptor numbers return to normal. This is called down regulation. Down regulation takes four to six weeks to occur, about the time it takes antidepressants to help people feel better.

"What is depression doing to my brain?"

You may remain unconvinced that depression has a physical cause. Even if you believe that depression is caused by psychological factors or a weakness of spirit, the physical changes in the brain in depression are undeniable. That is not to say that these changes are the cause of depression. They could be a result of having depression. It is also possible that there may not be one cause. There could be many different types of depressions with different physical or psychological roots.

The most consistent physical changes scientists have observed are:

- Reduced NT levels in the brain.
- Changes in the number of NT receptors in the brain and their ability to function properly.
- Reduced activity and signs of atrophy in several areas of the limbic system in the brain.

While these changes have been observed in most people with depression, not everyone will have all of the above abnormalities. This makes it hard to point to any one as a definitive cause of depression or to use them as a means for diagnosis.

Low levels of NTs may account for the symptoms associated with depression, such as problems with sleep, appetite, energy, concentration, memory, and motivation. Even symptoms not typically thought of as related to depression, such as body aches and pains, have been associated with decreases in NTs.

New imaging techniques that help scientists look inside the brain in more detail have shown which areas are less active and reduced in size with depression. Not only do neurons lose axons and dendrites that foster communication, but other brain cells are affected as well. One of these is called the glial cell, which helps provide support and nutrients to the neurons. While often thought of as having a lesser role than the neurons, glial cells actually make up nearly 90 percent of our brains and play a critical part in brain activity. They are also reduced in size and number in depression.

The parts of the depressed brain that have the most alterations in activity and show the most atrophy is in the limbic system. The hippocampus, which plays an important part in moods and memory, is less active and is almost 10 percent smaller in people with depression (see Photo 1). The prefrontal cortex, which helps with planning and attention, shows similar changes. This can lead to poor attention, memory

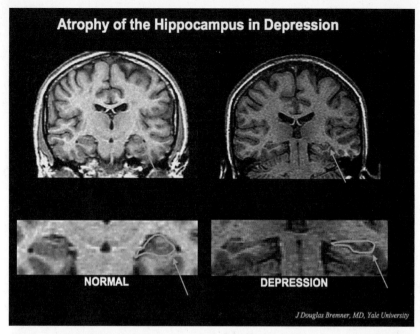

Atrophy of the Hippocampus in Depression

NORMAL

DEPRESSION

J Douglas Bremner, MD, Yale University

Photo 1. This MRI imaging scan shows the hippocampus, which is an important part of the limbic system that plays a role in memory and the body's emotional responses. In depression, the hippocampus can shrink in volume. With treatment, this reduction in size can be reversed.

difficulties, motivation problems, and trouble with initiative—many of the symptoms some experience. These problems linger even when depression starts to lift. This may be explained by a longer recovery time for these areas to return to normal functioning.

The amygdala generates emotions in response to emotionally charged events. If something happens that reminds you of a past bad experience, the amygdala will create a negative emotion. In depression, the amygdala is overactive causing it to shrink over time. The thalamus, which takes thoughts and sensory information to and from the cerebral cortex and helps create emotions, thoughts, and memories, is also overactive and changes in size with depression. Since this is a communication hub between the thinking and feeling part of the brain, an increase in activity could affect how you deal with emotional experiences.

What could cause parts of the brain to shrink or atrophy? One possibility is low BDNF and other neurotrophic factor levels. Since these chemicals help grow and nurture neurons, a decrease in their production may lead to fewer nerve cells. Low levels of 5-HT, DA, and NE have also been shown to reduce BDNF levels in the brain.

Another explanation for reduced brain size and activity is the overproduction of certain hormones or other chemicals that are designed to help the body function during stressful situations but are toxic when their levels are too high for too long. Two of these, cortisol and glutamate, are well known and important for normal brain function. Glutamate is a neurotransmitter and is dangerous when elevated. Some researchers blame glutamate for contributing to other diseases that destroy the nervous system like Alzheimer's, Parkinson's, and Huntington's diseases.

Cortisol is a "stress hormone" that is stored in the adrenal gland and released after a series of chemical events occur. The hypothalamus sends out a chemical, corticotrophic-releasing hormone or CRH, which tells the pituitary gland to release adrenocorticotrophic hormone or ACTH. This is the hormone that triggers the adrenal gland to release cortisol (see Figure 6). If any of these organs are not working properly, cortisol levels can be affected. Since cortisol helps with healing from injury and inflammation, medicines that work in a similar way such as cortisone or prednisone are effective in treating inflammatory problems such as arthritis and poison ivy. A brief

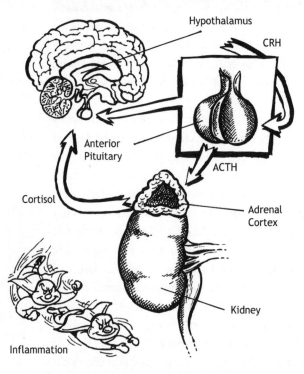

Figure 6. The brain reacts to stress by having the hypothalamus increase production of corticotrophic- releasing hormone (CRH). CRH signals the pituitary gland to produce more adrenocorticotrophic hormone (ACTH). ACTH tells the adrenal gland (sitting on top of the kidney) to make cortisol, which helps the body's stress response, including inflammation. Cortisol also signals the hypothalamus to shut off CRH production. In depression, CRH production is not regulated correctly and excessive cortisol levels, which may have negative effects on brain structures, can result.

increase in cortisone levels can be good for you when your body needs it but damages the brain when the levels are high for prolonged periods.

If learning how depression affects your brain depresses you, consider some good news. Most of these changes can be reversed when depression is properly treated. Scientists once thought that once neurons were damaged, they could not be repaired. We know now that in specific areas of the brain, damaged neurons can heal and new neurons can grow. Unfortunately, that does not occur in all areas of the nervous system. That is why people with spinal cord injuries and strokes often do not get back full function after the neurons are damaged. In the areas affected by depression, researchers have seen significant recovery. The earlier you get help and the better your depression responds, the greater your outlook for return of normal brain functioning.

"How can depression affect my physical health?"

Doctors have long observed that depression negatively impacts their patients' physical health. Depression can reduce survival rates from cancer, heart disease, stroke, diabetes, and many other chronic health conditions. Even illnesses such as asthma and arthritis might have worse outcomes when occurring with depression.

Does depression make the physical condition worse, or are people who are more likely to have a bad outcome from their illness more likely to get depressed? No one can say for sure, but having health problems and depression is a bad combination.

One possible explanation for this finding is that someone with depression may be less likely to follow her doctor's treatment recommendations. Memory and concentration problems might result in her forgetting to take her medication reliably. A cancer victim could feel so hopeless or defeated by his depression that he refuses aggressive chemotherapy or radiation. Someone with depression and diabetes or heart disease may not have the motivation to stick with a diet and exercise program that could improve their outcome.

There is other evidence, though, that depression itself affects the body in such a way that actually causes or worsens health problems. In other words, depression may not just be bad for the brain but also the body. Earlier in this chapter I discussed how depression is associated with an increased release of cortisol. Elevated levels of cortisol can affect your insulin levels and blood sugar. It can also lead to reduced muscle tissue and bone thickness, elevated blood pressures, and a less effective immune system needed to fight infections. Scientists have wondered whether having untreated depression for many years may put someone at a greater risk for heart problems, blood sugar abnormalities, autoimmune disorders, and inflammatory diseases.

Stress and depression can result in a surge of adrenaline and norepinephrine (also called catecholamines) into the body. These two chemicals are important in the "flight or fight" response, causing your heart rate to go up, breathing rate to increase, and blood vessels to constrict. These physical changes allow to you to respond quickly and efficiently to dangers such as an oncoming car or, in more prehistoric times, to a charging wooly mammoth. The downside to this protective response is that when it's turned on for extended periods of time (such as with stress or depression), one could increase one's chances of heart or circulation issues. Adding to this risk is the effect of depression on 5-HT, which works in the circulatory system regulating the body's response to injury. Platelets release certain proteins that help with clotting and cause blood vessels to constrict to limit the spread of the injury. Both of these are controlled in part by 5-HT and their ability to work properly could be impacted the longer depression goes untreated.

Depression also impacts the immune system. The body protects itself from harmful foreign objects—such as a bacteria or viruses—with an inflammatory response. One example of inflammation occurs when you get a bee sting and your skin reacts with redness, swelling, and itching. This normal reaction keeps you healthy but can be a problem when the immune system doesn't function properly. An overactive immune system can make the body attack itself as though it is a foreign object, putting someone at risk for diseases such as lupus, rheumatoid arthritis, fibromyalgia, asthma, hay fever, multiple sclerosis, and chronic fatigue syndrome, to name a few.

During inflammation, the body releases certain chemicals that facilitate the process. These chemicals can be measured in the blood indicating a high inflammation state. Cytokines are one group of these chemicals and are elevated in people with depression. One cancer drug is a synthetic variation of one type of cytokine called interleukin. This drug can cause depression in those who take it. Another protein called c-reactive protein is released when there is inflammation. It is higher than normal in depression. C-reactive protein is often checked during routine physical exams by your doctor to see if you are at risk for diseases like heart disease and strokes. Just as with other abnormal physical findings, no one knows whether these immune system alterations cause depression or are a result of having depression. Nonetheless, all this suggests that depression not only can make you feel bad emotionally but also physically.

There is good news for someone with depression who worries how these changes may affect their physical health. Depression is a treatable disease, and the human body has remarkable abilities to heal itself. As described in the section on changes in the brain ("What is depression doing to my brain?" on page 76), taking an early, proactive, and aggressive approach to getting well prevents or reduces any negative on impact on your wellbeing.

Lucy's Story Continues

Lucy, under the encouragement of her therapist and friend, decided to talk with her medical doctor about antidepressants. She shared her skepticism about taking "an artificial drug" to treat depression.

"First of all, isn't this just masking the underlying problem?" she asked. "How do antidepressants work? Don't they make you feel happy when you really aren't? And there seem to be so many of them! Do all antidepressants work the same? Or are they somehow different? What antidepressants are available for me to take?"

"How do antidepressants work?"

We know some of what antidepressants do in the brain but cannot say for sure that these actions explain why they treat depression. The FDA requires every antidepressant to state on its label that "the exact mechanism of antidepressant effect is unknown." For many years, researchers suspected that antidepressants worked by restoring the levels of NTs, the suspected cause of depression. This idea still has legs to stand on, but new theories have emerged which may explain the antidepressant effect more precisely.

Antidepressants work on one or more of the three different mechanisms neurons use to regulate NT levels:
- Reuptake pumps.
- Monoamine oxidase.
- Autoreceptors.

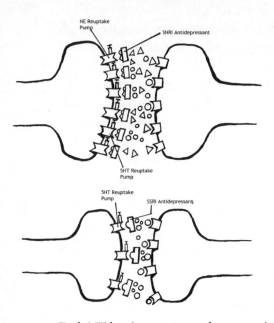

Figure 7. Serotonin reuptake inhibitors (SSRIs) work by blocking just the serotonin reuptake pumps, allowing more serotonin to be available for use. Serotonin-norepinephrine reuptake pumps (SNRIs) block both serotonin reuptake pumps and norepinephrine reuptake pumps, making more of each neurotransmitter available.

Reuptake pumps are proteins located on cell membranes. They recycle NTs by pumping them back into the presynaptic neuron. Each NT has its own reuptake pump; i.e., a serotonin reuptake pump, norepinephrine reuptake pump, and dopamine reuptake pump. Many antidepressants block one or more of these reuptake pumps, resulting in higher levels of NT. Medicines that block serotonin reuptake pumps are called selective serotonin reuptake inhibitors, or SSRIs. Those that block serotonin and norepinephrine are called serotonin norepinephrine reuptake inhibitors or SNRIs (see Figure 7).

Figure 8. The monoamine oxidase enzyme breaks down serotonin, norepineph-rine, and dopamine. When a monamine oxi-dase inhibitor antide-pressant is given, this enzyme is blocked and neurotransmitters are no longer broken down. This means more NTs become available.

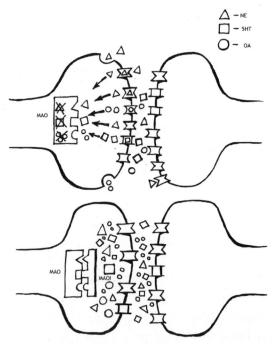

Monoamine oxidase is an enzyme that regulates monoamines levels by breaking down excess neurotransmitters the brain doesn't need. One class of antidepressants, MAOIs, works by blocking this protein. This results in an increase in the levels of 5-HT, DA, and NE (Figure 8).

A third mechanism for controlling NT levels is through autoreceptors. They are receptors that detect the available levels of NT. When NT levels are adequate, the autoreceptor instructs the neuron to stop making and releasing them. Some antidepressants block autoreceptors from detecting the levels of NT. This results in more NT being produced.

In certain people, one of these actions may be more effective or important than another. Perhaps antidepressants work in different ways in different people with different types of depression.

"Do all antidepressants work the same?"

Although antidepressants work in a variety of ways, certain medicines share common actions. This has led researchers to classify antidepressants by how they affect different NTs and NT receptors. However, the more we learn about these medicines, the more we realize that they do not always fit neatly into one class. This is relevant to your treatment because you or your doctor may assume if you do not respond to one medicine in a class that you are more likely to fail another from the same class. This is often not the case, since there are important differences that distinguish one drug from others in the same class.

The classes are labeled by their primary effect on NTs. Prozac, for example, blocks the reuptake of 5-HT through its effect on the reuptake pump and is classified as an SSRI. It was later discovered to also block NE to a smaller degree. Medicines classified as SSRIs can affect other NTs, but remain in this class since their primary impact is on 5-HT. The more we learn about each medication, the more the classification systems seem inadequate and confusing. While some of these other actions may be inconsequential, they could explain why some people respond or tolerate one medication better than another in its class.

"What antidepressants are available for me to take?"

Currently, there are seven major classes of antidepressants. Below is a current list of the different classes of antidepressants and the most common medications currently used that fall within each class. The medicine is listed by the generic name with the U.S. brand in parentheses.

Why Do Antidepressants Take So Long to Work?

If depression is caused by low levels of NT, then you should feel better as soon as those levels return to normal. The amount of NTs starts increasing within 24 to 48 hours of starting medicine, but antidepressants typically take four to six weeks to work. Why should improvement take so long? One possible explanation is a phenomenon that happens to receptors called *down regulation*. Up regulation is an increase in postsynaptic receptors that occurs as NT levels drop. Down regulation is a return to a normal number of receptors when NT levels increase and takes about four to six weeks. (See page 75.)

Down regulation is also seen with autoreceptors. Antidepressants block the presynaptic autoreceptors from determining NT levels. In response to being tricked into thinking that there is too little NT available, the autoreceptors down regulate. With fewer autoreceptors, there is less feedback to the neuron to slow down NT production. This ultimately leads to an increase in NTs over time. Down regulation of autoreceptors also can take several weeks to occur, explaining the delayed effect of antidepressants.

Another possible explanation is that increasing NT levels triggers a series of actions that result in the depression response. One of these actions could be an increased production of neurotrophic factors, such as BDNF. This may explain how areas of the brain reduced in size and activity with depression can return to normal when depression is treated. In Chapter Five I discuss non-medicine interventions that may also increase BDNF. In the future, scientists may be able to develop new antidepressants that bypass increasing NT levels and work directly on another of these actions. Such a medication could work faster, be more effective, and have fewer side effects than those we have today.

Although I mentioned the delayed effect of antidepressants, a small number of people do feel better in a day or two. Some may experience a placebo effect in which they feel better because they convince themselves that the medicine is helping before it really does. Others may be benefiting from an increase in NTs alone. Those who improve only after several weeks on medicine may be responding when down regulation occurs or neurotrophic factors have time to take effect.

Appendix D "Starting Dosing Characteristics of Most Commonly Prescribed Antidepressants" and Appendix E "Commonly Prescribed Antidepressants by Side-Effect Risk" detail the mechanism of action in more detail for each medication, available forms and doses, dosing range, and common side effects. There are other medicines used to treat depression outside the United States but those not approved by the FDA are not included.

Selective serotonin reuptake inhibitors (SSRIs): They work by blocking the serotonin reuptake pump, keeping the serotonin in the synapse between neurons around longer. They often affect other serotonin receptors that can lead to unintended side effects such as nausea, sleeping difficulties, and anxiety. They are the most common class prescribed because they are easy to start, usually well tolerated, and physicians are most familiar with them. Many are available in generic form, making them accessible and affordable.

- Citalopram (Celexa)
- Escitalopram (Lexapro)
- Fluoxetine (Prozac)
- Paroxetine and paroxetine controlled release (Paxil and Paxil CR controlled release)
- Sertraline (Zoloft)
- Fluvoxamine and fluvoxamine controlled release (Luvox and Luvox CR controlled release)*

   *This medicine is an SSRI and, though not FDA approved in the U.S. for depression, is prescribed for depression in many other countries. It is FDA approved for obsessive-compulsive disorder. Fluvoxamine CR (Luvox CR) is also approved for social anxiety disorder.

Norepinephrine dopamine reuptake inhibitors (NDRIs): There is only one medication commonly used in this class, called Wellbutrin (buproprion). It blocks the DA and NE reuptake pump, causing an increase in the levels of DA and NE without impacting 5-HT.

- Bupropion (Wellbutrin)
- Bupropion sustained release (Wellbutrin SR)
- Bupropion extended release (Wellbutrin XL)

Serotonin norepinphrine reuptake inhibitors (SNRIs): These medications came to market after the SSRIs and block the reuptake of both 5-HT and NE. They have become increasingly popular and have been helpful to many who have not responded to SSRIs. Since pain perception is regulated through NE and 5-HT, some SNRIs may help manage pain associated with certain medical conditions such as fibromyalgia and diabetic peripheral neuropathy. There is some research suggesting that medicines working on multiple neurotransmitters may be more effective than single mechanism drugs but other evidence refutes this.

- Duloxetine (Cymbalta)
- Venlafaxine (Effexor)
- Venlafaxine extended release (Effexor XR)
- Venlafaxine ER
- Desvenlafaxine (Pristiq)

Monoamine oxidase inhibitors (MAOIs): This is an older class of medicine that blocks monoamine oxidase, preventing the breakdown of the monamine neurotransmitters NE, DA, and 5-HT. Some depression types seem to preferentially respond to MAOIs and some doctors believe they are among the more effective medicines on the market. They are not commonly used today because of the risks of serious, and possibly even life threatening, reactions if mixed with certain types of foods and medicines.

- Tranylcypromine (Parnate)
- Phenelzine (Nardil)
- Isocarboxazid (Marplan)
- Selegiline transdermal (EMSAM)

Tricylic antidepressants: This is the oldest class and includes three chemically related families of antidepressants—secondary amines, tertiary amines, and tetracyclics. Practically, they can all be grouped together since they work on blocking 5-HT and NE in varying degrees. The medicines differ mainly on effects they have on other receptors that may or may not be important for treating depression but can impact their side effect profiles. They can vary with regards to activation, sedation, dry mouth, weight gain, and a number of other side effects. When studied in comparison to newer medicines such as SSRIs, they tend to do as well or better but usually have more side effects.

- Amitriptyline (Elavil)
- Clomipramine (Anafranil)
- Doxepin (Adapin, Sinequan)
- Imipramine (Tofranil)
- Trimipramine (Surmontil)
- Desipramine (Norpramin, Pertofrane)
- Nortriptyline (Pamelor, Aventyl)
- Protriptyline (Vivactil)
- Amoxapine (Asendin)
- Maprotiline (Ludiomil)

Serotonin modulators: You may find this class of antidepressants identified by other names. These medications block the postsynaptic receptor 5-HT2A which helps the mood and anxiety enhancing receptor 5HT1A work better. They also block the reuptake of 5-HT and NE to a small degree. One of the commonly used medicines in this class, trazodone (Desyrel), is sedating and is frequently used as a sleep aid, even though it is not approved for that use.

- Nefazodone (Serzone)
- Trazodone (Desyrel)
- Trazodone extended release (Oleptro)

Serotonin norepinephrine modulators: These medicines block the presynaptic receptor alpha 2 which is a NE receptor. They also have selected effects on certain serotonin receptors. The commonly prescribed medicine in this class, mirtazapine (Remeron), also works on a variety of serotonin receptors including 5-HT2A, 5-HT2C, and 5-HT3. Because these receptors can cause changes in other NT levels in addition to 5-HT, this medication can increase 5-HT, NE, and probably even DA levels.

- Mirtazapine (Remeron)

If you made it through this whole chapter, consider yourself awarded an honorary degree in neuroscience. The rewards of such a degree mean that you will be able to make better sense of new discoveries about depression and its treatment when you hear of them. More importantly, this information helps you in deciding how to approach treating depression in the here and now. Anyone deciding when they should get help and what steps they should take must understand the potential impact that depression can have on the brain and one's physical health. If you do decide to take an antidepressant, Chapter Four gives you insight into reasonable expectations when starting medicine.

Chapter Four

What Can I Expect When I Start Antidepressants?

Lucy's Story Continues

" **I** understand a little better now why you suggested that I try an antidepressant. I saw the doctor and he made a good argument that maybe my depression won't go away with what I've tried so far," Lucy reported to her therapist, Elaine.

Elaine responded, "But you haven't started taking it yet?"

"Maybe depression can be physically harmful to the body, but I am afraid of developing other problems if I start an antidepressant. I told him I would think about it and get back to him," Lucy said.

Elaine replied that there are risks anytime you take a medicine, but from her experience people rarely develop serious problems with antidepressants. At the worst, she could develop side effects or the medicine might not work. Lucy felt reassured when Elaine said, "If you don't like it or it doesn't help, stop."

Lucy agreed to give it a try, but wondered about the next step, "My doctor went over all the different medicines. There are so many. How will he know which antidepressant to put me on?"

Once you have decided to start taking an antidepressant, you need to know what to realistically expect. If you have never taken an antidepressant before, you probably wonder how the medication will make you feel, how long it takes to work, and what side effects you may experience. If you have been on antidepressants in the past, you may wonder whether the medicine will work as well or better than what you have taken previously. Will you have more or fewer side effects than you had with past medicines? Antidepressants often cause immediate effects that are different from those you may experience once you have been taking them for a longer period of time. This chapter focuses on what to expect within the first few weeks of treatment. Part Two of this book (beginning on page 103 with Chapter Six) addresses issues that are more likely to arise once you have been on antidepressants for an extended time.

Any one person's experience starting on an antidepressant can differ greatly from another's. You may respond to the medication quickly with few, if any, problems, while others may improve less dramatically and have to navigate through more side effects. Fortunately, antidepressants, as a class, are usually well tolerated, and most people can start them with relative ease. However, you may not care much for how you feel on the first medication you take and need to try several before you find the one that works best for you. Your chances of successful treatment will improve if you know what to expect and develop strategies in advance for managing any problems, should they occur.

This chapter discusses:

- Ways to help you and your doctor decide which medicine to try.
- When and how to start your medication.
- Most common side effects and how to deal with them.
- How you should expect to feel.
- Whom you should tell, and how to manage reactions from others.

"How will my doctor know which antidepressant to put me on?"

Choosing an antidepressant is a decision you and your doctor should make together by weighing the pros and cons of the available options. More than 30 commonly used medications are on the market today, and none has been conclusively shown to work better than another. With experience, doctors develop personal preferences about which antidepressant works best for which symptom or patient type. Sometimes these preferences are supported by findings from research studies, and sometimes they evolve from what a doctor observes over time in her own patients. Another important factor in a doctor's antidepressant choice is what possible side effect she thinks you might experience. For example, she might start you on a medicine that is more likely to make you sleepy and calm if you are have trouble sleeping or are experiencing a great deal of anxiety. She would be more likely to give you an antidepressant that often activates or energizes if you experience low energy or sleep excessively.

Patients often ask their doctor, "What is the best medication to treat depression?" The answer is, "Whatever works best for you." You may read or hear about some research study comparing two different antidepressants that proved one worked better than the other. These are usually single studies, almost always funded by the pharmaceutical company that makes the "superior" antidepressant. There are subtle ways that companies can structure the design of a study to give their medicine an edge. They may use a certain study population that favors their drug, or they may dose the competing medication lower than their own. Many doctors who were visited by pharmaceutical representatives during the aggressive antidepressant marketing campaigns in the 1990s recall being shown a study demonstrating that drug A worked better than drug B (by the Drug Company A, of course) and the following week being shown a study with the complete opposite result funded by Drug Company B.

Other factors that may go into your doctor's decision-making process include:

- A specific antidepressant has been shown to work in depression in addition to helping another condition you may have, such as panic disorder or post-traumatic stress disorder.
- You have a close blood relative who responded to a certain medication.
- You require a medicine that can be safely taken with other medicines you are on.
- You have another medical condition, such as liver or kidney disease, which limits the use of certain antidepressants.

Make sure your doctor chooses your medicine for the right reasons. Some physicians may not be fully informed on all the newest antidepressants available and might only prescribe one or two different medicines they are familiar with. Others tend to use whatever antidepressant is in their sample closet. They may believe antidepressants are all the same and are not aware of the important, but subtle, differences between them. Because of cost or pressure from insurance companies, a doctor may only use generic medicines first. While this may save you money and prevent the doctor's office from the headaches of time-consuming prior authorizations, you may not get the medicine that would work best for you.

You may have heard good things about a particular medication or have seen a seductive advertisement for an antidepressant. If you ask your doctor for an antidepressant by name, your doctor may simply comply with your request. Rarely, a doctor may give a patient a certain medicine because he likes the pharmaceutical representative or company that promotes the product. Those who oppose aggressive promotion of medication believe that this happens more often than it really does. The vast majority of doctors do what they believe is best for their patients. Pharmaceutical company promotion may get doctors to try a medicine with their patients but, if time after time it does not live up to the hype, they will stop using it.

Jane's Story Continues

Jane, in searching for the answers to her many questions about starting on antidepressants, became frustrated with the lack of scientific precision on the subject. As a physics professor, she wanted to find more consistent information. It seemed that every doctor she spoke with had a different method for initiating medication. They were vague when she asked what she should expect and seemed to qualify their responses to her questions with, "Everyone is different."

She told her last doctor, "I can handle most things as long as I know what to expect. I feel more comfortable when I have a detailed plan of action. There seem to be so many different methods to starting antidepressants. What dose do I start on and what time of day do I take it? When will I start feeling better? What will I feel? How will I know if it's working?"

"What dose do I start on and what time of day do I take it?"

Pharmaceutical companies have guidelines for starting antidepressants that are based on the research studies that led to the medicine's approval. These guidelines give doctors a starting dose, frequency of taking the medicine, and other recommendations to optimize safety and tolerability. Unfortunately, designers of these early clinical trials cannot always predict the best way to use the medicine in non-research settings.

Research subjects may accept certain side effects more readily than "real world" patients will, since they have volunteered to be experimented on, are often getting paid for their participation, and receive free treatment. For example, if the starting dose is too high and causes nausea, a research patient may keep taking the medicine until the side effect goes away, whereas most other people would stop. When the medicine is approved, the recommendation may be to start at the higher dose since few people stopped taking the medicine in the study.

After doctors have sufficient experience with the medication, they usually develop a prescribing style that they believe works best for their patients. The pharmaceutical companies are not allowed to instruct doctors to do anything not done in the study, even if that becomes standard medical practice over time. Changing the FDA guidelines or labeling on a medication is not an easy process and requires substantial scientific evidence.

One example in which labeling differs from standard practice is with one of the newer antidepressants, duloxetine (Cymbalta). The guidelines are to start at 20 mg twice a day or 60 mg once a day. Most doctors who have used this medicine know that many patients do better starting at 30 mg a day and may stay on this dose for an extended period of time before ever increasing the dose. The "art of medicine" is reconciling between the science, labeling, and what really works.

Some doctors prefer to stick rigidly to FDA guidelines or are required to in an office setting such as a health maintenance organization (HMO), where prescribing is dictated by certain protocols. Others are driven by their own experience. Patients can usually benefit from their doctor's experience unless his practices fall so outside the normal usage of the medicine that you are unlikely to get better or are at risk for serious side effects.

If you are sensitive to medication side effects, your doctor can use a lower-than-normal starting dose. The downside to this approach is that you may still experience side effects, and it may take longer to feel better. Make sure your doctor increases the medicine to an effective level if you are not responding to the lower dose within four to six weeks. Some patients ask their doctor to start at a high dose in hopes that they will get better faster, but there is no evidence that this will speed up your recovery time. In fact, this can be unsafe and lead to more side effects.

Another conservative starting strategy you can use, if your medicine is a scored tablet, is to cut the pill and take half for a few days before increasing to the whole dose. This allows you a trial period to see if you tolerate the medicine without problems. When a tablet is scored, it means the active drug is equally dispersed in both halves, so half the pill means half the dose. Pills that are not scored may not have the active drug equally distributed. This means that when you cut them, you have no idea how much medicine you are getting. Controlled or extended-release medications cannot be safely cut because the medicine is designed to be slowly released. There can be serious—and possibly dangerous—side effects if the medicine is released faster than intended. While some of these medicines will identify themselves as having a slow-release mechanism such as Wellbutrin XL (extended release) or Wellbutrin SR (sustained release), others do not, such as duloxetine (Cymbalta) or desvenlafaxine (Pristiq). Medicines that can be safely cut are listed in Appendix I on page 288.

Some antidepressants are available in liquid form. This is a great option for those who have trouble swallowing or can only tolerate very small dose changes at a time. These formulations can be expensive and insurance companies may be reluctant to pay for them. There is also more room for dosing errors with liquid medication.

Most antidepressants can be taken any time of the day, as long as you are consistent with taking it at that same time every day. You do not want to take it in the morning one day and evening the next. Often people choose a certain time either because it is most convenient or because of the medicine's side-effect profile. If you find the medicine activating, you may prefer to take it in the morning to give you energy and avoid trouble sleeping. A sedating medicine would be better at night to help you sleep and avoid daytime sedation. Doctors usually tell their patients to take a medicine at a certain time because they can anticipate the side effect but there are always the exceptions to the rule. For example, a medicine that typically makes people sleepy might give you too much energy. Some medicines are supposed to be given twice a day, but your doctor may feel it is safe to take once a day. If you are concerned about taking an antidepressant with your other medicines, check with your doctor first. Most antidepressants can be safely taken with many other types of medication, but be sure to ask your doctor about the specific medications you are taking.

Appendix D "Starting Dosing Characteristics of Most Commonly Prescribed Antidepressants" lists the most commonly prescribed antidepressants with the recommended starting doses and whether the medicine can be safely cut or is available in liquid form. There are also some suggestions for what time of day a medication is typically best tolerated, as well as more conservative dosing strategies for those who prefer to start low and go up slowly. Again, be sure to discuss this with your doctor so he can determine the correct dosing schedule for you.

"When will I start feeling better?"

Most people with depression have felt poorly for a while and are anxious for quick relief of their symptoms by the time they decide to start an antidepressant. Unfortunately, these medications do not work right away. If your depression has gotten to the point that you cannot function at work or home, those several weeks it may take to get better can seem much longer. Some people do feel better within a few days of taking an antidepressant but the vast majority do not notice any significant relief for at least two to four weeks. Possible reasons for this are discussed in Chapter Three in the section on how antidepressants work.

You should expect to feel at least 50 percent better within four to six weeks of taking the right medicine at the right dose. Full recovery may take up to 12 weeks. Some symptoms can even take longer than 12 weeks to fully resolve, such as concentration and memory difficulties. Symptoms that do not go away even though the depression has mostly lifted are called residual symptoms. Managing residual symptoms is discussed in Chapter Six.

In some cases, an immediate improvement in one or more of your symptoms may be due to a side effect, not an antidepressant effect. A sedating antidepressant may help you sleep better as soon as you start taking it. Your mood could be starting to improve somewhat because you are sleeping better. An activating medicine could give you more energy, but not necessarily because your depression has improved. Taking an antidepressant that is not fully treating depression but helping because of side effects is generally not a good idea, since these effects will eventually wear off. Sometimes a side effect that helps in the beginning of treatment becomes problematic later on. If your sleeping improves because your depression has resolved, you may not want a medicine that continues to make you sleepy.

Sometimes doctors will prescribe non-antidepressant medications for people with depression. This may be because these medications provide more immediate symptom relief, or because the patient's condition has been misdiagnosed. One class, called the "benzodiazepines," includes medication such as alprazolam (Xanax), clonazapine (Klonopin), lorezepam (Ativan), or diazepam (Valium). They are prescribed due to their calming effect. They help with anxiety, agitation, and sleeping problems, but they do not actually treat depression. They may even numb you emotionally. While the rapid effect is welcomed, these medicines can be highly addictive, especially if taken for extended periods. They also quickly lose their effectiveness, resulting in the need to take higher and higher doses for the same benefit. If you have been on a benzodiazepine, don't expect the same fast result when starting an antidepressant. Be careful of taking something for short term relief that in the long run may be detrimental to your health.

"What will I feel? How will I know if it is working?"

Depression is often described as similar to being at the bottom of a deep well, and the medicine is the rope that you need to pull yourself out. When an antidepressant works properly, you should experience improvement in emotional symptoms such as sadness, anxiety, and hopelessness, as well as in any physical symptoms such as sleep, appetite, and energy disturbances. Antidepressants are not "happy pills," as some people mistakenly believe. Hopefully, once you feel better, you will be able to do the things you need that actually make you happy. You will also be in a better position to make changes in your life to reduce the chances of your depression returning. The medicine, like the rope in the well, does not do the work for you. Some people who are looking for a quick and easy solution to their depression jump from medicine to medicine. They do not get better until they realize and undertake the life changes they must make to bring on their recovery.

When you are on antidepressants, you still feel emotions. If someone close to you passes away, you will feel sad. If you are mistreated at work, you will get angry. You can still experience anxiety about finances or health concerns. The difference is, on antidepressants, you are able to better deal with these feelings. Without the fog of depression, you see options, are able to put things into perspective, and use your own resources to more effectively manage any problems you may face.

Undertreated Depression is Common

One 2003 study showed that only 52 percent of those who had depression were getting any treatment. Of those who were getting help, only 1/4 were receiving what would be defined as adequate treatment. In other words, there are a whole lot of people not getting treated or getting minimal treatment and, most likely, not getting better.

Not Doing What the Doctor Ordered?

Did you know that 25 percent of people who are prescribed antidepressants either do not fill the prescription or stop taking them after two weeks? Approximately 35 percent of those taking antidepressants stop after two months.

If you are not going to take your medicine, or if you choose to stop taking it shortly after starting, let your doctor know why. If you have unanswered questions, she may be able to address those. She can also let you know her concerns if you do not take them and maybe even be able to give you some alternatives.

Frank's Story Continues

Frank took his prescriptions to the pharmacy and showed the samples to the pharmacist. "My doctor gave me these and said try them for a few weeks before getting the prescription filled. What do you know about this stuff? What side effects should I expect? I'm sure that doctor isn't telling me everything."

"What side effects should I expect?"

Antidepressants as a class are usually well tolerated. No medication, including those sold over the counter, is free of side effects. Yet, clearly, the risk of not treating depression is far greater than any risk from taking antidepressants. Fortunately, most side effects that occur early in treatment are not particularly bothersome and tend to lessen over time.

The most common problem seen when first starting an antidepressant is either sedation or activation. You might welcome a sedating medication if you have trouble sleeping, or an activating one if you feel like you are low on energy. If these side effects distress you, there are some strategies to manage them. First, make sure you take a sedating medicine before bed or an activating one when you wake up. Usually, the time of day you take the medicine has little impact on how well it works at treating your depression. You can also try reducing the dose temporarily to see if your body adjusts, although this may delay your recovery time. Your doctor can give you a sleeping medication or anti-anxiety medicine for a little while to help. Taking another pill just to manage a side effect is not ideal; hopefully, this is a short-term solution. Switching antidepressants is always an option if the sedation or activation persists and continues to be bothersome.

Antidepressants are known to affect the digestive system and can lead to side effects such as diarrhea, constipation, and nausea. Similar to sedation and activation, gastrointestinal problems are usually temporary, mild, and easily manageable. Nausea is the most common and is more often seen with antidepressants that work on serotonin and norepinephrine. Nausea usually resolves on its own after the first week. Lowering the starting dose, or eating a small amount of food before taking the medicine, may help until the side effect goes away. If you develop any problems with constipation or diarrhea, most over-the-counter treatments can help. Some gastrointestinal disorders, such as irritable bowel syndrome, are worsened by stress and depression and actually improve with antidepressants.

Other typical initial side effects are dry mouth, dizziness, and sweating. Most people do not find them disturbing enough to quit taking the medication. Sugar-free sour lemon drops or gum can help with dry mouth, as can several over-the-counter preparations available at most pharmacies, such as Biotene.

One rare side effect after starting an antidepressant that could be a cause for concern is feeling more depressed. There have been isolated cases of people wanting to die or hurt themselves early in treatment. Some studies have shown that this is more likely to occur if you are under age 25. Unfortunately, the media has reported on this as though anyone under 25 is taking a huge risk by using antidepressants. In reality, the chances of this happening are rare and, as long as you watch for signs of feeling worse and contact your doctor immediately, you can prevent any harm. Those who are not aware of this risk may not think to call their physician or stop the medicine, and assume they are getting worse for no reason. There is more on this in the special section on child and adolescent depression.

Why would antidepressants make someone feel worse? There are a few theories. One idea is that the depression itself is getting worse and the medicine has simply not yet had a chance to work. Some people with depression may have a type of manic-depression or bipolar disorder, even if they have not yet had a manic episode. In those cases, antidepressants can be activating and cause irritability and worsening moods. Mood stabilizers are a better and safer treatment option in those people.

Another rare side effect of antidepressants can be akathisia, in which you experience a sense of inner restlessness and trouble sitting still.

Anyone who has developed akathisia and was not aware of it might feel more distressed, leading to a worsening of their depression. Their doctor might conclude that they need to take more antidepressant since they feel poorly, and so they raise the dose. This would only make the symptom intensify. A few medications help treat akathisia, and, usually you only have to take them for a short while since akathisia typically gets better over time.

Make your doctor aware of any side effect you experience so that she can determine whether it is normal and whether it will likely resolve. Any sudden worsening of mood or very uncomfortable side effect may warrant an after-hours phone call to your doctor. You should not stop taking your medicine abruptly on your own without medical supervision.

There are other side effects that become more noticeable after being on the medicine for longer periods of time. These are discussed in Chapter Nine along with solutions for managing them.

Frank's Story Continues

A fter listening about possible side effects, Frank asked, "Will my insurance cover this antidepressant?"

The pharmacist responded, "Your insurance will cover part of it but you have a high co-pay since there is no generic version available."

When Frank heard the cost, he called his doctor's office immediately and told the nurse, "I went to get the medicine and it was so expensive. Is there a generic I can take or is there one my insurance will cover better?"

"I went to get the medicine and it was so expensive. Is there a generic I can take or is there one my insurance will cover better?"

If you pay for your medicine out of pocket and it is not yet available in a generic version, you may experience sticker shock. Antidepressants are not cheap, but they are usually more affordable than medicines used to treat other medical conditions. The reason new medicines are so expensive is because of the cost of bringing them to the market. Pharmaceutical companies spend hundreds of millions of dollars to research and develop a medication, and many of these medications never even get approved for use. The company has only 17 years of patent life, including the time it takes to research its safety and effectiveness, to recoup its costs and turn a profit. Once approved, the medicine may be on the market for only a few years before it is available in a generic formulation and other companies can manufacture it and sell it.

Generic medications are inexpensive and require fewer insurance hassles, including prior authorizations. Also, generic medicines have been around for a longer time so many doctors are familiar and comfortable with prescribing them. A potential disadvantage is that doctors and patients have observed that some generic medicines do not work as well as the brand. Generic medicines are allowed to have 20 percent variation in blood levels from their brand counterpart. This variation, or possibly a difference in quality in the manufacturing process of generic pharmaceutical companies, could explain differences in effectiveness. While some pharmacists, insurance companies, and generic manufacturers deny there is any difference between brand-name and generic drugs, increasing numbers of reports suggest the contrary, particularly with certain types of medicines.

If your doctor wants you to take an antidepressant that is not available in a generic form, she can usually provide samples for you to try first. Your doctor may have free or discounted trial coupons or you may find them on the Web site of the pharmaceutical company that makes the medicine. If the medicine works well, you can switch to a different generic medication, should cost be an issue, or decide that the benefits are worth the cost. At least you now have a frame of reference for how you can feel on an effective antidepressant. Most pharmaceutical companies have medication-assistance programs (applications are available on their Web sites) for anyone falling below certain income levels. Insurance companies commonly lower co-pays on newer medicines over time if the medicine is shown to be particularly helpful or if the pharmaceutical company negotiates a good deal with them. You can also check into other insurance companies' coverage should you have the opportunity to change insurers later on.

Gaining FDA Approval of a New Drug Isn't Easy

The application that pharmaceutical companies fill out to get a new drug approved by the U.S. Food and Drug Administration can be up to 100,000 pages long and take up to 2½ years to review.

"Who do I have to tell that I am starting an antidepressant?"

You should notify your other doctors when you start taking an antidepressant so that they are aware of all your health issues and can make sure there are no possible adverse interactions with any other medicines you take. Anyone else you choose to tell depends on how comfortable you are with sharing this information and whether you believe they will be supportive. Depression often affects relationships with family, friends, or co-workers, but whether you choose to tell them you are starting an antidepressant requires careful consideration. Hopefully, they will welcome the news that you are doing something positive to feel better. Sometimes family members or close friends can provide useful feedback on their observations as you start medication. There may be positive or negative changes that you are not aware of since it is hard to be objective about your own feelings.

Unfortunately, not everyone will be supportive and encouraging, and you may want to rethink sharing this information with those people. Those who do support you may expect unrealistic changes in your personality or your interactions simply because you are taking antidepressants. These could include qualities about yourself that you do not feel need changing. When you start an antidepressant, there is a risk that people you have conflicts with will say that your depression is the reason for problems in the relationship, freeing them of having to make any changes themselves. You should set realistic expectations with those individuals in advance about what you hope will change with medication treatment.

What about telling your employer? Antidepressant use may have precluded you from working in certain types of jobs in the past, but that is hardly ever the case nowadays. There are now laws in place to protect you from discrimination for mental-health treatment in the workplace. People in a few occupations, such as airline pilots, are still required to report if they are taking "mood altering" medications and could even be prohibited from working in that job as long as they take them. Some professional licensing boards require you to disclose that you receive mental-health treatment but it will not impact your ability to work in that field. You should check with your local government agencies, licensing board, if applicable, or human resource department for the rules of disclosure as they apply to you and your job.

Some people voluntarily tell their boss or co-worker if their behavior or performance at work has been affected by their depression. They hope to be supported in their efforts to get better. Some employers are very understanding, and others are not. If there is ignorance or prejudice in your workplace around mental-health problems, you could find yourself mistreated and ostracized. Despite any legal protection you are entitled to, your employer may find legal loopholes to prevent them from getting into trouble. You should have a good feel for the reaction you will receive before you decide to share this information.

Remember that any medicine that affects the brain can slow your reflexes or reaction time as a possible side effect. If you have a job in which you operate dangerous machinery or an occupation in which slow reaction times can put you or others at risk, you must let your employer know if you are experiencing such problems with the medicine. Those side effects should go away shortly. If they do not, you may need to discuss other medication options with your doctor.

Chris' Story Continues

Chris was excited to hear about a new antidepressant that seemed to work differently from others he had tried. He was determined not to be too optimistic, since he had high hopes in the past that were dashed when his symptoms returned. His doctor explained in detail how the medicine worked and how to gradually increase the dose until he got to the right level.

He remarked to his doctor, "I understand you don't have much experience with this medicine because it's so new. Some of the reading I've done says that doctors

Some Medication May Not Work as Well as Claimed

The FDA does not typically care much about a failed study showing a new drug did not better than a sugar pill. They care more about having enough positive studies. One popular antidepressant, citalopram (Celexa), had three out of five studies submitted to the FDA that failed to show a difference from placebo. Failed trials are not typically published in scientific journals. So some medications may not work as well as they say.

have to try these medicines on their patients many times before they really know how to use them."

The psychiatrist responded, "That's true, but I have talked with other physicians who have had success with this medication."

Chris asked, "So we will start at the dose the pharmaceutical company recommends and see what happens? When will I know whether to change the dose or try something else?"

"When will I know whether to change the dose or try something else?"

Doctors differ on how they decide whether to change a medication or increase the dose if you don't respond. Patients who do not feel better after a few days on a new medicine will occasionally call their doctor with complaints that nothing has happened yet. While four to six weeks is the typical time frame it takes to improve, many people notice some change within the first or second week. This early progress may be modest, but is an indication that, over time, the medicine will help.

If there is absolutely no improvement after six weeks, the likelihood is low that staying on the medicine, or even increasing the dose, will do much good. You should probably consider a different antidepressant. There are a few exceptions to this rule:

You are experiencing unusually high stress: If you are experiencing a significant life change, such as a loss of job, divorce, or recent death of someone close, you may not be able to sense much improvement from an antidepressant. You may need to wait until the emotional intensity of your situation settles down before determining whether the medicine works.

Your starting dose is inadequate: Your doctor may have started you on a dose that is too low. He might not be familiar with the proper dosing, may have deliberately put you on a low dose to avoid side effects, or he may have worried about drug interactions with other medicines you are take. You need to at least get to a therapeutic dose before deciding whether the medicine is the right one.

You metabolize drugs quickly: Some people have a genetic predisposition to eliminate certain medicines quickly from their body. Also, you may be taking another medicine that speeds up the body's metabolism of your antidepressant, so you may need a higher dosing than normal. There are ways to test your genetic makeup to see if your metabolism of a specific drug is slow, normal, or fast. You or your doctor should check whether other medicines or nutritional supplements you are taking will affect how you metabolize the antidepressant.

Make sure that any positive change is from the antidepressant effect, and not a side effect. For example, sedation can help you sleep better, but it doesn't mean the medicine is helping your depression. These side effects typically wear off over time and do not help with other symptoms of depression. If there is small but real improvement, you may simply need a higher dose. The recommended dosing guidelines do not apply to everyone. Plenty of people need lower doses and others require higher doses.

After reading this chapter, you should be well prepared to start on an antidepressant. Remember, people's experience starting medication can vary, and you may need to make adjustments based on your individual needs. Most problems you could encounter are easily managed if you know what to do. If you are not convinced that you want to start an antidepressant yet, Chapter Five gives you an overview of some proven non-medication strategies you can try. Even if you have decided to take an antidepressant, incorporating some of these into your treatment program can only help to speed your recovery and improve your chances of getting off medication sooner.

Are There Alternatives to Taking Antidepressants?

Chris was ready to leave his psychiatrist's office when she surprised him with the following question, "Have you ever seen a therapist?"

He was not sure why she would ask, given that he told her repeatedly that nothing that "happened" in his life to make him feel depressed.

"I did see a counselor for a couple of weeks and it didn't really help."

"What kind of therapy was it?" she asked.

"There are different kinds of therapy?"

"Yes, many."

"What's supposed to happen when I see a therapist? I went two times and each time I left feeling worse than when I went in," Chris told her.

He added, "If depression is a physical disease, how can talking about your problems help? When I got on the right medicine before, I felt great. I think I just need to find something that will work like that again."

Up to this point, I have focused on depression, how it affects the brain and body, medication options, and what you might expect when starting an antidepressant. However, even if you agree that you are depressed, you may still not be convinced that you want to take an antidepressant. There are a number of alternative treatments you can consider.

This chapter reviews some of the better studied and more commonly used non-medication options:

- Psychotherapy and other types of counseling.
- Nutritional supplements.
- Light therapy.
- Diet.
- Non-traditional healing practice such as yoga, meditation, and acupuncture.
- Exercise.

If any of these or other approaches you try are not helpful, you can always reconsider whether to take an antidepressant. Many of these treatments can be used in conjunction with antidepressants to improve your response. Some people on antidepressants may not do well unless they incorporate some complementary therapies into their regime.

"If depression is a physical disease, how can talking about your problems help?"

Talking therapy can be traced back to the Persians in the ninth century, but it did not become a mainstay of treatment for mental-health problems until Sigmund Freud, the most recognizable name in the mental-health field, developed some of his revolutionary theories.

There is a great deal of misunderstanding about psychotherapy. Therapy, when done correctly, is far more complex than just talking about your problems or regurgitating the events of your past. It can be hard work at times, but it can produce dramatic and long-lasting change. Many people think of therapy as it is portrayed in the media—lying on a couch as a gray-bearded, pipe-smoking gentleman wearing an aged, tweed jacket nods at regular intervals as you ramble on about faded childhood memories. Others imagine therapy to be similar to what they see on talk shows where the all-knowing, television therapist can hear about someone's psychological issues, uncover the origin of the problem, and generate a comprehensive treatment plan in 50 minutes. Neither scenario accurately portrays what happens in most therapists' offices.

Different therapies are based on one or more of the many psychological theories of depression. If depression does have psychological roots, it does not invalidate that there are physical changes in the brain with depression. Perhaps these biological changes are not the cause, but the consequence of getting depressed. Improving your psychological well-being through therapy or other lifestyle changes may reverse these changes without the use of medicine. Yet, some mental-healthcare providers believe in psychological causes of depression but still feel medicine is necessary in addition to therapy.

Most theories about psychological causes of depression were developed through studying human behavior, by therapists interacting with patients, or by using animal models to learn about responses to different types of stress or environmental changes. Freud believed that depression is a result of losing someone or something real or imagined in your childhood. He based this idea on his observation that depression was similar to grief. Grief then leads to anger turned inward, which evolves into self-hate, self-criticism, and guilt.

Cognitive therapists believe that depression develops from a negative view of oneself. When something bad happens, automatic negative thoughts are triggered, creating feelings of hopelessness and sadness. An interpersonal therapist sees depression as a consequence of poor interpersonal relationships that lead to rejection from others. Humanistic psychology teaches that depression occurs when people are unable to self actualize and achieve their goals. Animal behavioral experiments have shown that animals experience a phenomenon called learned helplessness when they discover they have no control over an unpleasant situation (like an electric shock given to a rat in a cage). They become apathetic and depressed.

Psychological theories of depression are complex and cannot be adequately explained in a few sentences. There are volumes of books dedicated to these ideas. It is more important to realize that depression is understood in many ways other than simply chemical imbalances in the brain. Therapy may give you some insight and coping skills necessary to overcome any psychological causes or barriers to getting better.

"There are different kinds of therapy?"

While there are hundreds of different therapies, only a few are frequently used in practice. Most therapists incorporate a variety of styles when treating their patients. Some examples of different styles include:

Psychoanalysis: This is one of the first well-developed psychotherapies. It is based on Freud's theory that we have unconscious memories and feelings that we are not immediately aware of but that shape our feelings and behaviors. This therapy requires an extensive time commitment and is geared to understanding yourself in great psychological depth. You will most likely find yourself lying on a couch and not getting much feedback initially from the analyst. One of the techniques is for the therapist to help you interpret transference—feelings you may have toward someone (usually the therapist) that really come from feelings toward someone in your past. When you are more aware of your unconscious thoughts, you are better able to control them.

Psychoanalytic psychotherapy: This is based on similar concepts as psychoanalysis, but with less focus on interpreting transference. The goal is still to look for insight into why certain behavior and feelings occur. This is less time intensive and is usually more problem-focused. And you probably won't be lying on a couch.

Cognitive therapy (CT): Based on the principal that our thoughts affect our feelings, this form of therapy involves identifying and overcoming negative thought patterns. For example, you may think that you are incompetent at your job because your boss points out a few mistakes on a report. You learn to figure out which situations in your life trigger these negative thoughts and replace them with more positive ones. This is an active therapy that may involve reading or homework outside the sessions. CT is usually brief and symptom focused. There are types of CT such as cognitive processing therapy (CPT) you may hear about that have been developed and studied for other conditions such as post-traumatic stress disorder (PTSD).

Interpersonal psychotherapy (ITP): Like cognitive therapy, ITP is also structured and brief, often lasting for 12 to 16 sessions. The focus is on how relationships affect your mood and how to change negative patterns in your interpersonal interactions. Therapists often use an ITP manual to guide the therapy.

Behavior therapy (BT): BT is most effective for changing behavior patterns and is more commonly used for conditions such obsessive compulsive disorder or eating disorders than for depression. The goal is to learn new, healthy behaviors and unlearn old, destructive ones. There is less attention to the cause and more to methods of controlling the behaviors. For example, a fear of heights may be treated by slowly going to higher and higher floors of a building which, over time, reduces anxiety.

Supportive psychotherapy: This therapy is useful for someone who is less interested in where certain feelings and behaviors come from and more concerned with problem solving and receiving support from the therapist. There is more focus on everyday issues with a goal of alleviating symptoms.

Therapy depends a great deal on the human interaction between the patient and the therapist, making it hard to study and prove its effectiveness. CT and ITP are brief and very structured, which makes them easier than psychoanalysis or psychoanalytic psychotherapies to validate and compare to other treatments like antidepressants. CT and ITP have been shown to work as well as antidepressants in mild to moderate depression and better than supportive therapy. CT alone may do slightly better than ITP alone in severe depression, but neither works as well as medication. CT and ITP with medication help more than medication alone.

"What is supposed to happen when I see a therapist?"

Therapy is not a quick fix and does not usually work as it is portrayed in the movies where some forgotten traumatic memory is uncovered and all your problems instantly melt away. Don't expect your mood to lift after every session. Therapy is an active process in which you have to work with the therapist to understand why you have certain feelings and behaviors and learn how you can change them.

Your therapist may need several sessions just for information gathering. He will want to learn about your background, understand the problems you are experiencing, and then determine a plan of action. A good therapist is supportive and reassuring but also has an obligation to help you get better. As a result, you may hear things from the therapist about yourself that may not be pleasant, which is hard if you are already feeling down about yourself. Unconditional support might make you feel good immediately but it does not help you in the long run.

If you hear something you disagree with, challenge your therapist. Therapists are not always correct in their interpretations or recommendations. A good therapist should create an open environment for that kind of dialogue.

Some suggestions for making therapy more useful:

- Be clear about your goals and address those with the therapist.
- Make sure the type of therapy you are undergoing is best for your condition.
- Commit to at least four to six sessions before deciding that the therapist or therapy is not right for you, unless there is something very out of the ordinary in his or her practice.

- If the therapist does something that bothers you, such as being late or cancelling appointments, confront him or her about how it makes you feel rather than just being angry or quitting. These conflicts, and how you handle them, can be useful therapeutic experiences.
- Avoid quick cures such as hypnosis (which is useful for other conditions), or fad therapies such as "recovered-memory therapy" for depression. They usually do not produce lasting change.
- Your insurance may only pay for certain types of therapy or for only a limited number of sessions. You may need to pay out-of-pocket to get the right treatment.
- When you share so much of yourself in therapy, it can create an intimate relationship with the therapist. Make sure you stay within proper boundaries of a therapeutic relationship such as by not having social conversations, inquiring too much about the therapist's personal life, or seeing each other outside of a professional setting.
- If you decide to quit therapy, discuss it during a session and have a plan for how and when to stop.

Lucy's Story Continues

As Lucy thought more about taking an antidepressant, she wondered whether she could try additional alternative treatments first. She had seen a naturopathic doctor for several years, but never fully shared with him the severity of her symptoms. She felt embarrassed to tell him and feared he would say she wasn't working hard enough to get better. With the encouragement of her therapist, she decided to share just how badly she felt.

The doctor's open-mindedness to medication surprised her, though he preferred she continue to try alternatives first.

"Before you decide, let's reevaluate what you're doing now. Even if you do take an antidepressant, you can still do many things to help yourself."

Lucy responded, "I've been using St. John's Wort. What about other natural supplements? I heard about taking amino acids and fish oil. Can changing my diet help depression?"

"I've been using St. John's Wort.
What about other natural supplements?"

There is a growing interest in using natural medicines or supplements to treat all kinds of physical ailments including depression. However, despite common perception, "natural" does not necessarily mean safer or better than conventional treatments. Many natural supplements are untested and unproven. They could also do harm by delaying your start with more proven therapies. The longer depression goes untreated, the harder it can be to treat.

Some natural medicines or supplements are derived from plants, herbs, and animals, such as St. John's Wort or omega-3 fatty acids. Others, like melatonin, may be synthesized in a laboratory just like prescription medicines, though they replicate natural hormones in the body. Vitamins and amino acids are also promoted as alternative therapies.

These products are not held to the same standard as conventional medications by government regulatory agencies such as the FDA. They are considered dietary supplements and the manufacturers are not required to prove their effectiveness in controlled research studies as they are with prescription medicine. Because of the prolific use of natural therapies, there is a growing interest in studying these products. Unfortunately, without the deep pockets of the pharmaceutical industry, funding is limited. An agency established within the National Institute of Health, called the National Center for Complementary and Alternative Medicine (NCCAM), is conducting some of these studies. Even if a study has been done and a product was shown not to work, it can still be promoted and sold.

The potency and purity of these products varies greatly between different manufacturers. In other words, you do not always know how much of what you are getting. Suggested dosing can differ from brand to brand. If a product was tested in a clinical trial, the recommended dose on the bottle can differ from the amount used in that study. This makes it difficult to know if you are taking a safe or effective amount. The NCCAM Web site (www.nccam.nih.gov) reviews current research findings and can provide some guidance on proper dosing. Another site, www.consumer-labs.com, reviews the quality of specific products.

Though some physicians disapprove of these treatments, a growing number incorporate them into their practices. These doctors may be good resources from which to learn which products are higher in quality. Naturopathic physicians, pharmacists, and chiropractors are often familiar with the more reliable products and manufacturers. Be wary of healthcare practitioners selling products in their office because they may be biased toward the products they make money on. They may be good products, but they may be more expensive than you can obtain elsewhere. If you currently take, or are considering using, such products, let your doctor know to make sure there will be no dangerous interactions with any other medicine you take.

The following are some of the more common natural medications and supplements used to treat depression:

St. John's Wort (SJW): Derived from the SJW flower or Hypericum Moseranum, this centuries-old product is one of the more popular natural treatments. Dozens of studies have shown that SJW is helpful in mild to moderate depression but less effective in more severe depression. SJW may work by increasing serotonin, but it affects many other chemicals in the brain as well. It can have dangerous interactions if you are taking other medicines, especially other antidepressants, but it has relatively few side effects when used alone. Dry mouth, dizziness, and constipation are the most common side effects. The recommended dose is between 900 and 2,000 mg divided into two to three times per day dosing. This can get expensive.

Omega-3 fatty acid: This is a lipid, or fat, that is found in many plants and animals and plays an important role in inflammation and the body's immune response. There are three types of omega-3 fatty acids—DHA, EPA, and ALA—and each has different functions. Omega-3 has been extensively researched and shown to help many medical conditions, including heart disease, autoimmune disorders, depression, and bipolar disorder. In fact, countries with high omega-3 consumption typically have low rates of depression. Supplements may have different amounts of DHA, EPA, and ALA. EPA may be more important for helping mood. Experts recommend at least 750 mg of EPA a day for depression or bipolar disorder. Omega-3 studies use as much as 1.5 to 6 grams of omega-3 a day. ALA is available in flaxseed and other supplements, but many people cannot convert ALA into the more useful EPA and DHA.

SAMe: This is a synthetic form of a compound found in most living cells of mammals and plays a role in synthesis of neurotransmitters and in communication between cells. SAMe has been used to treat conditions such as depression, liver disease, and osteoarthritis. The recommended dose by mouth is around 400 mg but better results were seen in studies with doses up to 1,600 mg per day and when taken by injection. Like SJW, this can be expensive at high doses.

Folic acid: Low levels of folate (vitamin B9) and vitamin B12 levels may cause depression because of their role in making 5-HT, DA, and NE (see Glossary or Chapter Three). You are likely to respond better to an anti-depressant if your folate levels are in the normal to high range or you add folate when taking an antidepressant. One form of folate supplements, L-methylfolate, is able to get into the brain more easily than other forms and helps with synthesis of neurotransmitters. L-methylfolate (Deplin) is available as a prescription medicine but it is considered a medical food. It is approved for the dietary management of low folate levels in depressed patients and improves antidepressant response. There is no evidence that it treats depression alone.

Many other natural supplements are touted as having an antide-pressant effect. DHEA is a synthetic version of a steroid produced in the body that is used to produce your sex hormones—estrogen and testos-terone. DHEA is advertised to help your sex drive, memory, and mood. Using DHEA can be risky because of its possible effect on hormone lev-els and the results from studies have not been as impressive as for other natural products.

There is also a growing interest in using pharmacy-compounded hor-mones such as testosterone, progesterone, and bio-identical estrogen (derived from plants) to help with mood, particularly in post-menopausal women. This is controversial because of the potential dangers associated with taking hormones, limited proof of effectiveness, and lack of FDA regulation. Other products such as tryptophan, melatonin, kava kava, and valerian are used for certain symptoms associated with depression such as insomnia and anxiety but not for depression itself.

If you are going to use any type of supplement, do it under a trained healthcare professional's supervision since there are risks. Make sure you are getting a high-quality product and taking the right amount.

"Can changing my diet help depression?"

Unhealthy dietary habits can cause depression and depression-like symptoms, such as low energy, poor concentration, sadness, and decreased motivation. North American and European diets that include fast food, red meat, refined sugars, soft drinks, white bread, and unrefined carbohydrates have been associated with higher rates of mood disorders and other health problems. Countries with historically low rates of depression see a dramatic rise when they start to import fast-food restaurant chains and processed foods from western countries.

Inadequate intake of necessary vitamins, minerals, and other important organic compounds such as vitamin B, magnesium, or omega-3 can also be a depression risk factor. This can occur through poor dietary choices or gastrointestinal problems that prevent proper absorption. If this is the case, changing what you eat or taking nutritional supplements could reverse symptoms. If you are not experiencing a nutritional deficiency, there is little evidence that dietary changes alone will treat depression. A change in diet, though, can improve how you feel physically and emotionally and may help any other treatments work more effectively.

Vitamin and mineral deficiencies are easy to diagnose with a simple blood test. There are three types of B vitamins that are most closely related to mood problems:

Vitamin B12 (cobalmin): This is found in whole grains and animal protein, but, even with proper dietary intake, some medical conditions prevent proper absorption. This includes Crohn's disease, history of intestinal surgery, alcoholism, and pernicious anemia. Vegetarians may not get enough B12 because they avoid eating meat.

Vitamin B6 (pyridoxine): This vitamin helps synthesize neurotransmitters and may be low if you have an intestinal problem that prevents absorption. Women taking estrogen or birth control pills are also at risk for low B6. Sunflower seeds, yeast, wheat germ, and raw foods are good sources of B6.

Vitamin B9 (folate): Low folate levels have been associated with depression and poor response to antidepressants. High amounts of folate can be found in leafy vegetables (lettuce, spinach), vegetables (broccoli, peas, beans), and fortified cereals.

Although some people report feeling better when taking additional vitamin B, these supplements have not been proven to treat depression when blood levels are in the normal range. However, adding more vitamin B–rich foods to your diet is not harmful and makes for healthier food choices. Vitamin B supplements could be dangerous if taken in excessive amounts.

Magnesium is a mineral critical for normal body and brain functioning. Low levels are thought to cause symptoms such as fatigue, concentration problems, and anxiety. Magnesium supplements are promoted as having an antidepressant effect, but there is no evidence that they work if your magnesium level is normal. In fact, too much can be dangerous, so check with your doctor before taking magnesium supplements. Magnesium-rich foods include wheat germ, avocados, and certain nuts like almonds and cashews.

Low levels of Vitamin D have been linked to a variety of health problems including bone loss, immune disorders, fatigue, depression, and heart disease. The exact role of Vitamin D in depression is unclear but may be related to changes in the production of neurotransmitters. Only recently has testing for Vitamin D (a simple blood test) become more commonplace by the healthcare community and a surprisingly high number of people are found to have a low level. This may be a result of a reduced exposure to sunlight (which increases Vitamin D). There is no evidence that Vitamin D supplements help depression if your levels are normal, but may provide some relief of symptoms if you are deficient.

Increasing omega-3 fatty acid consumption is one of the best-studied diet changes shown to improve your physical and emotional health. Dietary sources of omega-3 include cold-water oily fish such as salmon, anchovies, sardines, and herring. Other fish, like tuna or swordfish, also contain omega-3, but in lesser amounts. Many fish contain high amounts of mercury which can have detrimental effects on your health. Most nutritionists recommend eating fish no more than twice a week for that reason. High-quality omega-3 supplements are typically mercury-free.

Non-fish sources of omega-3 tend to contain mostly the ALA form. Many people have trouble converting ALA to the EPA and DHA forms, which are more beneficial in mood and other health disorders. Good dietary sources of ALA are flaxseed, kiwifruit, chia, and a variety of nuts including hazelnuts, walnuts, and pecans.

Are Antidepressants Fishy?

Rates of depression are 60 times higher in New Zealand (where the average consumption of seafood is 40 pounds per year) compared to Japan (where a person consumes nearly 150 pounds of seafood each year).

Omega-6 (linoleic acid) is another important fatty acid that helps promote inflammation (omega-3 is anti-inflammatory). A healthy balance between omega-6 and omega-3 levels is important for physical and mental well being. Omega-6 is found in large quantities in oils from certain seeds and nuts including sunflower, cottonseed, corn, and safflower. Refined soy oil, which is in many processed foods such as packaged snack foods, fast foods, and sweets, is also rich in omega-6. People living in North American and Europe consume a ratio of omega-6 to omega-3 that is 15 to 25 times to one. A healthy ratio is considered closer to two to four times to one. Countries with high omega-6 to omega-3 ratios have high rates of depression, dementia, inflammatory diseases, and other health problems.

Reducing your ratio of omega-6 to omega-3 takes a few simple steps. First, avoid processed and fast foods rich in soy oil. Palm, coconut, canola oil, and extra virgin olive oil are preferable for cooking and salad dressing. Also, try to obtain milk, cheese, and meat from grass-fed animals (not grain-fed). You can also decrease omega-6 levels by eating fewer grains and more fruits and vegetables.

Reducing or eliminating caffeine, sugar, and alcohol could also have a positive impact on your mood. Caffeine is a powerful stimulant that, if discovered today, would probably require a prescription to obtain. While caffeine improves energy, concentration, and may even provide a small mood lift with moderate consumption, high usage can produce irritability, mood swings, and significant withdrawal symptoms when abruptly stopped. Studies have shown that people with depression consume more caffeine than those without depression.

Sugar also provides a quick boost in energy and mood but can lead to an abrupt drop in both within an hour or two. Populations with high sugar consumption have higher rates of depression. Sugar intake has

An Argument for Better Prison Food

At the 2006 Nutrition and Health Conference sponsored by the University of Arizona's College of Medicine and Columbia University's College of Physicians and Surgeons, Dr. Hibbeln cited a study showing that violence in a British prison dropped by 37 percent after omega-3 oils and vitamins were added to the prisoners' diets.

been associated with a decrease in BDNF (discussed in Chapter Three) and in endorphins, which are pain-relieving, mood-elevating chemicals in the brain.

Alcohol is a depressant that can reduce neurotransmitter levels. While some health benefits are reported with moderate alcohol use, such as with red wine, no one knows how much alcohol it takes to cause or worsen depression.

Some health food stores promote taking amino acid supplements such as tryptophan, tyrosine, and 5-HTP as mood enhancers. Your body uses these amino acids to manufacture neurotransmitters, but there is no evidence that adding more amino acids to your diet, unless you are deficient in them, helps treat depression. Much of this hype is geared to selling nutritional products, amino acid testing services, or supplements. There are even questions about the validity of some of the amino acid blood tests used by non-traditional healthcare providers.

There is no need to undergo some complicated and unproven antidepressant diet you may hear or read about. You can easily avoid bad food choices by preparing your own meals and not keeping unhealthy products at home. Adjusting to a healthy diet can take a few weeks since your body may be used to the taste and feeling you get when eating foods high in sugar, saturated fats, or enriched wheat products. You may benefit from seeing a nutritionist to help you overcome personal stumbling blocks toward healthy eating habits.

Jane's Story Continues

Jane excitedly called her doctor when she read an article about the body's natural rhythms and how they are affected by light. She always dreaded the winter months because of how bad she felt during winter. For years, she planned a regular trip to the Caribbean during Christmas to help her mood.

"I've been reading about all these other ways to treat depression that bring the body into more balance. Does light therapy really treat depression? How about yoga, meditation, or even acupuncture? These seem more natural than taking a pill."

"Does light therapy really treat depression?"

Exposure to light plays an important role in your body's natural circadian rhythm and neurotransmitter production, both of which can be altered when you have less exposure to light. This explains why some people get more depressed in the winter months. Light therapy has been shown to be effective for seasonal affective disorder (SAD), or the "winter blues," and may have some benefit in non-seasonal depression as well. You'll have to invest in a light box and make the time commitment to give yourself adequate light exposure. It is safe and inexpensive with few side effects. The standard recommended exposure is to a 10,000-lux white florescent light for 30 minutes each day.

All varieties of light boxes are available in pharmacies and on the Internet. There is no prescription required. Some use different types of bulbs, allowing for shorter exposure times, or are advertised as more effective than the traditional florescent bulbs. You can even build your own box. If you have a history of eye problems, check with your doctor about excessive light exposure. Light therapy can trigger manic episodes in people prone to bipolar disorder.

Negative ion therapy is similar to light treatment but has not been studied as extensively. Some people say they feel better in natural settings where negative ions are found in high concentrations, such as in forests or near oceans. The treatment involves exposure to a negative ion generator which may increase serotonin levels. Small studies have shown that it may work as well as antidepressants in SAD but there is not enough evidence at this time to advocate for its use. There seem to be few side effects associated with this therapy.

"What about yoga, meditation, or even acupuncture?"

A number of healing practices, such as yoga, meditation, and acupuncture have been used for thousands of years for physical and mental well-being. They are gradually becoming more mainstream in western culture and have been promoted as helping treat depression and other mental-health disorders. Some small studies show that they can improve mood. These studies have few subjects, are poorly controlled, and do not compare the practices with medication treatment. They also do not seem to work as quickly as medication.

Yoga has been shown to increase GABA, a neurotransmitter in the brain that helps with mood and anxiety. Acupuncture is based on the theory that the body has an energy force, or ch'i, that intersects at 12 points, and depression occurs when one of these points is blocked. Acupuncture works by opening those blockages. Meditation has been used to treat depression and other health problems by improving mindfulness of one's body and surroundings. While all of these practices have been shown to be safe when done properly, some doctors have suggested that people with more severe forms of depression and other mental-health problems should avoid meditation and yoga with a meditation focus.

Frank's Story Continues

"Frank, you have to exercise more," Dr. Gregory said during their last appointment.

"I know, I'm a little heavier than I should be, but I dropped some weight already."

The doctor commented, "Not just for weight loss. You told me you're reluctant to take medicine. Exercise can help treat depression if done correctly."

Frank asked, "I know exercise is good for me but how can it help my mood?"

Popular Alternatives

Seventy percent of the world's population uses alternative treatments, as does 25 percent of the population in the United States. In 2007, more than $34 billion was spent on alternative health products and practitioners in the United States.

> "The sovereign invigorator of the body is exercise, and of all the exercises walking is the best."
> —Thomas Jefferson, Former President of the United States

"I know exercise is good for me but how can it help my mood?"

The antidepressant effects of exercise have been studied for many years. In fact, exercise may be as effective as medicine in mild-to-moderate depression. The results are less impressive in individuals with more severe depression. Medication usually works faster, but the benefits of exercise may last longer. Getting someone with depression to dedicate themselves to a rigorous exercise regimen is one of the biggest obstacles to its use, since lack of energy and motivation are symptoms of depression.

Exercise works best for depression when done with sufficient intensity and frequency. While even minimal physical activity reduces depression symptoms, rigorous exercise produces the most robust effect. One study showed significant improvement with 35 minutes of fast walking five times a week or 60 minutes three times a week, but far less change with 15 minutes of walking five times a week or stretching three times a week. Exercise appears to increase BDNF, neurotransmitter levels (5-HT and NE), and endorphins—all of which are associated with improvement in mood.

You can make responsible decisions to treat many types of depression without taking medication. Make sure you use non-medication therapies that have been proven to work. Many scams promise quick and easy results. Even if they seem to be based on scientific fact, investigate before spending your time or money on such approaches. Remember that natural treatments or supplements are not always safe and can be expensive. Delaying treatment with something that is more likely to work carries a risk as well. Many non-medication treatments can be used in addition to medication to help you feel better and, hopefully, improve your chances of getting off medicine.

Chapter Six

Is This as Good as It Gets?

Although it took longer than she expected, Jane noticed she slept better and could get up more easily in the morning since starting the antidepressant several months ago. She also no longer dreaded leaving her house. At work, one of her teaching assistants commented, "You seem more relaxed lately. I haven't seen you smile this much in a while." Jane felt pleased with the improvement but felt a little self-conscious that her depression had been so obvious to others.

Although Jane's anxiety spells became less frequent and intense, she felt disappointed that the anxiety had not gone away completely.

She told her doctor, "I'm certainly much better than when I started the medicine, but I don't feel as good as I did before I got depressed. Is this as good as it gets? How can I tell if this is what the medicine should do?"

This section of the book deals with issues that come up midway on your journey to overcoming depression. If you started an antidepressant, you have, hopefully, made it through any initial bumps in the road. The first medicine your doctor gave you may have worked great with few or no side effects. Or, you could be one of the many people who had to try several different medicines until you found the one that works best for you, and with the fewest problems. After 8 to 12 weeks on an antidepressant, you should be feeling significantly better. With perseverance and a bit of luck, any side effects you experienced should have resolved or you have been able to manage well despite them. This chapter focuses on tools to help you determine how well you are responding to the medication and provides techniques to optimize your treatment.

The differences before and after starting medicine seem more obvious in the first few weeks of antidepressant therapy because the experience of being depressed is fresh in your mind. Once you have been on medicine for a while and many of your symptoms resolve, it may be harder for you to tell whether you are doing as well as you should. There is no blood test or brain scan that can tell you that you are depressed and, similarly, there is none to confirm that depression has completely gone away. Your doctor has to rely on your answers to a series of questions about ongoing symptoms, just as she does when trying to diagnose depression.

As our understanding of depression treatment has evolved, the focus of treatment has shifted from simply getting people better to getting people well. As a result, current research explores how to use existing treatments more effectively and works to develop new therapies with the goal of helping you achieve a full recovery.

This chapter looks at approaches you and your doctor can take to assess what, if any, symptoms may persist despite treatment. It also reviews some strategies to optimize your current treatment. Issues addressed in this chapter include:

- The difference between doing better and getting well.
- Methods for determining if the medicine is working well.
- Reasons why symptoms may persist even though you are on medicine.
- What you can do to help make the medicine work better.
- Common antidepressant augmentation strategies.
- Other treatment options if nothing seems to help.

"How can I tell if this is what the medicine should do?"

Based on results from antidepressant research studies, you should notice at least 50 percent improvement in the first four to six weeks if you are taking the right medicine at the right dose. Government drug-regulation agencies like the FDA only require that an antidepressant relieve at least 50 percent of your symptoms with a statistically greater likelihood than a dummy pill, or placebo, for drug approval. Consequently, these studies do not always give us the information we need to be able to achieve 100 percent improvement (or as close as possible) with the medicine.

In a depression study, *response* is defined as getting at least 50 percent better. *Remission* is defined as getting well. Researchers have created scales to rate your symptoms and they agree that certain scores on specific validated depression scales indicate that your symptoms are gone, or pretty close. If you have a high depression score, such as 30, on a commonly used scale like the Hamilton Depression Scale (HAM-D), and then receive a score of 15 at the end of a study, you are considered to have *responded* to the medication. The problem is that even a score of 15 is too high and means you are still fairly symptomatic. Typical scores on a Ham-D to qualify for a depression study range from 15-25 but can go much higher.

Similarly, a score of 7 or less on the HAM-D means you are in remission but some symptoms may remain. Not everyone agrees on which number you must fall below on any given scale to be considered *remitted*. For example, some may consider a score of 8 or 10 or less on a HAM-D as being remission. In one trial you might meet the criteria, but not in another.

Another limitation to these scales is that each emphasizes certain symptoms and omits other important ones. One scale may only rate sleeping too little but not evaluate whether you sleep too much. For example, the HAM-D rates more physical changes such as energy level, interest in sex, and anxiety symptoms such as heart racing, stomach upset, and rapid breathing than another commonly used scale, Montgomery Asberg Rating Scale (MADRS). MADRS gives more weight to emotional symptoms of depression like feeling down on yourself or sadness. This means there is no all-inclusive, fool-proof measurement tool that determines whether you are optimally treated.

The best thing you can do to assess how you are doing and to help your doctor make the right decision for your care is to develop your *own scale* that tracks *your* particular symptoms and functioning. Chapter Two describes common symptoms of depression but there may be others that you experience. Figure out what changes you have noticed about yourself since the depression began and which areas of your life have been affected, such as work, home, hobbies, or relationships. Write them down and rate the severity on a scale of 0 to 5. If you are comfortable involving family or friends, they may be able to give you some feedback on what they have noticed. Rate any change as you continue with treatment. See Appendix J "Sample Mood Diary." You can also find free mood charts online on sites such as www.takingantidepressants.com or www.medhelp.org.

Depression–The Sequel

In patients whose depression went away and then returned, those with residual symptoms relapsed three times faster than those without.

" I noticed you're much less negative in our last few sessions, and it sounds like you are getting out of the house more. I know you don't feel much change with the antidepressant but do you notice anything?" Elaine asked at the end of the therapy hour.

Lucy said, "I feel more optimistic. I'm not sure whether it's the medicine. Maybe just deciding to take medicine means I'm starting to get serious about getting better. I still eat too much and love my sleep. You said my overeating and sleeping are signs of depression. But if the medicine is working, why do I still have these symptoms? Are there some things I can do to make the medicine work better?"

"But if the medicine is working, why do I still have these symptoms?"

Many people taking an antidepressant experience significant improvement yet continue to have some ongoing symptoms. In clinical studies (funded by pharmaceutical companies), typically 50 to 70 percent of people taking an antidepressant respond, while only 30 to 45 percent remit. An important study, STAR-D, conducted in 2006 and funded by the National Institute of Mental Health (not a pharmaceutical company), compared different medication treatments after failure to respond to one antidepressant trial. More than 4,000 people with depression were started on citalopram (Celexa), a commonly used antidepressant, and, after 12 weeks, researchers found that only 28 percent of subjects remitted.

Residual symptoms are those symptoms that persist despite overall improvement. They are often less frequent and severe but can still impact your work, home, and social life. If you have taken time off from your job due to depression, you may be feeling well enough to return to work. Not until you get back into the routine do you notice you are still having lingering difficulties with concentration and decision making. These residual symptoms could affect your job performance. You may be functioning well at work and home but still not want to get back into your exercise routine or hobbies.

Studies show that residual symptoms are associated with a higher risk for relapse and recurrence of depression. Some doctors believe that if you take antidepressants repeatedly and do not remit, you are more likely to develop treatment resistance similar to taking an incomplete course of an antibiotic for an infection. When the infection is not completely treated, the bacteria causing the infection can develop a resistance to the antibiotic, prolonging or worsening the infection. While the exact mechanism of developing resistance with antidepressants may differ from that of antibiotics, a similar result may occur—the medicine does not work as well.

Carefully monitor any problems that have not resolved since taking an antidepressant. Some may be residual symptoms of the depression, but other problems may be explained by other reasons, such as being misdiagnosed, having a co-existing medical or additional psychiatric condition, a side effect from another medicine you are taking, or longstanding personality traits. If a symptom comes from any of these, antidepressants are unlikely to treat them.

The difference between treating a symptom coming from the *state* of your depression verses a personality trait is that the former is far more likely to respond to medication than the latter, which may require a non-medication intervention, like therapy. Typical depression symptoms, such as low self-esteem, pessimism, or low motivation can all be part of one's personality even prior to having depression. Personality traits can lead to depression, or they can result from having depression for many years. Either way, the medicine may treat depression but not help those particular symptoms.

Risk factors for residual symptoms of depression include:

- Not taking the medicine regularly.
- Using too low of an antidepressant dose.

Charlie Brown on Depression

"This is my depressed stance. When you're depressed, it makes a lot of difference how you stand. The worst thing you can do is straighten up and hold your head high because then you'll start to feel better. If you're going to get any joy out of being depressed, you've got to stand like this."

—Charlie Brown

- Abusing alcohol or drugs.
- Needing an additional medication or intervention, such as therapy.
- Experiencing a severe life stressor, such as a relationship problem or job stress that interferes with the antidepressant's effectiveness.
- Taking the wrong antidepressant.

"Are there some things I can do to make the medicine work better?"

If you don't respond to the medication or experience ongoing residual symptoms, make sure you are taking the antidepressant exactly as prescribed at the correct dose. Many people forget to take medicine from time to time, especially if there is not a noticeable problem shortly after missing a pill. Medicines that have to be taken more than once a day or under certain conditions, such as with or without food, are more frequently missed. Unfortunately, skipping as little as one pill a week can impact how well the medicine works.

Most antidepressants can be taken any time of the day, but they are sometimes prescribed at a specific time of day to minimize side effects. For example, a sedating antidepressant is more likely to be prescribed at bedtime even though the timing of the medicine has no impact on its antidepressant effect.

To improve your medication compliance:

- Ask your doctor if you can change the time you take the medication. You may be more likely to remember it at another time of day, such as breakfast or when brushing your teeth.
- If you take more than one medicine, use a pill box to organize them all in advance.
- Set a pill reminder on your cell phone or watch.
- If you were told to take the medicine more than once a day, ask if you can take all the doses at one time in the day safely or whether there is an extended-release version.
- Ask your doctor how to take the medicine if you realize several hours later that you have forgotten it.
- Have an emergency stash (sometimes your doctor can give you samples) in case you forget to refill the prescription on time.
- Make sure you always have refills on the bottle and a follow-up appointment with your doctor before they run out.

Dosing an antidepressant too low is another common reason for an incomplete medication response. A medication can be prescribed at the usual recommended dose, but you may require a greater amount because of your metabolism or body size. Studies are designed to get people 50 percent better (and not into remission), which means that doses used in trials may be lower than what some people need in order to get well. Government agencies restrict pharmaceutical companies from telling doctors to use more than was shown to be safe and effective in their studies. For example, the recommended dosing of venlafaxine XR (Effexor XR) is up to 225 mg per day, but doctors commonly write for doses of 300 to 450 mg. Some doctors stick to official prescribing guidelines, but others who have more expertise and a greater comfort level using more than the suggested dosing go much higher. Occasionally a pharmacist may question an unusually high dose, because it is their job to make sure the doctor did not make a mistake. Some insurance companies may resist paying for higher doses but, in most cases, the doctor can get it authorized. Always consult your doctor if there is any question about dosage, and never adjust your dosage on your own without consulting your doctor.

Make sure you have been correctly diagnosed. Symptoms such as trouble sleeping, difficulty concentrating, or poor energy can be seen in other psychiatric disorders in addition to depression. If you suffer from other symptoms not commonly seen in depression, let your doctor know so that he can determine whether your diagnosis is accurate. For example, post-traumatic stress disorder (PTSD) can look similar to depression but often includes flashbacks or nightmares of a traumatic event. This distinguishes it from depression. Often people will have depression with another psychiatric diagnosis. Sometimes antidepressants treat both, such as in the case of generalized anxiety disorder (GAD) or panic disorder (PD). Other conditions, such as attention deficit disorder (ADHD), require an additional medication to successfully manage each. Psychiatric conditions that are commonly seen together are listed in Table 6-A "Common Psychiatric Disorders Co-Occurring with Depression" (on page 136).

Depression and alcohol or substance abuse frequently occur together. You can not always be certain whether the alcohol or drug problem triggered the depression or is a consequence of the depression. Doctors often hear from depressed patients that alcohol or an abused drug helps them feel better or manages an ongoing symptom. For example, someone might report using alcohol for sleep problems or marijuana to blunt anxious feelings. In reality, alcohol and drugs worsen depression over time and lessen the effectiveness of antidepressants. Alcohol and drugs can be seductive to someone with depression because they provide some immediate relief of symptoms, and a person may be unaware of the more gradual negative effects.

Medical issues can lead to residual symptoms. Chronic pain worsens depression, lowers BDNF levels (see Chapter Three), and diminishes antidepressant response. Drops in sex hormone levels (estrogen, progesterone, and testosterone), such as seen in post-menopausal women and in men over the age of 40, can worsen depression and related symptoms such as energy, concentration, and sex drive. Fluctuations in blood sugars in someone with diabetes can lead to mood swings or changes in energy level. Asthma, emphysema, or other respiratory problems can make someone feel short of breath, weak, and anxious. Autoimmune and neurological disorders can cause many symptoms similar to depression such as fatigue, low motivation, poor concentration, and even feelings of sadness and despair.

Review any other medications you take that may contribute to residual symptoms and decrease antidepressant responsiveness. They can also have side effects that mimic depression symptoms. Asthma medications, decongestants, and attention deficit medications can make people feel anxious and have trouble sleeping. Some heart medicines, such as beta blockers, can cause fatigue. Other medicines that can trigger or worsen depression include:

- Steroids.
- Narcotic pain medications.
- Interferon for Hepatitis C.
- Birth control pills.
- Isotretinoin (Accutane) for acne.
- Varenicline (Chantix) for smoking cessation.
- Finasteride (Propecia) for hair loss and enlarged prostate.

Many people with depression also take sleeping pills or anti-anxiety medication, which provide some immediate relief until the antidepressant begins to work. The goal is to be able to wean you off those medications once you are better since they are not intended for long-term use. If you notice worsening sleep or anxiety whenever you stop them, you might incorrectly assume that the depression has not remitted. However, it may actually be that you have developed a physical dependence on anti-anxiety or sleeping pills, which causes withdrawal, not residual depressive symptoms. In that case, you must gradually taper yourself off rather than abruptly discontinue them. You can also substitute non-habit-forming alternatives, such as over-the counter melatonin, ramelteon (Rozerem), or trazodone (Desyrel) for sleep. Buspirone (Buspar) or gabapentin (Neurotin) are often prescribed as non-addictive alternatives to help with anxiety. Coming off high doses of anti-anxiety or sleep medicines can be dangerous and may require a doctor's supervision. Withdrawal symptoms from those types of medications typically do not last more than one to two weeks. Be sure to consult your doctor on the safest way to come off of any medication that you are physically dependent on.

Consider whether any residual symptoms may be normal emotional reactions to life stressors. Antidepressants are not designed to numb you to your surroundings. Even if your depression has remitted, you will still experience difficulties with moods, anxiety, sleep, concentration, or energy during significant life events such as relationship conflicts, job stress, loss of a friend or family member, or financial problems.

Frank's Story Continues

Frank and his wife, Candace, told the doctor about the changes they both noticed since Frank started the antidepressant months ago. Candace found Frank far less irritable. She even started to look forward to his coming home from work. But when the doctor asked if there were some things that hadn't improved, she responded, "He still spends more time on the couch than he ever did before. He isn't back in the garden either."

"I'm just tired," said Frank. "I'm getting older and my body doesn't work the way it used to. The medicine has taken a lot of that edge off, and I'm happy to stick with it, but I don't want to take more or try a different medicine."

The doctor responded, "Sometimes adding another medicine can help with ongoing symptoms. In your case, this could give you more energy or motivation. It's a common practice and easier than trying to change the medicine you're currently taking since you do feel better."

"Another medicine?" asked Frank. "I don't even want to be on this one." The doctor smiled when he heard Frank say to his wife jokingly on his way out, "I

Common Augmentation Medicines

The following are medications frequently added when one antidepressant is only partially effective:

Antidepressant: Medicine Class

- Buproprion: Norepinephrine dopamine reuptake inhibitor
- Mirtazapine: Serotonin norepinephrine modulator
- Nefazodone: Serotonin modulator
- Trazodone: Serotonin modulator
- Amitriptline: Tricyclic
- Imipramine: Tricyclic
- Desipramine: Tricyclic

Non-Antidepressant Psychiatric Medicine: Medicine Class

- Buspirone (Buspar): Anti-anxiety
- Lithium (Lithobid, Eskalith): Mood stabilizer
- Aripiprazole (Abilify): Atypical antipsychotic/mood stabilizer
- Quetiapine (Seroquel/ Seroquel XR): Atypical antipsychotic/mood stabilizer
- Olanzapine (Zyprexa): Atypical antipsychotic/mood stabilizer
- Risperdone (Risperdal): Atypical antipsychotic/mood stabilizer
- Ziprazadone (Geodon): Atypical antipsychotic/mood stabilizer
- Lamotrigine (Lamictal): Mood stabilizer
- Methyphenidate (Ritalin): Attention Deficit Disorder
- Dextroamphetamine (Dexedrine): Attention Deficit Disorder/Narcolepsy
- Mixed amphetamine salts (Adderall): Attention Deficit Disorder

Non-Psychiatric Medicine: Medicine Class

- Pindolol (Visken): Blood pressure
- Thyroid (Cytomel, Synthroid, Armour thyroid): Thyroid Disorders
- Ropinirole (Requip): Parkinson's disease
- Pramipexole (Mirapex): Parkinson's disease
- Modanfinil (Provigil): Narcolepsy

think he gets paid based on how many pills his patients take."

When Frank brought the prescription to the pharmacist, Frank asked, "My doctor wants to add another medicine to what I already take. Is this typical?"

"My doctor wants to add another medicine to what I already take. Is this typical?"

Combination therapy, or augmentation for depression, is a common treatment approach when one antidepressant has helped but there are still ongoing symptoms. Other medical conditions frequently require more than one medicine for adequate disease management such as high blood pressure, asthma, or diabetes. Medicines with different mechanisms of action can work synergistically to maximize benefit. Taking an additional medication to treat depression is not very appealing, especially to someone who may already be reluctant to take an antidepressant. Augmenting your antidepressant with another medicine can turn response into remission and may allow you to reduce the dose of your current medicine. The downside to this approach is the cost of another drug, risk of added side effects, and possible drug interactions. There is very little research on augmentation strategies, leaving doctors to rely on word-of-mouth practices from respected peers and their own clinical experience to guide them. Some augmentation practices have become so commonplace that they are generally accepted as standards of care, despite the lack of research to support them.

In the STAR-D study described earlier in this chapter, research participants who did not remit were switched to one of seven treatments—changed to one of three different antidepressants, changed to cognitive therapy alone, augmented with one of two other medicines, or augmented with cognitive therapy. The study was designed to see if any one of the seven different strategies worked better than another. The results showed that all approaches worked about the same and helped an additional 20 to 30 percent of participants. Other augmentation strategies were studied at later phases of the study including adding lithium, or thyroid medicine, or changing to an MAOI. No approach stood out as superior to another but all were helpful to some.

The most common medication augmentation strategy is to add another antidepressant. Doctors typically use a medication with a different mechanism of action from the antidepressant you already take. Since SSRIs and SNRIs are the most common antidepressants prescribed, buproprion (Wellbutrin), mirtazapine (Remeron), or a tricyclic are often used as augmenting agents.

Most augmenting medications are chosen because of a desired side effect from the medicine. Buproprion is activating so it is used when residual symptoms are low energy, poor concentration, and lack of motivation. Mirtazapine and tricyclics, with some exceptions, tend to be more sedating and help improve appetite, so they are used when someone reports trouble sleeping, poor appetite, or high anxiety. On rare occasions, a doctor may add an SSRI to an SNRI to get a little more of the anti-anxiety effects from increasing serotonin but some doctors question the utility of this since the two classes are so similar.

Non-antidepressant psychiatric medicines are also used for augmentation. Many such medicines are indicated for bipolar disorder or manic-depression. They do not treat depression (except bipolar depression) when used alone, but they are helpful when added to an antidepressant. There are more studies looking at the augmenting effects of lithium, a bipolar medication, than any other medicine, since it was the most commonly used until a few years ago. Now, with so many more options available, lithium is not used as much because of its effects on the kidneys and thyroid gland, the need for regular blood monitoring, and potential toxic effects if too much is taken.

The new generation anti-psychotic mood stabilizers are considered by some to be "broad-spectrum psychotropics" because they target many chemicals and receptors in the brain. They are increasing in popularity

Is More Merrier?

A 2010 study from Mojabai et al looked at office-based psychiatry practices compared 1996 to 1997 prescribing trends with those of 2005 to 2006. The use of two antidepressants nearly doubled from 8 to 16 percent.

among doctors as effective augmenting agents. Aripiprizole (Abilify) and quetiapine XR (Seroquel XR) are two such medications that are FDA approved as add-on therapy in depression if you are not fully responding to your current treatment. Pharmaceutical companies that make similar types of medicines are looking to get their medicines approved for this use as well. Some researchers question whether the benefits—which were not as dramatic in the studies as doctors have observed in selected patients—are worth the risks of possible increases in blood sugar and cholesterol, weight gain, and motor movement problems that can be seen with medicines from this class.

Buspirone (Buspar) is an anti-anxiety medicine that is also given as an augmentation agent. The few studies with buspirone show more impressive results than most doctors see in their patients. Stimulants, prescribed for attention deficit hyperactivity disorder (ADHD), are used in depression as well, but some doctors question whether the benefit is because of symptom relief, particularly with energy and concentration, rather than actually treating the underlying depression. A small number of studies demonstrate that some non-psychiatric medications, such as those used to treat thyroid problems, Parkinson's, and high blood pressure, can help antidepressants work better.

One of the most commonly recommended non-medication augmentation approaches is psychotherapy. Many doctors prescribing antidepressants prefer that their patients see a therapist because it helps them monitor how their patient is doing with treatment. Many doctors also believe that therapy helps you feel better and improves your chances of eventually being able to stop antidepressant therapy. Proving that psychotherapy actually boosts the effectiveness of medicine has not been easy and many studies show mixed results.

The STAR-D trial showed that adding cognitive therapy when someone is partially responding to medicine did as much as adding another antidepressant. Another frequently referenced 1999 study looked at treating people with chronic depression for two years or more with a form of cognitive therapy alone, an antidepressant—nefazodone (Serzone)—alone, or medicine and therapy combined. Both therapy and medicine alone worked the same, but a far greater number improved when given both. Some other studies show different conclusions—that therapy works as well as medication but adds little benefit when combined with medicine. Therapy has been shown to help resolve life stressors, social functioning, and relationship difficulties, as well as improve overall compliance with treatment. These changes could help overall outcome.

"What can I do if nothing helps?" Chris asked his doctor. He had noticed some positive changes the first few weeks with the new medicine, but this seemed to level off. He admitted that he felt better than when he took nothing, but he was disappointed at not being where had hoped to be in his recovery. He felt discouraged. He wasn't ready to give up on the medicine just yet, but wanted to know if his doctor had a game plan, just in case.

He had done plenty of reading about other treatments for depression that hasn't responded to medication and wanted to hear what his doctor thought about these options.

"What can I do if nothing helps?"

For some, overcoming depression is as easy as taking a pill a day. Others improve without medicine by making lifestyle changes, using alternative treatments, or actively engaging in therapy. More often, people choose a combination of medication and non-medication treatment options. If taking a variety of antidepressant and augmenting agents and trying a number of non-medication treatment options fail to sufficiently help, what is left to do? Fortunately, most people who take action to overcome depression successfully do so. A small group, though, suffer from treatment-resistant depression (TRD). The definition of treatment-resistant varies considerably because so many treatment options are available that it is difficult to say when you have tried enough. There is currently one medication approved for TRD: Symbyax. This is actually two medications in one—fluoxetine (Prozac) and olanzapine (Zyprexa)—and is also approved for bipolar depression. There is some data to suggest that there is a unique synergy when you use these two medicines together.

The oldest and best-studied treatment for TRD is ECT. ECT has been proven to work in severe cases of depression, bipolar disorder, and psychotic disorders by inducing a brief seizure with a small amount of electricity. Mentioning ECT as a treatment option generates a strong reaction from many people, based on its portrayal in books and film as a harmful and, at times, punishing therapy. When first used many years ago, there were some serious side effects, including memory loss and bodily injury, because anesthesia and muscle relaxers were not given. With new anesthesia techniques, the treatment is very safe and, with changes in the type and duration of seizures, the risk of memory problems is greatly reduced.

ECT works faster than most other treatments, and the results can be dramatic. No one knows why it helps. The idea developed from the observation that people with epilepsy who also had depression felt their mood lift after a seizure. Although this may sound strange, ECT is actually one of the more natural treatments because seizures are common and can occur from a head injury, a seizure disorder such as epilepsy, alcohol or drug intoxication/withdrawal, a medication side effect, or in childhood from a high fever. ECT usually requires 6 to 12 treatments every other day and can be done in a hospital or as an outpatient. ECT is used only in severe situations where many other options have failed.

Another non-medication option for TRD is transcranial magnetic stimulation (TMS) in which a magnetic pulse is applied to the skull, triggering electrical activity in targeted areas of the brain. TMS, unlike ECT, does not require anesthesia or a seizure to be effective, making it safer and easier to administer. While TMS has been used for many years, the FDA only recently approved its use for depression in those who failed to respond to antidepressants. The treatment takes about 40 minutes and must be done five days per week for five to six weeks. Most insurance companies do not yet cover the procedure and each treatment is quite expensive because of the high cost of the equipment. The results are not as impressive as with ECT and you have the problem of, once getting well, staying well. More information is available from one of the manufacturer's of the TMS device at www.NeuroStarTMS.com.

A rarely used FDA-approved device to treat refractory depression is the vagus nerve stimulator (VNS), originally designed to treat seizure disorders. Some people have experienced very dramatic improvement with VNS. The studies have not shown huge improvements but, keep in

If You Think That Sounds Rough...

In Neolithic times, a treatment technique was used to treat mental illness called trephination, in which a hole was drilled into the skull to release unwanted demons. Trephination dates back to 6,500 BC France where skulls were found with trephination holes.

Table 6-A

Common Psychiatric Disorders Co-Occurring with Depression

Depression can be accompanied by other psychiatric conditions. Even though your depression may be well controlled with treatment, you can have other symptoms from another mental-health problem that is co-occuring. Here is a list of diagnoses and common residual symptoms:

- **Social Anxiety Disorder:** anxiety, social avoidance
- **Attention Deficit Disorder:** poor concentration, memory problems, procrastination
- **Generalized anxiety:** anxiety, sleeping trouble, irritable, physical symptoms
- **Post-traumatic stress disorder:** insomnia, avoidance, anxiety
- **Panic disorder:** anxiety attacks, avoidance, physical symptoms
- **Alcohol or drug addiction:** anxiety, sleep problems, physical symptoms, mood swings, irritability

mind that the study participants had some of the most difficult-to-treat depressions. The device is implanted into the chest wall and sends small, electrical pulses to the vagus nerve, an important nerve that runs from the brain, down the neck, and into the diaphragm. The vagus nerve controls many bodily functions including neurotransmitter release, breathing, digestion, and heart rate. Unlike the rapid results seen with ECT, VNS typically takes several months before noticeable improvement is seen. With VNS, depression comes back less frequently, and if it does, is often less severe. It is very expensive, involves a surgical procedure, and insurance has been reluctant to pay for the device and implantation. More information is available from the manufacturer of the VNS at www.vnstherapy.com.

Once you are on an antidepressant, you need to continually monitor your progress and let your doctor know what has and has not improved. Remember that getting better is not enough. Your goal is to get well. Make sure you do everything you can to allow the medicine to work effectively and, if necessary, consider adding an additional medication, or changing the antidepressant, when residual symptoms persist, even if you find some benefit. Taking the least amount of medication will not help you achieve the goal of eventually taking no medication.

There can be many factors contributing to why you only respond partially to an antidepressant and you may be tempted to make changes on your own based on something you have heard or read. You should not do anything without the consent and guidance of your healthcare provider. Make sure that if your doctor does change your medication regime she gives you a good explanation for how she came to that decision. You do not want to prematurely stop what you are doing or unnecessarily add medications that may not be needed. The good news is that, unlike a few decades ago, you have many options to reach your goal of a complete recovery.

Chapter Seven

How Safe are Antidepressants?

Lucy picked up a few books on antidepressants and read some concerning things about possible risks with taking these medications. She is well aware of the differing opinions on whether antidepressants are safe. At the natural foods grocery store and other places she shops, Lucy runs into people all the time with strongly negative attitudes about conventional medicine. She bought these books to try to get a balanced viewpoint about risks with antidepressants and a little reassurance about her decision to take medicine.

After reading them all, she decided to email her doctor, whom she saw as a pretty straight shooter, rather than try to sort through all this on her own. "Are antidepressants safe? Are there any dangerous side effects I should know about?"

All medications carry some risks, and antidepressants are no exception. However, the risks of untreated or inadequately managed depression are far greater than those of the antidepressants. Fortunately, serious side effects with antidepressants are rare, but they do occur. You can prevent any significant problems by knowing what those risks are and what to do should you experience any such problems.

Government regulatory agencies, such as the FDA, require that new medications go through a rigorous scientific review process to assess their overall effectiveness and safety. Pharmaceutical research studies only give us a narrow picture of a medication's true risks and benefits, because the number of patients participating in these studies is relatively small and the studies are usually short in duration. Pharmaceutical companies are required to continually collect information about any serious problems associated with a medicine after it is approved for general use and make that information available to doctors and patients. Some very popular medications have been pulled from the market for safety reasons because of this reporting system.

Pharmaceutical companies are required to warn patients and doctors of all possible medication risks. These companies are held liable if there is a possible link between a medication and a bad side effect that they did not adequately inform the public about. This explains why more than half of a 30-second television advertisement for a medication is devoted to listing all the possible side effects you could experience. These monitoring and warning systems are far more sophisticated than in the past and should give you some sense of comfort about any medication you take.

People have more concerns about the safety of antidepressants than they do about medicines used to treat most other medical illnesses. Some of these concerns are generated by the occasional unsubstantiated news story about the overprescribing of antidepressants, the dangers associated with these medications, and pharmaceutical companies' betraying the public trust by hiding safety data. Antidepressants provide easy targets for attention-grabbing news stories because so many people take these medicines, and there is a long-standing negative bias about mental-health treatment. The slew of unfavorable portrayals of psychiatric illness and treatment in film and literature reinforce such biases.

Granted, there have been mental-health treatments in the past, like in all areas of medicine, which, while well intentioned, had adverse outcomes. Nowadays, there are far better methods to study new medical therapies and regulatory agencies provide more aggressive oversight to prevent harmful treatments from being used. Antidepressants, as a class, are some of the best-studied medications on the market and have a long track record of being monitored for safety since their arrival in the late 1950s.

This chapter addresses serious problems that can occur when taking an antidepressant as well precautions you should take if you are on other medications or have specific health issues. These include:

- Possible serious side effects.
- Risk of increased suicidal thoughts, worsening depression, or violence.
- Medical risks associated with antidepressant treatment.
- Drug interactions between antidepressants and other medication.
- Long-term risks of antidepressants.

"Are there any dangerous side effects I should know about?"

As a whole, antidepressants are relatively safe medications. The exception to this is the older generation of antidepressants, the tricyclics and MAOIs, which, if not taken correctly, could have very serious physical side effects. In fact, if you take more than prescribed, you could develop a life-threatening reaction. In contrast, the newer generation of antidepressants, such as the SSRIs and SNRIs, are unlikely to cause any serious injury, even with a fairly significant overdose. However, you should never take more than prescribed and, if you or someone you know does, you should contact your doctor immediately or go to the nearest emergency room. There can always be rare, unexpected reactions with an overdose of any medication.

Despite an overall high side-effect burden compared to the newer generation antidepressants, doctors still prescribe tricyclic antidepressants because they are inexpensive and uniquely effective for certain types of depression. Tricyclics are safe when taken as prescribed. However, if taken in too large of quantities, tricyclics can cause heart rhythm changes that could be fatal. No one knows how much is too much, and it may depend on what other medicines you take and whether you have an underlying heart problem.

MAOIs are also very effective antidepressants and are often used for people who have tried several other antidepressants without success. As a class, they carry the greatest risk. Certain medicines and foods must be avoided if you take an MAOI to prevent a possible, life-threatening increase in blood pressure (see Table 7-A "Sample List of Foods to Avoid with MAOIs" on page 141). If you experience a severe headache, flushing, or confusion, you should go to an emergency room as soon as possible since these could be signs of severe blood pressure changes from an MAOI reaction. Some people do not stick rigidly to the MAOI diet but still never experience a problem, while others are exquisitely sensitive. Everyone is encouraged to comply with the diet because you can never predict how sensitive you may be. If MAOIs dramatically improve the quality of your life, the dietary restrictions are a minor inconvenience.

A rare problem that can occur with the newer antidepressants is *serotonin syndrome*. If you are on a high dose of a serotonin antidepressant or take one or more other medicines that also impact serotonin levels, you may be warned by your doctor or pharmacist to watch out for signs of serotonin syndrome (see Table 7-B "Medicines that Can Cause Serotonin Syndrome" on page 142). This includes diarrhea, nausea, vomiting, and

Table 7-A

Sample List of Foods to Avoid with MAOIs

- Aged cheeses, some processed cheeses (cottage cheese, cream cheese, pot cheese, and ricotta cheese are allowed)
- Chianti, vermouth, sherry, red wines, tap beer, nonalcoholic beer and wine
- Broad (fava) beans
- Sauerkraut
- Italian green beans
- Snow pea pods
- Soy products, especially soy sauce and tofu
- Aged or cured meats
- Caviar
- Liver
- Concentrated yeast extract, brewer's yeast, yeast supplements, yeast paste (marmite), miso (commercial leavened products with baker's yeast are allowed)
- Acidophilus and products with acidophilus
- Any food that is not fresh, overripe, close to expiration date

Sample List of Medicines to Avoid with MAOIs

- All serotonin antidepressants
- Demerol
- Cold preparations
- Cough medicines with decongestants
- Sinus medications
- Nose drops or nasal sprays
- Hayfever medications
- Diet pills
- Amphetamines

This list is not meant to be comprehensive.

Table 7-B
Medicines that Can Cause Serotonin Syndrome

- **Antidepressants:** SSRIs, SNRIs, MAOIs, tricyclics, mirtazapine, St. John's Wort
- **Antiparkinson Medications:** Amantadine, bromocriptine, carbergoline, levodopa, pergolide, selegiline
- **Migraine Medications:** dihydroergotamine, naratriptan, sumatriptan, zolmitriptan
- **Ilicit Drugs:** cocaine, ectasy, LSD
- **Other:** sibutramine (Meridia, weight loss), tramadol (Ultram, pain reliever), meperidine (Demerol, painkiller) or dextromethorphan (cough medicine).

feeling flushed. In more severe cases, you can experience an elevated heart rate, changes in blood pressure, confusion, trouble with coordination, muscle rigidity, and hallucinations. If you stop taking the antidepressant— and any other medicine that could be contributing—shortly after these symptoms start, you can prevent the syndrome from progressing. On rare occasions, someone will develop serotonin syndrome on very low doses of a serotonin antidepressant. However, most doctors that prescribe a lot of antidepressants, even in very high doses and with other serotonin-impacting medicines, hardly ever see serotonin syndrome, and the vast majority of cases that do occur are mild and resolve quickly.

Chris' Story Continues

Chris likes to read the little warning labels that come with his medication. Despite no formal medical training, he prides himself on how well he can understand most of the technical information on those little labels.

When reading about his antidepressant, Chris was surprised by the big, boxed warning that antidepressants have a risk of increasing suicidal thoughts in children and young adults. Although he was older than those at risk, he felt concerned because he did previously have thoughts of wanting to die and found them frightening. He did not want to experience that again. That's why he wanted to be on antidepressants in the first place. He always took special notice when he saw news reports about antidepressants, especially stories about someone on antidepressants becoming violent.

He asked his doctor, "I've been reading that antidepressants can make you feel worse or even suicidal. What about these stories I hear about people getting violent on antidepressant?"

"I've been reading that antidepressants can make you feel worse or even suicidal. What about these stories I hear about people getting violent on antidepressants?"

Suicidal thoughts can occur with more severe depressive episodes. These thoughts can range from a wish that you were no longer alive to actually planning out, or making, a suicide attempt. Antidepressants have been reported to trigger or worsen suicidal thoughts in a small number of people who take antidepressants. No one knows for sure what, if any, link exists between the medication and these thoughts. Nevertheless, there are warnings on all antidepressants encouraging you to watch carefully that your depression doesn't get worse or that you don't start to experience thoughts of wanting to die or hurt yourself.

Patients often feel reluctant to discuss thoughts of suicide with their doctor because they fear their doctor "will think I'm crazy," or that they will be involuntarily committed to a psychiatric hospital. Doctors with experience treating depression realize having these thoughts does not necessarily mean you would act on them. Usually suicidal thoughts remain just thoughts. Hospitalization is an option when someone is at a point where they can no longer control these thoughts and need more aggressive intervention. If you can assure your doctor you are not a danger to yourself, she will not send you to a hospital if you do not want to go.

Few people with depression actually attempt, or successfully complete, suicide, but when it does occur, the results are tragic. The impact of suicide on one's family and friends is emotionally devastating and leaves the survivors with feelings of confusion, guilt, and profound loss. In most cases, the person who attempts, or does commit, suicide is unwilling to fully participate in treatment, and there is little that anyone can do in those situations.

Many people who do commit suicide never told anyone they were struggling with such thoughts. It is common to hear from people who know someone who has attempted, or completed, suicide that they were completely shocked their loved one could have done such a thing. On the other hand, there is also no truth to the myth that if someone talks about suicide they will not act on these thoughts. Anyone who shares that they are experiencing suicidal ideations, even in a casual manner, must be taken seriously and be evaluated by someone trained in this area. If you are open and forthcoming with your doctor or therapist, he will better understand the seriousness of your depression and be able to get you the help you need to be safe.

The little we do know about a possible link between antidepressants and suicide comes from the clinical studies comparing the effectiveness and safety of antidepressants with those taking a placebo (dummy pill). The greater incidence of suicidal thoughts and behaviors observed in these studies occurred in children, adolescents, and adults under the age of 25. There were no completed suicides in any of the child studies. In those over 24 years old, there was no statistically significant increase observed, and there was actually a decrease in suicidal thoughts and actions in adults over age 65. One review of more than 380 studies with nearly 100,000 adults treated with antidepressants found no link between suicidal thoughts or behaviors and antidepressants.

There is an ongoing debate about the meaning of these research findings. First, the phenomenon is hard to study because there are so few actual suicide attempts during antidepressant studies. There are many other factors that can contribute to an increase in suicidal thoughts, such as family issues, work or school problems, drug or alcohol use, or relationship conflicts. This makes it hard to know what role, if any, the medication played.

Secondly, the earlier research studies labeled any thought or act of self-harm as "suicidal." In reality, some people have thoughts of hurting themselves because of feelings of anger or sadness without wanting to die. They may engage in an act of self-harm to get someone's attention or to get revenge. Recent antidepressant studies are doing a better job using measures to separate out an actual suicide attempt from acting out or attention-seeking behavior.

There are a few possible explanations for the antidepressant and suicide link. In some cases, people wait so long to get on medication that suicidal thoughts could develop as a result of their depression worsening while the antidepressant simply has not yet had time to help. They may associate the thoughts with the medicine because the thoughts developed after starting the medicine. Another explanation could be that those who feel worse with antidepressant treatment may have an unidentified bipolar (manic-depression) disorder. Research suggests that antidepressants are not beneficial in treating bipolar depression (except under certain conditions) and may make someone with the disorder feel worse.

A side effect sometimes seen with antidepressants, called akathisia, an uncomfortable feeling of restlessness and agitation, has been associated with increased thoughts of suicide. The introduction of fluoxetine (Prozac), initially heralded as a miracle pill in the early 1990s, was soon followed by a small number of reports of people who had started the medicine and made suicide attempts. Researchers later determined that some of these people may have developed unrecognized akathisia that led to even more depression and anxiety. Before doctors knew this could occur, some people who developed akathisia were told to increase their medication dose because they assumed the depression was not responding to the current dose. This only made them feel worse. Now that doctors are aware of akathisia, they can give medication to treat it or change the antidepressant to one without that side effect.

When antidepressants first came to market, doctors noticed that a few people made suicide attempts soon after starting medicine. Some researchers at the time speculated that early in treatment there is a window of vulnerability. During this time, the antidepressants can give someone an increase in energy and motivation which may allow them to act on suicidal thoughts before the medicine had a chance to actually improve moods and feelings of hopefulness. Finally, it is possible that, for a small number of people, antidepressants trigger something in the brain that can elicit suicidal thoughts.

Doctors have mixed feelings about the warnings that antidepressants can worsen depression and trigger suicidal thoughts. The benefit of these warnings is that it has increased awareness of the seriousness of treating depression and using antidepressants. The newer generation of antidepressants, starting with fluoxetine (Prozac), were introduced as safe alternatives with relatively few side effects as compared to the tricyclics and MAOIs. This led some healthcare practitioners into a sense of complacency about prescribing antidepressants. The suicide warnings remind doctors to educate patients about any and all risks, particularly emergence of suicidal ideation, and that doctors should closely monitor patients during treatment. The downside to such a warning is that it may dissuade someone from taking an antidepressant when they could benefit from it. The incidence of suicide among children increased (after a 12-year decline) after the suicide warning was put on antidepressants. One possible explanation may be that the warnings have led to fewer people in this age range taking antidepressants.

You and your doctor should discuss what to do in the event you begin to feel worse or develop thoughts of harming yourself. If you are aware that this can happen when taking antidepressants, you will know how to handle the situation and can prevent any problems. A bad outcome is more likely when someone doesn't realize that such thoughts may be caused by the medicine and they don't get immediate help. If you experience such thoughts, contact your doctor immediately. He or she will most likely recommend that you stop or change your antidepressant. You can often switch antidepressants, preferably to a different class, and not experience the same problem. Some people have even been able to stay on the same antidepressant at a lower dose and do well. Doctors sometimes use mood stabilizers or other types of psychiatric medications (that are not antidepressants) with good results.

Every so often a news story emerges about someone who committed an act of violence and is (or was) taking an antidepressant or other psychiatric medicine. The media suggest that there could be some causal relationship between the medicine and the violent behavior. The reality is that very few people with depression become violent or aggressive. On the rare occasions this does occur, the person is most likely to have severe psychotic symptoms in which they lose touch with reality.

There is no evidence that someone not predisposed to an act of violence will commit some heinous act of aggression if he starts taking an antidepressant. An exception may be if the person has a bipolar disorder which is not adequately managed and they are put on an antidepressant. The antidepressant could trigger a manic or mixed episode with possible psychotic features. Even in the unlikely event that the medication were to cause anger and aggression to the point that the person loses control, there would be other warning signs including worsening sleep, irritability, racing thoughts, and irrational behavior.

In reality, these individuals almost always have other significant factors that put them at risk for these behaviors. They usually have a history of violence, impulse control problems, access to weapons, or alcohol abuse or drug problems. In addition to depression, they most likely have other psychiatric problems such as bipolar disorder, schizophrenia, or an underlying personality disorder. In many of these cases, it is later found that the person failed to take the antidepressant or other psychiatric medication.

Attributing homicidal thoughts to antidepressants because of isolated cases in which someone on an antidepressant becomes violent is similar to linking a cholesterol medicine to heart attacks because someone on a cholesterol lowering drug is more likely to develop heart problems. The disease that the medicine is treating, not the medicine itself, is the greater risk factor. Nonetheless, if you, or someone you know, has a history of aggression and violent behavior and you notice that these feelings intensify on an antidepressant, let your doctor or therapist know immediately and they can intervene.

Frank's Story Continues

Frank looked at all the medicines the pharmacist handed him. "You know I have a lot of health problems. Is this antidepressant safe with all my medical problems and my other medicines?"

The pharmacist responded, "As long as the doctor who prescribed the antidepressant knows all about your medical problems and medicines, it should be okay. There aren't too many medical problems that would prevent you from being able to take an antidepressant. My computer would tell me if any of the medicines you are on interact with one another and nothing is coming up."

"I guess if the computer says it's okay, it must be," said Frank. "For some reason though, that isn't very reassuring."

"Is this antidepressant safe with all my medical problems?"

Most antidepressants are safe to take if you have other medical problems. In fact, antidepressants are known to help reduce the physical and psychological burden of many health problems, including migraine headaches, inflammatory bowel disease, high blood pressure, diabetes, and Parkinson's disease, to name a few. However, there are a few precautions you should be aware of with some antidepressants and certain health problems. The kidneys and liver are responsible for how the body processes many antidepressants. In illnesses that impact the functioning of these organs, you may need to talk to your doctor about adjusting the dose of certain antidepressants.

If a medication appears to cause or worsen a health problem, regulatory agencies will sometimes put a warning on all the medicines in that class unless they are certain that the reaction is specific to that one drug. These class warnings are designed to inform you and your doctor about a possible risk that may not have been seen with the medicine you are on, but has been observed in related medications. The following are some class warnings on antidepressants. They have been observed with certain antidepressants but may not have been specifically linked to the medicine you take:

Narrow-angle glaucoma: This is the least common form of glaucoma (less than 10 percent of all cases) and is a disease in which fluid builds up in the eye. Most people with this type can still take antidepressants if the glaucoma is appropriately treated.

Increased bleeding: The SSRIs and SNRIs (antidepressants that affect serotonin levels) can put you at higher risk for bleeding problems since serotonin affects clotting. People with easy bruising, bleeding, or who are on blood-thinning medicines like aspirin, ibuprofen, naproxen, and warfarin (Coumadin) should be extra careful.

Hyponatremia: Low sodium levels in the blood can cause tiredness or confusion and could be dangerous to your health if untreated. It is rarely seen with antidepressants but it can happen. People with severe kidney failure, heart failure, who drink abnormally excessive amounts of water, or who are on water pills such as furosemide (Lasix) are most at risk.

Rash/Allergic reaction: An allergic reaction usually starts as a rash but can develop into swelling or breathing trouble. You should go to an emergency room immediately if this occurs. There is no greater risk of allergic reaction with antidepressants than with any other class of medication. Some people are allergic to a dye in their medication and may be able to successfully take a different dose of the same medicine if the dyes are different. Some medications are related like citalopram (Celexa) and escitalopram (Lexapro) or venlafaxine (Effexor) and desvenlafaxine (Pristiq). An allergic reaction to one can put you at a higher risk to react to the other.

Following are some warnings about possible medical side effects specific to certain antidepressants. These warnings may or may not affect your doctor's decision to treat you with that particular medicine depending on their level of concern.

Liver problems: Nefazodone (Serzone) has been linked to some cases of liver failure. Nefazodone is still used with great caution and careful monitoring of liver function. Duloxetine (Cymbalta) has been associated with liver problems in people who have preexisting liver damage or are heavy alcohol users.

Urinary retention (difficulty urinating): Tricyclic antidepressants and duloxetine can cause urinary difficulties. In fact, they have been prescribed as treatments for incontinence because of this effect.

Seizures: There is an increased risk of seizures with buproprion (Wellbutrin), clomipramine (Anafranil), and maprotiline (Ludiomil). Bupropion is more likely to cause seizures if you have a history of head trauma, seizures, or head injuries.

High blood pressure: Venlafaxine (Effexor) can put you at increased risk for elevated blood pressure. It is much more likely to occur with higher doses, or with the immediate-release formulation, rather than the extended release (Effexor XR).

Low blood pressure: Both tricyclics and MAOIs can predispose someone to a drop in blood pressure. This can make you feel weak, dizzy, and lightheaded.

Priapism (painful, prolonged erection): A rare side effect in men that is seen with trazodone (Desyrel). It requires immediate medical treatment.

You should also be aware of possible interactions between your antidepressant and any other medicines you may take. Known drug interactions are usually listed in the package insert that accompanies any samples you receive (assuming you can read the very small print on a very little sheet of paper), a printout from your pharmacy that dispenses the medicine, the drug manufacturer Web site, or any of the dozens of reliable Internet sites that review medications, such as www.pdrhealth.com or www.safemedication.com.

Some of the interactions listed are hypothetical or so extremely rare that doctors generally dismiss them. Keep in mind that some of these warnings are not designed to prevent these medicines from being used together, but rather to educate the doctor to be more cautious and to legally protect the drug manufacturer from liability if problems do occur.

In many cases, doctors prescribe medicines that have potential drug interactions because, in their experience, it is not a concern. One example is migraine headache medicines (many of them also work on serotonin), which doctors often prescribe to people taking antidepressants despite a warning about possible serotonin syndrome if you take the two together. Always check with your doctor if you hear about a possible interaction before stopping any medication you are taking to make sure the warning is a legitimate concern. Herbal medications such as St. John's Wort and yohimbine can interact with antidepressants. Natural therapies are often not listed in warning labels.

Some medicines can affect the blood levels of other medicines. As a result, you may need to adjust the dose of your antidepressant or another medicine you take with it. One example is using the antidepressants fluoxetine (Prozac) and amitripyline (Elavil) together. Sometimes amitriptyline is given in low doses to help with sleep or pain, but the fluoxetine can raise the amount of amitryptyline in your system to a dangerous level. Antidepressants have been known to affect the blood levels of people taking certain blood thinners (which could result in bleeding problems), anti-seizure medicines, and other psychiatric medicines. Your doctor or pharmacist should review all the medicines you take and tell you if there are potential interactions. Make sure all your healthcare practitioners know everything you are taking—prescribed or not.

Jane's Story Continues

Jane's close friend, Rachel, knows all about Jane's issues with depression. Rachel asked, "Are you still taking that antidepressant? Aren't you worried about taking it for so long? Do you think it can be harmful to your body in some way?"

Jane thought about Rachel's questions and, that night, went online to a medical Web site where you can ask questions of a medical expert. She typed in, "What are the risks of taking antidepressants long term?"

Within a few minutes, she received a response from the online doctor assuring her that antidepressants were safe to take for a long time. She also found that other visitors to the Web site responded to her question with a whole list of problems they, or someone they know, have had after taking antidepressants for a while. "Who do I believe?" she wondered.

"What are the risks of taking antidepressants long term?"

Many people wonder whether antidepressants are safe to take long term. Anyone with chronic or frequently recurring depression could find themselves on medicines for many years. Naturally, there are concerns that they may put themselves at risk for damaging their brain, liver, kidneys, or some other vital organ. As previously mentioned, most antidepressant studies are less than 12 weeks long and only a few extend past one or two years. What if you take an antidepressant for five, ten, or twenty years?

When taking a medicine for long periods of time, there is always the possibility of an unknown risk not detected in short clinical drug trials. Remember that antidepressants have been widely prescribed since the late 1950s, and there are people who have taken them consistently for several decades. If there was a significant risk of organ damage, cancer, or some other illness, there should have been evidence by now of those risks with

Differing Opinions

Tom Cruise, actor and member of The Church of Scientology, said in an interview with *Today* host Matt Lauer June 23, 2005:

"But what happens, the antidepressant, all it does is mask the problem. There's ways of vitamins and through exercise and various things. I'm not saying that that isn't real. That's not what I'm saying. That's an alteration of what—what I'm saying. I'm saying that drugs aren't the answer, these drugs are very dangerous. They're mind-altering, anti-psychotic drugs."

Brooke Shields, actor and author, said in *The New York Times* July 1, 2005:

"And comments like those made by Tom Cruise are a disservice to mothers everywhere. To suggest that I was wrong to take drugs to deal with my depression, and that instead I should have taken vitamins and exercised shows an utter lack of understanding about postpartum depression and childbirth in general. If any good can come of Mr. Cruise's ridiculous rant, let's hope that it gives much-needed attention to a serious disease."

antidepressants. Anti-antidepressant books and Internet sites frequently refer to the "addictive" qualities of antidepressants and some of the severe withdrawal symptoms or *discontinuation syndrome* as an indication of the dangers of taking these medicines long term. Discontinuation syndrome does not occur with everyone on an antidepressant and, while it can be uncomfortable for some, is not dangerous to your health. Chapter Eight is dedicated to this topic.

Researchers have raised concerns about whether taking antidepressants for extended periods of time could be associated with osteoporosis or thinning bones. No specific causal link has been established, and it may not be the medicine, but the depression itself, that is the risk factor. Poor nutritional intake, limited exposure to sunlight, and lack of exercise (all of which can occur in someone with depression) can predispose you to the condition as well. Some researchers have wondered whether taking antidepressants could actually predispose you to more depression later on. This idea evolved when people experienced a return of their depression after they came off their antidepressant. There is no strong evidence to date that taking antidepressants puts you at risk for more depression but there is data that shows untreated depression puts you at risk for more depressive episodes and a more difficult-to-treat illness.

In summary, antidepressants are generally safe, but there are some possible serious risks. You can avert any significant problems by watching out for early signs of a reaction and contacting your doctor if they occur. There can always be unknown risks of any medication you take for an extended period of time, but, after several decades of widespread antidepressant use, you should have a reasonable degree of reassurance about the safety of these medications. Remember that not treating depression aggressively and adequately carries its risks as well.

Chapter Eight

Are Antidepressants Addictive?

On the second day of her vacation, Lucy was watching the waves crash along the beach when she suddenly felt dizzy and lightheaded. She went back to her room and felt some tingling in her arms and shoulders. She wondered if she had eaten something the night before that wasn't sitting well with her and went to her pill box for some ibuprofen. At that point, she noticed she didn't have her antidepressant with her. In the excitement over her vacation, she had forgotten to pack them. She had missed at least three days.

She called her doctor and told him about her symptoms, "I haven't taken my antidepressant for three days. What should I do?"

"Don't worry. Those are probably symptoms from discontinuation."

"What's that? How do I know if I have discontinuation symptoms?"

"Some people get them when they miss or stop their antidepressant too quickly. Don't worry. It is not dangerous, just uncomfortable. Let me call a few pills into the local pharmacy there and I bet you'll feel better in a few hours."

Sure enough, her symptoms improved after a few hours of taking the medicine.

That night she shared the experience with her friend, "I know my therapist said these medicines aren't habit forming. If antidepressants aren't addictive, why do I feel so bad when I stop taking them?"

Some people fear that if they start taking an antidepressant, they may not be able to stop. This concern has been reinforced by reports of "withdrawal symptoms" when antidepressants have been abruptly stopped. The Internet is filled with stories written by people describing uncomfortable experiences when they have forgotten to take their medication or tried to come off antidepressants abruptly. Advocates against the use of medication to treat depression promote the idea that antidepressants are addictive or habit forming.

It's important to understand the difference between addictive medicines and those that cause discontinuation symptoms, which typically occur if you have been on medication for a while and then abruptly stop or miss several doses. While these discontinuation symptoms can be uncomfortable, they differ in many ways from the withdrawal syndromes seen with addictive medicines such as narcotic pain medicines or anti-anxiety medicines like alprazolam (Xanax).

You should be able to identify discontinuation symptoms in case you do experience them. Fortunately, these symptoms do not occur in everyone and, when they do, are typically short-lived and mild in intensity. Discontinuation symptoms are easily manageable and, in some cases, preventable, if you know what to do.

This chapter will help you:

- Understand antidepressant discontinuation syndrome and how it differs from withdrawal.
- Recognize discontinuation symptoms.
- Learn which antidepressants are more likely to cause discontinuation syndrome.
- Manage discontinuation syndrome when it occurs.

"If antidepressants aren't addictive, why do I feel so bad when I stop taking them?"

If you have been on your antidepressant for a while and skipped, stopped, or abruptly reduced the dose of your medication, you may have experienced the uncomfortable physical and emotional symptoms of antidepressant discontinuation syndrome (ADS). Up to 20 percent of those on antidepressants develop discontinuation symptoms. Though reported more frequently with the newer antidepressants, ADS is seen with the older tricyclic and MAOIs classes of medicines as well. The symptoms can range in severity from barely noticeable and mildly annoying to very disruptive and uncomfortable. Most people who do develop ADS find the symptoms mild, but, on rare occasions, it has been known to affect some to the point that they have been unable to go to work or had trouble getting out of bed for several days. Discontinuation is not harmful to your health, and there are no known permanent, lasting effects. No one knows why some people get it and others do not or why some people get it worse than others.

The exact cause of ADS is unknown and, because the syndrome is seen in different types of antidepressants with varying mechanism of actions, some researchers believe there could be several different causes. ADS may be related to antidepressant effects on the serotonin system. Suddenly stopping the medicine without allowing the body time to adjust can lead to a rapid decrease in serotonin levels or decreased sensitivity to the serotonin that is available. An abrupt drop in blood levels of antidepressants that affect NE could lead to sudden firing of NE neurons resulting in headaches, agitation, or restlessness. Some antidepressants, such as paroxetine (Paxil) and tricylics, block another neurotransmitter in the brain called acetylcholine, which is thought to cause different types of withdrawal symptoms seen with those medicines. If we knew why discontinuation occurred, we could develop better techniques to prevent or alleviate the symptoms.

Having withdrawal effects when you stop a medication does not mean the medicine is addictive. In fact, a number of different medications cause problems when abruptly stopped, including steroids, seizure medicines, and some high blood pressure pills. None of these is considered to be addictive. For a drug to be considered addictive, you have to develop tolerance (the need for more and more to get the same effect) and dependence. Dependence means you develop

Perception vs. Reality

A 1999 study in the Netherlands interviewing patients taking antidepressants found that of the 192 patients taking antidepressants for more than six months, approximately 30 percent believed that antidepressants are physically addictive, 43 percent thought that taking antidepressants made them dependent on their doctor, and 30 percent felt that if you started an antidepressant, you could not stop using them.

physical, emotional, and behavioral problems when the drug is quickly stopped. Although antidepressant doses must sometimes be increased to produce the same positive results, the mechanism is different from that seen with addictive drugs and is not considered by scientists to fit the definition of tolerance. You might think that there is dependence with antidepressants because of these withdrawal symptoms, but it differs in that the withdrawal is not physically harmful and does not lead to dangerous or destructive behavior. The dependence that develops with habit-forming medicines includes drug cravings and drug-seeking behavior. Neither of these is seen with antidepressant discontinuation.

Coming off an addictive medicine can be dangerous. You can experience severe sweating and temperature changes, racing heart, dilated pupils, extreme agitation, withdrawal seizures, and hallucinations. This is the reason many doctors hospitalize you if you have abused narcotic pain pills, sleep medicines, or certain anti-anxiety medicines. Some anti-anxiety and sleep medicines that are habit forming are prescribed with antidepressants to give you more rapid relief. Ideally, they should be used short term, but some people end up taking them longer. There is little risk of dependence, however, if they are given to you by a responsible physician and taken as prescribed.

Scientists have developed ways to determine whether a medicine is addictive by giving drugs in well-developed animal models and then analyzing the resulting behavior. Laboratory rats are taught to self-administer drugs by pushing a lever. They push the lever faster and more frequently if they receive an addictive medicine and the dose is continually lowered. They also push the lever that administers the addictive medicine and neglect the lever that gives them food. When the addictive drugs are stopped, laboratory animals develop characteristic behavior changes that indicate they are in withdrawal.

Scientists also study what happens when humans take a medication to see if it is habit forming. They monitor whether people report feeling high or euphoric and if they try to take more than they are supposed to. By all these measures, antidepressants are not abused in these animal models or when given to people. The ultimate test comes when a medication becomes commercially available. If there is street value among drug users, then the medicine is probably addictive. Antidepressants are not sought out as drugs of abuse and doctors do not find their patients taking more than prescribed.

"How do I know if I have discontinuation symptoms?"

Discontinuation symptoms vary considerably from person to person, but there are certain consistent complaints that doctors hear time and again from their patients. Common physical discontinuation symptoms include nausea, flu-like symptoms, "electric shock" sensations, headaches, unsteadiness, dizziness, and trouble sleeping. The more commonly reported emotional symptoms include anxiety, irritability, and mood swings. A host of other symptoms have been attributed to ADS, but there is no method to verify that all these are actually caused by stopping your antidepressant (see Table 8-A "Discontinuation Symptoms" on page 160).

Discontinuation from the tricyclic antidepressants is similar to that of the newer generation of medications, but may cause more problems with balance and movement, such as tremor, stiffness, and muscle rigidity. This may be explained by tricyclics' effects on the neurotransmitter acetyl-choline, which facilitates coordination and motor movements. The MAOIs are reported to have some of the most severe discontinuation symptoms, including aggression, agitation, difficulties with thinking clearly, muscle problems, and, in rare circumstances, psychosis. This may be due to MAOIs' unique effects on other receptor sites such as dopamine. If you are taking an MAOI, you should be extra careful about missing doses or stopping abruptly.

Many of the physical and emotional symptoms identified as discontinuation are identical to those seen with depression. When you stop your antidepressant, you cannot always tell whether you are experiencing discontinuation or a depression relapse. Typically, missing a few doses should not bring about the depression so quickly, but could precipitate ADS. However, some people are very sensitive to the antidepressant effects of their medication. They feel better within a few days of starting an antidepressant and can notice their depression returning after being off medicine within a day or two.

Getting back on the antidepressant will help you feel better, but does not tell you whether you are having ADS or a depression relapse. The only way to know if the symptoms are from discontinuation is to stay off the medicine and see if the symptoms improve over time. You risk that your depression will worsen and become more difficult to treat. Some people have both—depression relapse and discontinuation—when they stop their medicine. In that case, the symptoms from discontinuation gradually improve while the depression symptoms will likely worsen the longer you are off the medication.

Chris wanted to check on some other medication options to see if he could get even better results. He was interested in Effexor, which he heard was helpful for anxiety and depression. When he started researching the medicine on the Internet, he read several stories about people having a hard time getting off the medicine. There was clearly more written about this subject with Effexor than any other medicine he looked up.

On his next visit with his doctor, he asked, "Why are so many people having a hard time with that drug? Are some antidepressants more likely to have discontinuation syndrome than others? If I do take Effexor and stop it later, what can I do when I get these symptoms? Will I ever be able to get off the medicine?"

"Are there some antidepressants more likely to have discontinuation than others?"

Discontinuation effects are seen with every antidepressant, but they may be more common with certain medications. The newer SSRIs and SNRIs have more reports of discontinuation syndrome, but this may be because they are used more frequently than other antidepressants. The most reliable predictors of whether you will get antidepressant discontinuation syndrome are the length of time you are on the medicine, how high your dose is, and how quickly the medicine is eliminated from your body.

Medications with short half-lives, the time it takes the blood level of medicine to drop by half, have more withdrawal effects because the amount of the medicine in the body decreases quickly. For example, fluoxetine (Prozac), which has a five-week half-life, seems to have less discontinuation than other antidepressants such as paroxetine (Paxil) and venlafaxine (Effexor), which have half-lives of less than 24 hours. However, discontinuation is still seen frequently with extended- and controlled-release preparations of venlafaxine and paroxetine. This may mean that the half-life is still very short, even with these gradual-release preparations or that other characteristics of these medicines contribute to a higher likelihood of symptoms. Table 8-B (on page 161) lists antidepressants by their half-life and their discontinuation risk.

"...what can I do when I get these symptoms?
Will I ever be able to get off the medicine?"

When discontinuation occurs because you skipped your medicine, simply resume taking it and the symptoms should resolve within a few hours. If you have missed more than a week, your doctor may not want you to go right back to your previous dose level. You should check with your doctor to see if she wants you to start on a lower dose and slowly work your way back up. If you have run out of the medicine and not seen your doctor in a while, she should be willing to have the pharmacist give you a few pills to hold you over until you can be seen. Pharmacists occasionally give an emergency supply of a day or two if you cannot get in touch with your doctor and if you have been consistently refilling the medicine at that pharmacy. Ideally, you should have an emergency supply hidden somewhere in case this occurs.

Discontinuation effects may also develop if you have been switched to a generic formulation or a different manufacturer of a generic medicine you are taking. Since generic medicines can have 20 percent variability in blood levels, you may experience a dip in the amount in your body, leading to withdrawal. If possible, changing back to the medication from the original manufacturer is the best solution. This way you know if this is the reason for your symptoms and you run less of a risk of the depression returning with a lower dose. Pharmacists can usually order generic medicine from a different manufacturer, if you request it. You will most likely pay more for a brand medicine, but, if using insurance, the co-pay may not be significantly higher.

When trying to reduce the dose or come off your antidepressant, gradually tapering yourself down will help prevent discontinuation. Chapter Thirteen goes into more detail on developing medication taper schedules. Despite a slow taper, you may still have some uncomfortable symptoms. The most common strategies are to ride it out, since most discontinuation peaks within 24 to 72 hours and resolves within one to two weeks. You can go back on a lower dose for a short period of time until your body adjusts and then resume your taper with your doctor's approval.

Often discontinuation is minimized when you switch from one antidepressant to another, particularly if they are from a similar class. Some doctors switch their patients to fluoxetine (Prozac), which has a long half-life, and then taper them off the fluoxetine. It is often easier to gradually reduce and stop fluoxetine. If you are on a high dose of an antidepressant,

Table 8-A

Discontinuation Symptoms

- Dizziness
- Vertigo
- Lightheadedness
- Difficulty walking
- Nausea/vomiting
- Fatigue
- Headaches
- Insomnia
- Shock-like sensations

- Parasthesia (skin crawling, burning or pickling)
- Visual disturbances
- Diarrhea
- Muscle pain
- Chills
- Worsening depression; suicidal thoughts

you may have little trouble decreasing the dose initially but may develop more symptoms as you go down to the lower doses. For example, going from venlafaxine 300 mg to 150 mg is easy for most people but 150 mg to nothing is a lot harder. There are no medications, other than antidepressants, that consistently help, but some people report that over-the-counter diphenhydramine (Benadryl) alleviates some of their symptoms.

When you no longer need to take an antidepressant to treat or prevent depression, you will be able to stop taking them. Concern about discontinuation syndrome is not a reason to stay on antidepressants longer than needed. You can tell if you are more or less likely to have ADS if you have ever missed a dose or two of your medicine and noticed a problem. If you are very sensitive to coming off antidepressants, just go slowly. Remember that discontinuation is not dangerous and will resolve within a fairly short time period. The bigger concern when stopping your antidepressant is making sure your depression does not return.

Table 8-B

Half-Life, Active Metabolite and Discontinuation Risk of Commonly Prescribed Antidepressants

Generic Name	Brand Name	Half-life* (hours)	Active Metabolite**	Discontinuation Risk***
Amitriptyline	Elavil	9-12	yes	medium
Buproprion	Wellbutrin IR	12-30	yes	low
Buproprion Sustained Release	Wellbutrin SR	12-30	yes	low
Buproprion Extended Release	Wellbutrin XL	12-30	yes	low
Citalopram	Celexa	35	no	medium
Desvenlafaxine	Pristiq	11	no	medium
Duloxetine	Cymbalta	11-16	yes	medium
Escitalopram	Lexapro	27-32	no	medium
Fluoxetine	Prozac	84-144	yes	low
Fluvoxamine	Luvox	15	yes	medium
Fluvoxamine Controlled Release	Luvox CR	15	yes	medium
Mirtazapine	Remeron	20-40	no	medium
Nefazodone	Serzone	2-4	yes	medium
Nortryptline	Pamelor	18-35	no	medium
Paroxetine	Paxil	21	no	high
Paroxetine Controlled Release	Paxil CR	15-20	no	high
Sertraline	Zoloft	26	yes	medium
Venlafaxine	Effexor IR	3-13	yes	high
Venlafaxine Extended Release	Effexor XR	3-13	yes	high

*Half-life: the time it takes for the blood level to drop in half if the medicine is stopped. The likelihood, severity, and time to onset of discontinuation symptoms is related to medications with shorter half-lives.

**Active metabolites are compounds produced in the body when the medications are metabolized. They have some therapeutics effects as well. Medications with active metabolites may have longer half-lives and therefore less risk or severity of discontinuation.

***These are relative risks but actual risk of discontinuation can vary widely from person to person depending on the dose you take, length of treatment, your sensitivity to discontinuation, and how your body metabolizes that particular medication.

For more information on discontinuation risk of specific antidepressants, see Appendices G and H (pages 286 and 287).

Chapter Nine

Overcoming Side Effects

" I don't care how much less irritable I am on the medicine, this is no way to live," Frank told his doctor. Frank was referring to the effects of the antidepressant on his sex drive.

"I have no interest in sex since I've been taking this antidepressant. Is there anything I can do about it? My wife isn't complaining, but I know it bothers her. We used to have a good sex life. I didn't notice the problem when I first started the meds, but now it's pretty obvious."

Dr. Gregory responded, "Antidepressants can affect your sex drive and performance, but there could be other reasons, too. We can try some things to help and still keep your depression under control."

Most side effects from antidepressants occur early in treatment and typically disappear within a few weeks. However, you can experience reactions that do not improve over time and others that may not appear until after you have been on antidepressants a while. Fortunately, there are many different antidepressants on the market today with different side-effect profiles. With a little patience and persistence, you will most likely find one that works for you with few, or no, side effects. Medication reactions seen early in treatment often differ from those that develop after taking antidepressants for several months.

Chapter Four discusses the most common early side effects and ways to deal with them. In this chapter, I review problems that are more likely to occur after the first one or two months of taking an antidepressant. These medication problems seen later in treatment are rarely serious but may be bothersome enough that, if they persist, you would prefer to stop or change your antidepressant.

These side effects include:

- Sexual problems
- Weight gain
- Antidepressant apathy
- Sleep problems
- Fatigue

If you experience any of these, make sure that there are no other explanations for these symptoms before you assume that the antidepressant is the problem and stopping it is the solution. I will examine other possible causes and look at changes you can make to help overcome these symptoms. In most cases, you can stay on your medication if it is helping and successfully manage any side effects you may experience. If not, you can always switch to one of the many other antidepressants available and continue to receive the benefit of treatment.

"I have no interest in sex since I've been taking this antidepressant. Is there anything I can do about it?"

Antidepressants can affect sex drive, arousal, and performance in both men and women. However, not everyone on an antidepressant experiences sexual side effects. In fact, some people have reported that their sex life got better with antidepressant treatment. When moods are good, so are relationships and general interest in sex. Antidepressants can also affect neurotransmitters that regulate sexual functioning—like norepinephrine and dopamine—which directly improves drive and performance. Several antidepressants are prescribed specifically to treat sexual problems.

Sexual functioning is affected by physical well-being, emotional health, environment, relationships, partner attraction, religious background, and sexual attitudes.

While your antidepressant may contribute to sexual problems, stopping or switching medication does not always solve the problem if there are other issues at play. In fact, changing your antidepressant therapy could lead to a worsening of depression and even more difficulties with your sex life. A thorough assessment by your doctor or a therapist can help you sort through other possible causes of any sexual difficulties.

Discuss with your doctor whether you have any health problems or you take medicines that could contribute to sexual difficulties. Medical problems such as diabetes, heart disease, or abnormal hormone levels can impact sex drive and performance. Low levels of testosterone in adult men and women of all ages, and estrogen in women, can affect sexual interest and functioning. See a doctor who is knowledgeable in this area because hormone replacement can treat sexual problems but this is a new area and not all doctors are well versed in it.

Low libido can indicate that your depression is not being adequately treated. Depression can also impact intimacy with your sexual partner. People with depression can be withdrawn, angry, irritable, and less sensitive to the needs of others. The lack of motivation and interest, as well as social withdrawal, that often accompany depression, can result in not helping around the house, forgetting birthdays, and anniversaries, or making little effort to bring romance into their relationship. These behaviors can drive a wedge between you and your partner and can impact your sex life.

Relationship problems can serve as a stressor that leads to depression just as depression can lead to relationship difficulties. As depression improves, so do relationships, but restoring the physical intimacy can take time. If you are the one with the depression, let your partner know you are doing everything you can to prevent the depression from returning. If you are in a relationship with someone who has struggled with depression, it is common to feel some anger or resentment toward that person if they have not been physically or emotionally available. The most important step a couple can take is to open up the lines of communication and allow each person to express how the depression has affected them. This will go a long way to healing the relationship and, ultimately, physical intimacy.

Some people are fortunate to be in relationships that require very little effort to keep their sex life vibrant. Most relationships, however, require effort by both parties to constantly re-energize their physical and emotional connection. To improve your sex life, create a safe environment where you and your partner can safely talk about each other's sexual needs and make an effort to meet those needs within your comfort level. This

Sexual Problems Happen Even Without Antidepressants

Nearly 30 million Americans report having erectile problems and 52 percent of men form the ages of 40 to 70 years of age have some degree of erectile dysfunction. Estimates of women with low libido range from 25 to 43 percent.

often requires some give and take on both ends. Be creative and sexually adventurous. Everyone, at any stage of life, can benefit from learning more about ways of pleasing one's partner through couples counseling, books, movies, and the Internet.

All antidepressants can impact libido and sexual performance (the most common complaint being unable to achieve orgasm), but some are more likely to do so than others. Few studies directly compare the incidence of sexual side effects across different antidepressants. In the past, pharmaceutical companies downplayed the impact of their antidepressants on sex drive and performance. Early studies of SSRIs showed sexual side effects occurring in 2 to 10 percent of people taking them whereas later reports revealed rates as high as 30 to 70 percent, depending on the medication. Most of what we know about rates of sexual problems with each antidepressant comes from what doctors hear from their patients. Sexual functioning is partly regulated through the serotonin system, so the antidepressants with greater effects on that system, such as the SSRIs and SNRIs, tend to have more sexual side effects. Because the SNRIs also target norepinephrine, they may have fewer sexual side effects. The MAOIs and tricyclics seem to have less effect on sexual functioning than the SSRIs, while buproprion (Wellbutrin), an antidepressant that works on norepinephrine and dopamine, has been observed to have the fewest problems.

Some people who accidently, or intentionally, skip a few doses of their medicine, or stop taking it altogether, find their sexual libido and performance improve. This is one way to determine whether the medicine is the cause of the problem. In fact, doctors used to tell patients who experience sexual side effects to skip the medicine a day or two if they plan to have sex and then resume the medicine after. This approach has fallen out of favor because people would experience antidepressant discontinuation symptoms (see Chapter Eight) or notice their depression worsening. Also, it often didn't work. Sometimes missing as little as a few doses of the medicine can restore your sexual functioning to normal but often it can take up to one to two weeks before you see a noticeable difference.

Typically, the longer you are on the antidepressant, the greater the chance your body will adjust and sexual problems will lessen. Therefore, some doctors recommend a wait-and-see approach. Another strategy is to lower the dose of the medicine once you have been stable for at least six months. You may be able to maintain the benefits of the medicine and eliminate the side effects. There is a risk that the depression could return, and in those cases, doctors may lower the dose and add buproprion (Wellbutrin), which can improve sexual performance and also help maintain the antidepressant effect.

Though you should always consult your doctor before trying them, there are certain natural products and other medications that can sometimes help with antidepressant-induced sexual problems. These include:

Buspirone (Buspar): A non-habit forming anti-anxiety prescription medication that has been shown to improve libido and sexual performance. Most doctors have not found this to be as effective as studies suggest.

Sildenafil (Viagra), vardenafil (Levitra), tadalafil (Cialis): Erectile dysfunction medications indicated for use on men but have been shown to improve performance in women as well. They are less effective with improving sexual interest.

Pramipexole (Mirapex), amantadine (Symmetrel), and ropinirole (Requip): Medications intended to treat Parkinson's disease that can improve both sexual interest and performance by enhancing dopamine in the brain.

Methyphenidate (Ritalin), dextroamphetamine (Dexedrine), mixed amphetamine salts (Adderall): Stimulant medications that can improve sexual functioning through their effects on dopamine. Their use is limited because they can interfere with sleep, worsen anxiety, and are potentially addictive.

Avoid over-the-counter natural sexual enhancement products. They are untested and may be harmful since they often contain products that can impact your mood and interact with your antidepressant. Some examples are:

Yohimbine: A natural product that comes from a tree bark. It is found in many over-the-counter sexual enhancement products. Yohimbine can have dangerous interactions with antidepressants (particularly MAOIs) and can worsen depression and anxiety. Always consult your doctor before using products containing yohimbine.

Dehydroepiandrosterone (DHEA): A synthetic replication of a hormone produced in the adrenal gland and converted to testosterone. Most studies have shown that DHEA is ineffective as a sexual enhancement aid

**Eleven Foods Reported to Improve Libido
(Or So Goes the Rumor)**

The Web site www.askmen.com reports 11 foods that increase sex drive (there is no research to back this up as far as I can tell): celery, almonds, avocado, bananas, raw oysters, mangos, eggs, liver, figs, chocolate, and garlic (though this last one may affect your partner's interest).

and may be dangerous for your physical health because of its effects on hormone levels. Analysis of over-the-counter products with DHEA show that many of them contain such low amounts that they would be unlikely to help. Some products had no detectable levels of DHEA.

KyoGreen and arginmax: These are heavily advertised herbal treatments. The companies that sell the products conducted studies showing that they improved sexual functioning, but there was no placebo control group, making the findings scientifically invalid.

You can always change to another antidepressant. The risk is that the new medication will not work as well or may still produce sexual side effects. You could also develop other reactions that are more bothersome. Buproprion (Wellbutrin) is the least likely antidepressant to have associated sexual side effects, but some people who respond to the SSRIs and SNRIs do not feel it works as well on their depression. Furthermore, buproprion is not a preferred medication when anxiety is a major symptom. Nefazodone (Serzone) or mirtazapine (Remeron) have fewer negative effects on sexual functioning but have other potential problems associated with them, such as sedation and weight gain. There are some differences in risk of sexual side effects among the different SSRIs and SNRIs. Some people successfully switch within the class. Paroxetine (Paxil) is known to have the highest rates of sexual side effects whereas citalopram (Celexa) and escitalopram (Lexapro) are on the lower end of the spectrum. Much of this depends on the dose. Appendix E "Commonly Prescribed Antidepressants by Side Effect Risk" gives relative risk of sexual problems of the more commonly used antidepressants.

Jane's doctor commented during the physical exam, "You have put on a few extra pounds since your last visit. You aren't overweight and I don't think it's enough to be a concern, yet. Have you changed anything? Eating habits? Exercise routine?"

Jane answered, "I eat the same things I always have. If anything, I'm more active since I'm feeling better. I wonder if the antidepressant is affecting my weight. I read a lot on the Internet about weight gain with these kinds of medicines. I even thought about getting some of those diet pills I see advertised on television."

The doctor responded, "It could be the medicine, but not everyone gains weight with antidepressants, and I don't see much weight gain with the one you're on. Let's talk about some healthier ways of dealing with the problem rather than using diet pills."

"I know I've gained weight.
I eat the same things I always have."

Weight gain can be a side effect of any antidepressant. As with sexual side effects, the risk differs among the different medications. Weight gain can result from an increased appetite or a change in metabolism. Some people gain weight without changing their eating habits. Not everyone gains weight, so don't let that influence your decision on whether or not to take an antidepressant. If you do gain weight, you have many ways to control it. There are also antidepressants available that have very little risk of weight gain.

Most weight gain that does occur is not very significant and is usually more of a cosmetic issue. Unfortunately, today's society promotes unrealistic body images, so even modest changes can be unacceptable to both men and women. "I'd rather be thin and miserable than fat and happy," is a comment that doctors sometimes hear from their patients. On the other hand, in rare circumstances, the weight gain can become so pronounced that it could be a health concern, especially if there is a preexisting medical condition such as diabetes or heart disease. Under those circumstances, you may need to find an alternative medication or different type of treatment.

Of all the antidepressants, the tricylics seem to cause the most weight gain. This is one of the reasons doctors prescribe them so infrequently today. Mirtazapine (Remeron) is a newer-generation antidepressant associated with an increase in appetite and weight. It is an ideal medication for people with severe weight loss due to a medical problem. Buproprion (Wellbutrin) is one of the most weight-neutral antidepressants and can even precipitate weight loss. In fact, some weight-reduction programs use buproprion to treat obesity in people with, or without, depression. The more commonly prescribed SSRIs and SNRIs antidepressants, as a whole, seem to produce little to modest weight gain, but this can vary greatly among people. Paroxetine (Paxil) may stand out from the group as having the highest risk of weight gain. Appendix E "Commonly Prescribed Antidepressants by Side Effect Risk" rates antidepressants by risk of weight gain.

Some people are quick to blame their antidepressant for any weight gain they may experience, but other possibilities must be considered. The most common causes of weight gain in the general population are poor dietary habits and physical inactivity. If you eat too much of the wrong foods or don't get enough exercise, stopping or changing your antidepressant will have little effect on your weight and may cause your depression to worsen. Also remember that your metabolism slows down as you age, and you may not be able to stay at your present weight without changes in your lifestyle. A number of medical problems such as thyroid problems, diabetes, and heart problems can precipitate an increase in appetite or weight. Other medications, including steroids and diabetes drugs, can also lead to weight gain.

Some weight gain, particularly when seen early in treatment, may come from a normalization of weight. This occurs because many people lose weight when depressed as a result of being very anxious or having little interest in food. The metabolism slows down when food intake is reduced, similar to that seen with starvation diets. When depression improves and normal eating habits resume, the slow metabolism and increased caloric intake can cause a rapid weight gain. Eventually the body adjusts to its normal weight and metabolism over time.

Several studies show that weight gain with psychiatric medicines can be remedied with diet and exercise. Avoid fad diets that promise unrealistic results. They are often ineffective, unhealthy, and expensive. Most large, commercial weight loss programs such as Jenny Craig and Weight Watchers are safer alternatives with good track records of success. You can participate in most of their programs through the Internet, making them convenient and accessible. Seeing a nutritionist can help you to get a jumpstart in the right direction and maintain your adherence to a program. No diet works consistently for everyone, so you have to find the one you can most realistically follow and fits your lifestyle.

If you start a regular exercise and diet program and continue to find it difficult to lose weight, you can try certain medicines to facilitate weight loss. No medication is a magic bullet, and medication should not be used in lieu of making behavioral changes. They all have potential side effects as well.

Medications prescribed for weight loss include:

Buproprion (Wellbutrin): an antidepressant that can help depression, activity level, and weight loss.

Orlistat (Meridia): a prescription weight-loss medication that works by blocking fat absorption. It also sold over-the-counter as Alli. While orlistat is safe to take with antidepressants and can be used long term, you may experience stomach upset and diarrhea if you continue to eat high-fat meals while on it.

Topiramate (Topamax): an anti-seizure medicine known to decrease appetite. Many people find that the high dose required for weight loss can cause difficulties thinking clearly. It can be taken safely with most antidepressants.

Sibutramine (Meridia): a prescription appetite suppressant that works on serotonin. There is a risk of serotonin syndrome (see Chapter Seven) if mixed with serotonin antidepressants. Doctors will, on occasion, reluctantly add low doses to an antidepressant if weight gain is a significant problem and there are few other alternatives. Many possible serious side effects can occur with this medicine and it should be used cautiously.

Stimulant medicines are also used on occasion for weight loss. These include methyphenidate (Ritalin), dextroamphetamine (Dexedrine), mixed amphetamine salts (Adderall), and phentermine (Apidex). Ephedra, which is illegal in the United States, is a Chinese herbal product still found occasionally in many over-the-counter weight-loss preparations from overseas and is considered a natural stimulant. These medications and herbal remedies can decrease appetite and cause rapid weight loss, but most people develop a tolerance to them quickly as well. When you stop these stimulants, you will most likely regain the weight within a short period of time and may experience a short-term crash in energy and motivation. There is a high risk of abuse and dependence on these medicines. They can also worsen your moods, sleep, and anxiety. They can be dangerous to your physical health, affecting your heart and blood pressure. You should avoid these medications for weight control unless your doctor thinks there is a strong medical reason to use them.

Jane wrote down exactly what she told her therapist, Elaine, during their last session. At her doctor's appointment, she read off the paper, "I was afraid this would happen. I went to a funeral of the mother of a close friend and couldn't cry. That's not like me at all. I'm a very sentimental person. I even used to cry at those greeting card commercials. I'm not depressed, but I feel flat, like I've lost my emotions. If this is how antidepressants work, I don't want to be on them."

"I'm not depressed, but I feel flat, like I've lost my emotions."

When taking an antidepressant, you should still experience normal emotional reactions to life events. Antidepressants are not supposed to prevent you from being sad, happy, anxious, or angry when appropriate. People sometimes worry that taking antidepressants will numb their emotions. This is not the intended effect. However, some people do develop feelings of apathy or indifference as a side effect of antidepressants. This is called antidepressant apathy syndrome (AAS). AAS is uncommon and easily reversible with a few simple interventions.

AAS can occur with any antidepressant, but is seen more frequently with those medications that have the greatest effect on serotonin. The SSRIs have the highest risk followed by the SNRIs. Buproprion (Wellbutrin), tricyclics, and the MAOIs are least likely to cause AAS.

You may not be aware of AAS until later in treatment as your depression improves and you get back into your regular work routine, home life, and social activities. Someone with AAS may tell their doctor, "I don't cry at the movies like I used to," or, "I went to a hockey game with friends and couldn't get excited. That's not like me." AAS can result from taking more medicine than you need. A dose required to initially treat the depression may no longer be necessary to keep you well. In this case, lowering the dose could alleviate the feeling of apathy or indifference.

AAS symptoms can include social withdrawal, physical inactivity, or lack of motivation. These symptoms are also seen with depression. When doctors hear that their patients are having AAS symptoms, they may not be sure whether the depression has worsened or their patients are on too much medication. In the former case, you would increase the dose, whereas, in the later, you would lower the dose. Your doctor might choose to raise the dose as a test if she is not sure. If your symptoms get worse, you are probably experiencing AAS. The risk of lowering the antidepressant dose first is that you could experience a depression relapse.

Researchers believe that AAS may be caused by an overabundance of serotonin in the areas of the brain (i.e., frontal lobe) that control motivation, interest, and attention. The high levels of serotonin may also block the effects of dopamine, another neurotransmitter that regulates attention, motivation, and energy. In fact, one of the AAS antidotes is to add a dopamine-enhancing medication, such as buproprion (Wellbutrin), or stimulants, such as methyphendate (Ritalin) or dextroamphetamine (Dexedrine). If lowering the dose does not work, or the depression returns when you do so, you may need to switch to an antidepressant with less serotonin activity.

Chris' Story Continues

"I thought you said my sleeping would get better after I got on the right antidepressant. My depression is better, but I still can't sleep without sleeping pills. I still feel tired most of the day. Could this be from the antidepressant?" Chris asked during his recent follow up with the psychiatrist.

"You've taken sleeping pills a long time according to your records. Have you ever tried stopping them?" the doctor asked.

"Every time I forget to take them or run out, I don't sleep. I didn't take them on a vacation once and didn't sleep for four nights."

"You need to slowly come off the sleeping pills because your body is probably dependent on them by now. There are a few things we can try to get you sleeping more naturally. I bet this will help your energy too."

"My depression is better, but I still can't sleep without sleeping pills."

Sleeping too much or too little is one of the hallmark symptoms of depression. If you have difficulty falling or staying asleep, your doctor may prescribe a sleeping pill for temporary use until the depression improves. Ultimately, the goal is to sleep well on your own. While most people do sleep better after their depression is treated, antidepressants can affect your ability to fall asleep, stay asleep, or get good quality sleep. Some antidepressants can cause you to sleep too much. Sleep side effects usually occur early in antidepressant treatment and improve over time. Sleep problems can, however, persist or appear months into medication therapy.

Make sure the antidepressant is causing your sleep problems before deciding to change your medication regimen. Insomnia is an epidemic in modern society. Nearly 20 percent of the population has a nightly, chronic sleep problem. Medical problems, non-psychiatric medicines, poor sleep habits, depression, and other psychiatric problems can all contribute to sleep irregularities. Check with your doctor to see if you have any health conditions, or are on any medications other than the antidepressant, that could affect your sleep. Your sleep problems could also indicate that your depression is inadequately treated. Discuss with your doctor whether increasing, augmenting, or switching your current antidepressant medication would help (see Chapter Six).

Sleep disorders are a major contributor to sleep problems, and they are more likely to occur in people with depression. The two common sleep disorders are sleep apnea (SA) and restless legs syndrome (RLS). These can be diagnosed by doctors or clinics that specialize in sleep medicine. SA is a condition that affects 4 to 5 percent of the population and is characterized by breathing difficulties while asleep. Your sleep partner may notice you gasping for air in the middle of the night, even though you have no recollection of it. In some cases, people with SA stop breathing hundreds of times a night. If you are overweight or a heavy snorer, you are at greater risk for SA. This can lead to daytime fatigue or memory problems and can worsen your overall physical health. SA is easily treatable once identified.

Common descriptions of RLS are "creeping or crawling feelings" or "pins and needles" in the legs. It is an uncomfortable, but not necessarily painful, feeling that can impair your ability to fall and stay asleep. RLS affects nearly 10 to 15 percent of the population and can be caused or worsened by medical problems such as obesity, iron deficiency, and diabetes. Antidepressants and other non-psychiatric medicines can trigger

RLS as well. Many effective and safe treatments for RLS exist. Both sleep apnea and RLS are diagnosed by an overnight sleep study.

Poor sleep habits lead to poor sleep quality. Many people with depression develop bad sleep practices. This includes going to bed late, waking up late, taking sleeping pills, and getting little physical activity or exercise. Employ the following good sleep habits:

- Avoid stimulants, such as caffeine and nicotine, late in the day. Check any sodas or food products for caffeine content. Some vitamins and over-the-counter diet pills also contain caffeine-like additives, such as ma huang.
- Use your bed for sleeping and sex only. Avoid reading, working, or watching TV in bed, so that your mind associates your bed only with bedtime.
- Avoid naps or time in bed during the day.
- Engage in exercise and other physical activity regularly.
- Wind down at night. Don't start projects or emotionally charged conversations near the time you want to go to sleep.
- Avoid alcohol or illicit drug use. Many illegal drugs, such as marijuana, help induce sleep but do not produce good, restful sleep. You also run the risk of developing a physical and psychological dependence on them to sleep.
- Create a bedtime routine, such as warm bath, reading, or listening to relaxing music to signal your body that you will go to bed soon.
- Get up early in the morning even if you have not slept well, in order to keep a regular schedule.
- Don't exercise late at night.
- Make sure you have a comfortable bedroom and bed.

If your antidepressant is causing your sleep difficulties, you can try a number of strategies to restore your sleep patterns to normal. You may benefit from changing the timing of your antidepressant. If your antidepressant keeps you up at night, take it as early as possible in the morning. If your medicine causes you to sleep too late, take it earlier in the evening. Talk to your doctor first to make sure it is safe to change when you take the medication.

Other non-medication remedies you can try to help with falling or staying asleep include yoga, meditation, relaxation exercises, acupuncture, and natural sleep supplements. Melatonin, a synthetic replication of a naturally occurring hormone in the brain that regulates the sleep cycle, is a commonly used sleep aid. It is non-habit forming with few side effects and is available over-the-counter. The typical dose is 3 mg. Chamomile, tryptophan, valerian, and kava-kava are other natural treatments that reportedly have sleep-enhancing qualities. If you do decide to try any of these products, check with your doctor to make sure they are safe and will not interact with your antidepressant. These supplements are not well regulated and the quality can vary dramatically among different manufacturers. See Chapter Five for suggestions on using medication alternatives.

There are a number of over-the-counter (OTC) and prescription sleep aids on the market today. OTC medications such as Tylenol PM, Sominex, or Unisom usually contain antihistamines (diphenhydramine or doxylamine succinate). These can help put you to sleep but do not necessarily provide you a good quality sleep. They also can cause a morning hangover which can affect your mental sharpness and coordination.

Use of prescription sleep medication usage is growing rapidly. An estimated 30 million Americans take sleep medicines annually. All of the prescription medicines approved for insomnia have the potential for creating tolerance, withdrawal symptoms, dependence, and a worsening of insomnia when you try to reduce or stop them. One exception is remelteon (Rozerem), a medication that works on specific melatonin receptors in the brain. You have to use remelteon for several weeks before it starts to work and not everyone benefits from taking it. There is no dependence or tolerance with remelteon as seen with other sleep medicines. Some doctors start patients on both remelteon and a traditional sleeping pill, even though they are not approved to take together. They slowly withdraw the habit-forming medication as the remelteon begins to take effect.

A number of other psychiatric medicines are given to help people sleep, even though they that are not approved as sleep aids. They can be very effective for more difficult-to-manage insomnia and they have less risk of dependence and abuse. The risk of morning hangover, daytime sedation, and possible weight gain may be higher with these medications. Examples include:

- Trazodone (Desyrl): antidepressant
- Nefazodone (Serzone): antidepressant
- Mirtazapine (Remeron): antidepressant
- Amirtypline (Elavil): antidepressant
- Doxepine (Sinequan): antidepressant
- Quetiapine (Seroquel): mood stabilizer/antipsychotic

Rebound insomnia occurs with prolonged sleep medication use and is a phenomenon in which your sleeping problems get worse after you stop taking your sleeping medication abruptly. Rebound is more common with the habit-forming sleeping medications and can take up to one to two weeks to resolve. The best way to avoid rebound and dependence on sleeping pills is to use them as little as possible and try to tackle your sleeping problems with non-medication strategies. If you have to change your antidepressant because of ongoing sleep problems, look at Appendix E "Commonly Prescribed Antidepressants by Side Effect Risk" for a list of the energizing or sedating properties of different antidepressants.

"I still feel tired most of the day. Could this be from the antidepressant?"

Fatigue and low energy, both symptoms of depression, can also be a side effect of antidepressants. Health conditions, such as hormone deficiencies, diabetes, autoimmune diseases, heart disease, and infectious illnesses can also contribute to fatigue. Other medicines you may be taking, such as anti-inflammatory medicines, cholesterol-lowering drugs, and heart medicines can also affect your energy level. As with other side effects discussed in this chapter, check with your doctor to discuss whether your fatigue could be caused by something else before stopping or changing your antidepressant.

Fibromyalgia and chronic fatigue syndrome are two conditions in which low energy and fatigue are the primary symptoms. Both conditions are seen more frequently in people with depression than the general population. While these conditions have a fairly consistent set of identifiable features, they are hard to diagnose and are not recognized by all healthcare practitioners as legitimate illnesses. This may be due to the fact that scientists have yet to discover a cause for either of these illnesses (though there are many other recognized health problems for which the cause of the illness is unknown) and because of the high rates of depression in those who have these conditions. Some doctors believe that chronic fatigue and fibromyalgia are types of depressive illness with more physical than emotional symptoms. While antidepressants can help both conditions, there are non-depression medicines that are beneficial as well. This suggests that there may be a root physical cause for these conditions that has yet to be discovered. The FDA recognizes fibromyalgia as a real medical illness and has approved several medications specifically for its treatment. There is still no approved medicine for chronic fatigue syndrome.

Lifestyle changes that can improve your energy:

- Get plenty of good, restful sleep.
- Adopt healthy eating habits and possibly include nutritional supplementation with omega-3 oils and vitamins (see Chapter Five).
- Exercise, stretch, and take part in other physical activity on a daily basis.
- Take time to recharge yourself with hobbies, spiritual development, social events, reading, and other enjoyable activities.
- Avoid alcohol, illicit drugs, and quick energy fixes with sugar or heavy caffeine.
- Incorporate stress-relieving and energy-boosting activities into your routine, such as massage, yoga, or meditation.

If your antidepressant is contributing to fatigue and you don't feel more energy after making these lifestyle changes, talk with your doctor about adjusting your antidepressant regimen. You can try to lower the dose of your medication. If your depression is not responding as well to a lower dose or the fatigue is not better, your doctor may decide to keep you on the lower dose and add buproprion (Wellbutrin), an energizing antidepressant. Stimulants such as methyphenidate (Ritalin), dextroamphetamine (Dexedrine), or mixed amphetamine salts (Adderall) can also help. Stimulants should rarely be used because they can disrupt the sleep cycle, have a high risk of tolerance, and carry a high abuse potential. Modafinil (Provigil) or armodafinal (Nuvigil) are medications for narcolepsy, a condition of excessive sleepiness, that may improve daytime fatigue and have less abuse potential than stimulants. Ideally, you should try to avoid additional medications just to improve energy unless the fatigue significantly impacts on your day-to-day functioning and other strategies prove unsuccessful.

People sometimes experience many other reported side effects, but they are generally not very disruptive. Headaches, nausea, diarrhea, and constipation are side effects that may linger beyond the initial few weeks of treatment. Most OTC remedies work well for managing these complaints. If you have any other symptom not discussed here and wonder if it could be from the medication, check with your doctor. If you look on the Internet you will most likely find someone else attributing similar symptoms to the antidepressant you take. That does not necessarily make it true.

Government regulatory agencies like the FDA try to capture new side effects as the use of a medication grows, but they depend on doctors and pharmacists to report problems as they occur. Yet doctors and pharmacists are often reluctant to do so, unless the effects are very serious, because they don't always know for sure that the medicine is causing the problem, and reporting involves a lot of time and paperwork. You may not find any information on your symptom from reliable sources. If your symptoms are not commonly seen with your medication, the only way to be sure is to stop the medicine and see if it goes away. This should be done slowly and only with the consent of your prescribing doctor. Remember that most side effects can be overcome with fairly easy solutions, many of which do not involve taking another medicine.

Chapter Ten

What if My Medicine Stops Working?

Jane was having dinner with her friend Hannah, and the topic of their shared experiences with antidepressants came up. Jane spoke freely with her close friends about taking antidepressants, particularly Hannah, since she had also been treated for depression in the past.

Hannah said, "I'm so glad you're doing well. You know, when I took Prozac in the past, I felt great for several years, and then one day it just seemed to stop working. I went to my doctor and he told me I had 'Prozac poop-out.'"

As a scientist, Jane found it amusing that well-educated healthcare practitioners would use such a term. But she also became concerned that her own medicine could also "poop out."

Jane asked her doctor about developing tolerance to antidepressants. "I know people get used to medicines sometimes. It happened when I took sleeping pills. They no longer helped after a few weeks. Do antidepressants stop working for everyone over time? Why does tolerance occur? If I start to get depression symptoms again, does that mean I'm developing tolerance? I don't look forward to going through that depression again or the process of having to find an antidepressant that works."

When you get on the right medicine and your depression lifts, you are likely to feel a tremendous sense of relief, especially if you had a difficult time finding an effective antidepressant with few side effects. As a result, many people who are doing well on antidepressants worry that their medicine will stop working. They do not look forward to the prospect of dealing with another episode of depression down the road and having to search for an alternative medication.

Fortunately, most people who take their medicine correctly, and make the necessary life changes to prevent a depression relapse, do stay well. There are others who do everything they can to keep their depression at bay (including consistently taking their medication), but still suffer a relapse. This has led researchers to wonder whether people can develop tolerance, also called antidepressant poop-out.

If your depressive symptoms return, you cannot simply assume you have developed tolerance to the antidepressant and that it is no longer working. There may be other factors that account for the change in how you feel. Attributing any reemergence of symptoms erroneously to a lack of medication effectiveness could lead you, or your doctor, to prematurely adjust or change medicine when better alternatives may exist. This chapter looks at the phenomena of antidepressant tolerance and what to do should you begin to re-experience depressive symptoms. This includes answering the following questions:

- What is antidepressant poop-out, or tolerance?
- How likely are you to experience tolerance to your antidepressant?
- How can you differentiate tolerance from other causes of depression relapse?
- What can you do to feel better again?

"Do antidepressants stop working for everyone over time? Why does tolerance occur?"

Many medications can become less effective the longer you are on them for a host of different reasons. Bacteria can become resistant over time to an antibiotic. Diabetes and high blood pressure medicines can sometimes stop working as the disease progresses and different treatments are required. Birth control pills are known to lose their effectiveness if you start taking certain other medicines with them. With sleeping pills, narcotic pain relievers, stimulants, and anti-anxiety medication, physical changes often occur in the body after a while that can render the medicine less effective. You may have to increase the dose several times to get the same effect and, eventually, you might find they stop working altogether.

Tolerance to antidepressants is estimated to occur in up to 20 percent of people who have successfully responded to an antidepressant. No one knows why some people become tolerant and others do not. There may be several different causes depending on the person, the medication, and the type of depression. Each of these may require a different intervention.

Antidepressant tolerance is sometimes referred to as tachyphalaxis or, the less technical term, antidepressant poop-out. Tachyphalaxis means "rapid protection" and takes place when the body changes in response to the effects of a medication over time. Tachyphalaxis can occur through several different mechanisms. One way tachyphalaxis occurs is when a medicine works by releasing certain chemicals that become depleted over time. An example of this is the medication epinephrine, which treats heart failure by forcing the body to release chemicals that make the heart work more efficiently. After just a few doses, the body's store of those chemicals is depleted and epinephrine is no longer effective until these chemicals are restored. Some researchers have speculated that antidepressants may stop working if the brain becomes depleted of certain neurotransmitters or the amino acids and other chemicals needed to make the neurotransmitters.

Tolerance can also develop as your body learns to more effectively process and eliminate the medicine. Your liver and kidneys metabolize many of the medicines you take and, over time, become more efficient at getting rid of the drugs from your system. If this occurs with your anti-depressant, the blood level of your medication can drop even though your dose has not changed. This could render the antidepressant less effective.

Some antidepressants only work when a certain amount is in your body. This is called the therapeutic window. Too little or too much med-icine can be equally ineffective. You could experience tolerance to your antidepressant if the level of the medicine falls outside the therapeutic window. Some medicines, like tricyclic antidepressants, have a narrow therapeutic window. This means you have to take just the right dose for the medicine to work.

What is Your Risk of Becoming Tolerant to Your Antidepressant?

Don't look in the scientific literature for an exact answer to this question. Rate of tachyphlaxis are reported to occur anywhere from 9 to 45 percent in those taking antidepressants.

Nortryptyline (Pamelor) is a tricyclic antidepressant metabolized by the body into several different compounds. One of these metabolites is known to worsen depression. This may explain why you can feel worse if you take too high a dose. Your doctor can check your blood levels if you are on a tricyclic antidepressant and can tell if you are taking too much or too little.

The newer—and more commonly prescribed—SSRIs and SNRIs do not seem to have a similar therapeutic window. This means that checking the blood level with these medicines does not provide any useful information about whether you are taking the right amount. Some of the SSRIs may also have metabolites that build up in your body over time that can negatively affect your response. The antidepressant citalopram (Celexa) has a metabolite, r-citalopram, that can reverse the serotonin-enhancing qualities of the medicine. This could mean that too much of the medicine could cause a high level of r-citalopram, reducing its effectiveness.

Fluoxetine (Prozac) has a metabolite that helps depression by increasing serotonin levels. It also has a long half-life (four to five weeks), which means that it lingers in the body for a long time even when you stop taking the medicine. If too much of this metabolite accumulates as you continue to take fluoxetine, you could get an overabundance of serotonin, which could precipitate antidepressant-induced apathy, fatigue, or other side effects that could resemble depression.

Some researchers have observed that the body can change when exposed to a medication for extended periods of time, and these changes can render the medicine less effective. With antidepressants, evidence suggests that the neurons may adapt over time to the increased neurotransmitter levels from the medicine by manufacturing fewer neurotransmitters. The neurotransmitter receptors can also become less sensitive to the available neurotransmitters.

"If I start to get depression symptoms again, does that mean I'm developing tolerance?"

Reemerging depressive symptoms do not necessarily mean you are becoming tolerant to your antidepressant, or even that your depression is returning. If you assume the problem is the medicine, you may make unnecessary medication changes or fail to recognize another medical issue that could be affecting your health. A number of other possible explanations exist to explain the changes in how you feel.

You may be experiencing medication side effects that mimic depression symptoms.

While most side effects typically appear soon after starting on a medicine and usually improve over time, some can develop later in treatment. These include fatigue, sleeping difficulties, changes in appetite, restlessness, and anxiety. If you experience any of these, you may have trouble determining whether they are a result of medication side effects or from your depression coming back.

One explanation for the development of side effects later in treatment is that the medicine can build up in your body over time. Many people on antidepressants eventually increase their dose at some point if they believe they have any residual symptoms or simply want to see if they will benefit from taking more. As previously mentioned, metabolites can accumulate the longer you take certain medicines (such as with fluoxetine), possibly leading to the development of serotonin apathy syndrome (see Chapter Nine) or other side effects that mirror depression. If you increase your dose in response to these feelings, those side effects will only get worse.

You may be taking an additional medicine or have a health condition that's affecting your antidepressant.

You could be on a medicine for another health problem that can affect the absorption or overall effectiveness of your antidepressant. If adding a new medicine causes your antidepressant blood level to drop, you could experience a depression relapse. If a new medicine causes your antidepressant level to increase, you could get side effects that mimic depression, such as antidepressant apathy, agitation, or sedation. Alcohol and some illicit drugs can also affect the absorption and blood levels of some antidepressants.

Some medical conditions can impact the effectiveness of antidepressants. Stomach or intestinal problems, including irritable bowel syndrome or delayed gastric emptying, as sometimes seen with diabetes, can reduce the amount of drug absorbed. Liver or kidney disease can affect the processing and elimination of particular antidepressants. Certain medical procedures, such as gastric bypass surgery, can alter antidepressant blood levels. If you notice any mood changes, check with your doctor to see if there are any medicines or health issues that may explain the change in your antidepressant response.

Your symptoms may be from a medical problem.

You may have had an extensive medical examination when you were first diagnosed and treated for depression, but new health problems can develop later on. A number of medical illnesses can cause symptoms similar to those seen with depression, such as low energy, decreased interest, sleep problems, or difficulty concentrating. The more common medical conditions that mimic depression are reviewed in Chapter Two. You may need a physical exam, blood work, or other diagnostic testing to figure out if something else is going on, causing you to feel worse.

Your symptoms may not be depression, but simply normal emotional or physical responses to stress.

If you are under undue pressure at work, or going through relationship or family problems, you could experience sleeplessness, anxiety, or other depression-like symptoms. This does not necessarily mean your depression is coming back. Some people believe they should be able to effortlessly handle stress and conflict if they are on an antidepressant. However, antidepressants are not intended to numb your emotions, and they do not prevent normal reactions to challenging life events. Some people with longstanding depression, who are on antidepressants, have difficulty determining if their response to stress is normal or a sign of re-occurring depression. Reviewing your condition with a mental health-care professional may provide some perspective on whether you should revisit your medication or try stress-reduction strategies first.

The quality of your medication has changed.

Most medications on the market today are manufactured under tightly regulated conditions, ensuring a high-quality and consistent product. Licensed and reputable pharmacists make sure that medicines are properly stored and are not used past their expiration dates since medications can lose their effectiveness if taken too long after they are manufactured. Unreliable pharmacies, especially unregulated ones online or overseas, may give you poor-quality, expired, or improperly stored products, which could explain the change in your medication response. You also want to check carefully whether the shape or color of your pill is different from what you took before to make sure you are receiving the correct medicine.

You could also be taking a less effective generic version of your antidepressant. Some people have noticed they do not feel as well when they switch from a brand-name medicine to a generic version. Additionally, doctors have observed that some of their patients do better with generic medicine from certain manufacturers than others. This could be because generic medications are allowed to have 20 percent variability in blood levels from their brand-name counterpart. Differences in the manufacturing process could also account for the disparity. A meticulous pharmacist can often identify poorly manufactured generic versions of medicines.

Switching back to the brand version, or changing back to your previous generic manufacturer (the generic pharmaceutical company name should be on your pill bottle), could help you feel better again.

You may be experiencing a new or different type of depressive episode.

As discussed in Chapter Two, there are many types of depression, and they can generate different symptoms, course of illness, or response to treatment. If you were successfully being treated for a melancholic depression but now experience symptoms more consistent with atypical or bipolar depression, your antidepressant may no longer be effective. This would be akin to someone having a lung infection that responds to a specific antibiotic, but then developing another infection from different bacteria that the same medicine cannot treat.

Rather than a relapse of your previous depression, you could be experiencing a completely new episode. This is important because we know that staying on the antidepressant that treated your most recent episode prevents it from returning. But we know very little about how effective antidepressants are at preventing new episodes. A new episode of depression may require a completely different intervention from your previous depression.

The Unwanted Gift That Keeps On Giving

Depression is a chronic, recurrent illness in 50 to 80 percent of people with depression.

Depression can also worsen over time and require higher antide-pressant doses or a different type of treatment. A similar phenomona is seen commonly with other chronic medical conditions such as heart dis-ease or diabetes. As the illness progresses, additional or alternative thera-pies are often needed. Fortunately, there are plenty of options available should this be the case.

If your medicine has stopped working, you may not have had a true antidepressant response in the first place.

From clinical research studies, we know that 30 to 45 percent of people who unknowingly take a placebo (dummy pill) experience an improvement in their depression. In other words, they feel better because they think are supposed to feel better (more on placebo in Chapter Twelve). The problem with the placebo effect is that the bene-fits do not usually last, and the depression often returns. A small body of research supports that some people who feel better after taking an antidepressant actually have a placebo response. When the placebo effect wears off, the depression comes back. In this case, you could respond by trying a higher dose that may give a true antidepressant effect or by taking a different medication.

There is no way to know if you got better because you thought you were taking something that would help and willed yourself to improve. People who experience very quick and robust improvement soon after starting an antidepressant are more likely to be placebo responders than those whose depression relief is more gradual over the course of several weeks. However, some true medicine responders do dramatically improve after just a few days.

Chris' Story Continues

Chris is well aware that depression can come back even if you take an antidepressant. He recalls his first antidepressant trial, in which he had such a dra-matic improvement and expected the effect to last as long as he stayed on the medicine. He also remembers the disappointment he felt when he slowly began to slip back into depression.

He feels great on his current medicine, but worries that he might not continue to do well.

At his most recent doctor appointment, he asked, "Is there a way to prevent becoming tolerant to antidepressants? What do I do if the antidepressant stops working? If the depression starts to come back, I want to do something early before it gets too bad."

"What do I do if the antidepressant stops working?"

If your depression comes back despite taking an antidepressant, there are several things you can try to get back on track. These include:

- Changing your antidepressant dose.
- Adding another medication.
- Switching to a different antidepressant.

If you know why your medicine no longer seems to work, it is much easier to choose the most successful strategy. However, in many cases, you, or your doctor, may not be sure why you stopped responding. Sometimes you need a little trial and error to best determine what will help.

Doctors usually first try to increase your antidepressant dose, unless you are already on a high dose or experience too many side effects. If you have tried increasing the dose and did not notice any benefit, going up even more is unlikely to help. However, if you notice some improvement with one increase, you may benefit by taking even more. Some doctors stick rigidly to the pharmaceutical companies' dosing guidelines and are reluctant to go higher. Other doctors, particularly those with expertise in treating depression, are comfortable prescribing more than the recommended amounts in some cases.

The dosing guidelines come from clinical research studies on the medication that the pharmaceutical company submits to government regulatory agencies that approve the medicine. Higher-than-recommended doses may not have been evaluated for safety, or they may have been shown to be ineffective or unsafe. However, as doctors gain more experience with medicines over time, they find that certain people do better on higher doses than the research suggests. An experienced doctor can often identify who may respond to these dose increases with limited risk.

Increasing the dose of the medicine can help by overcoming any adaptations your body may have made to the medicine over time or by increasing the available amount of drug if your blood level has dropped. Another possible benefit is that certain medicines begin to

Two is Better than One?

One study of 237 patients interviewed at a depression clinic found that those on venlafaxine or a tricyclic antidpressant (both work on two or more neurotransmitters) had a 3.7 percent risk of developing tolerance, while those on SSRIs, which work on one neurotransmitter, had a 14 percent risk.

target different neurotransmitters at higher doses. For example, venlafaxine (Effexor) works primarily on serotonin at low doses but begins to affect norepinephrine levels (and sometimes dopamine) as the dose exceeds 150 to 225 mg. Similarly, paroxetine (Paxil) is primarily a serotonin medicine until your dose is increased to 30 to 40 mg. Some evidence suggests you are less likely to develop tolerance on antidepressants that work on multiple neurotransmitters.

If you are feeling worse because a build-up of the antidepressant in your body is causing side effects or antidepressant-induced apathy, you may do better when your dose is decreased. In fact, some people in this situation who stop taking their antidepressant describe feeling better than they did when they were taking it. In that case, you could still be getting the antidepressant effect—which may last for several weeks—but no longer have side effects, which usually resolve soon after stopping the medicine (more on this in Chapter Fourteen). The risk with this strategy is that, if you lower your medicine too much or stop it completely, the antidepressant benefits eventually wear off and the depression returns. Instead, if you are on too much medicine, a better strategy would be to reduce the dose so you are taking enough of the medicine to treat the depression but not have too much in your system that it causes an excessive accumulation in your body.

Medication augmentation is another common approach to managing antidepressant tolerance. Adding another medicine can target additional neurotransmitters that your current medicine does not. It can also boost the effect of your current antidepressant without having to increase its dose. This is particularly useful if you are already on a high dose of an antidepressant or have side effects that worsen if the dose is increased. Augmentation medicines can be selectively chosen to target particular symptoms. If you experience trouble with motivation or energy, you can add a medicine that is more activating or energizing. If you experience insomnia or restlessness, you can add a medicine that is more calming or sedating. Augmentation also allows you to continue on your existing medicine, which may still provide some benefit.

The downside to augmentation is that any new medicine may have its own share of side effects, and it can be an additional financial burden. Also, some people do not like the idea of having to take several different medications and worry about the overall impact on their long-term health. If you do develop other problems or additional side effects with augmentation, it may be hard to tell which medicine is causing the difficulties.

Augmenting agents are reviewed in Chapter Six. These include, but are not limited to, other antidepressants, mood stabilizers, stimulants, Parkinson's disease medicines, and hormones. There is little research looking at natural treatments to help with antidepressant tolerance. If you are already on one of the more commonly used SSRIs or SNRIs, you could benefit from adding a medication that increases the neurotransmitter dopamine. Persistent elevations of serotonin, which can occur with prolonged use of serotonin antidepressants, can reduce dopamine levels over time. Dopamine helps regulate attention, concentration, motivation, and energy. Medications known to increase dopamine levels include the antidepressant buproprion (Wellbutrin), Parkinson's disease medications such as bromocriptine (Parlodel), amantadine (Symmetrel), ropinirole (Requip) or pramipexole (Mirapex), or the mood stabilizer aripiprazole (Abilify). The response to any one of these medicines is highly variable from person to person. Potential side effects can include agitation, restlessness, and sleepiness.

Stimulants, such as dextroamphetamine (Dexedrine), mixed amphetamine salts (Adderall), and methphenidate (Ritalin), are another class of medicines that increase dopamine. They work quickly and effectively, but tolerance develops rapidly and they often require higher and higher doses to get the same effect. People with a predisposition to addiction have a greater potential to abuse stimulants because of their mood-elevating effects. They can have negative effects on heart rate and blood pressure and may worsen anxiety, insomnia, and irritability. They should be used selectively and with great caution.

Mood stabilizers are used to treat bipolar disorder or manic-depression, but they can also help with recurrent depression. No mood stabilizer is approved for management of antidepressant tolerance, but aripiprazole (Abilify) and quetiapine extended release (Seroquel XR) are indicated to treat partial antidepressant response. Quetiapine seems to have some antidepressant and anti-anxiety properties that could be related to its active metabolite that increases norepinephrine levels. Olanzapine (Zyprexa) is approved for treatment-resistant depression in conjunction with the anti-depressant fluoxetine. Other mood stabilizers are currently being studied as single treatments, or add-on therapy, for depression and may receive such approval in the future. Ziprasidone (Geodon) has been shown to increase serotonin and norepinephrine levels to the same degree as some antidepressants. Lamotrigine (Lamictal) is a medicine approved for preventing future manic or depressive episodes in patients with bipolar disorder. It is sometimes used off-label to treat bipolar depression and is prescribed by some doctors to help treat non-bipolar depression as well. Lamotrigine may provide some protection against future depressive episodes. Lithium, one of oldest and best-studied bipolar medicines, is often added to boost the antidepressant effect with depression relapse.

Some researchers believe that if you are having breakthrough depression and respond to a mood stabilizer, you may either have bipolar disorder or some variant of the condition. Recurrent depressions could be a type of cyclical mood disorder similar to bipolar disorder that responds to mood stabilizers. These theories may explain why mood stabilizers work but such theories have not been proven. Antipsychotic medicines (many of the mood stabilizers already mentioned are also antipsychotics) may help if there are psychotic symptoms associated with the depression. While more severe psychosis includes paranoia, hallucinations, or delusions, subtle psychotic symptoms include trouble thinking clearly and confusion. The main risk posed by mood stabilizers or antipsychotics is side effects. Some mood stabilizers require regular blood monitoring to maintain safe levels. Antipsychotic/mood stabilizers often require checking for negative effects on cholesterol, blood sugar, and lipids. Antipsychotics can have long term problems with abnormal motor movements as well.

Hormone supplementation is an effective means of treating depressive symptoms. The most commonly used hormone is thyroid supplementation. T3, or triiodothyronin (Cytomel), may work better in depression than T4, or tetraiodothyronin (Synthroid). Some research indicates that thyroid augmentation helps partial antidepressant responders, even when the thyroid blood levels are normal. While there is less evidence of thyroid benefits in managing antidepressant tolerance, it is still a commonly used strategy. Endocrinologists are often reluctant to encourage thyroid augmentation if your levels are normal because of the risk of thyrotoxicosis (excess thyroid levels), which can be dangerous. A few doctors prefer using Armour Thyroid, a thyroid extract from cows or pigs, because they think it is more effective in treating depression than the synthetic T3 or T4. However, its use is controversial and is considered to be more difficult to regulate for quality and consistency. Some argue it can be dangerous if used improperly.

Sex hormones are also added under certain conditions when antidepressant treatment loses effectiveness. This includes estrogen, progesterone, and testosterone. They are only safe and effective if your levels of any of these hormones are lower than normal. There are significant risks to using hormone supplementation, so it should be monitored carefully by a healthcare provider experienced in this area. Some post-menopausal women have been shown to response better to antidepressants when on hormone replacement. If you take hormone replacement for too long or start too long after menopause, you may face a higher risk of developing certain types of cancers. Testosterone supplementation can help both men and women when their level is low, but it carries significant health risks as well.

Many people switch to a different medicine altogether if they feel their medicine is no longer working. This is a reasonable approach if you have not tried many other medications, are currently on a high dose, or experience unpleasant side effects. Typically, doctors switch you to a medicine with a different mechanism of action from your current antidepressant. The most common change is from the frequently prescribed SSRIs to a SNRI. There are people who develop tolerance and change to a different antidepressant. If someone develops tolerance, changes to a new antidepressant, and still does not improve, they may respond to the previous medication that stopped working after being off of it for a while. No one has been able to explain why this occurs.

"Is there a way to prevent becoming tolerant to antidepressants?"

There are no proven methods to reduce your risk of developing tolerance to antidepressants. Most doctors recommend that their patients incorporate healthy lifestyle practices (see Chapter Five) into their daily routine. This includes a healthy diet, exercise, psychotherapy, and stress reduction. Also, avoid alcohol intake or any illicit drugs. If you have had depression for a long time and are just now beginning to feel well again, you may find a tendency to involve yourself in too many activities. This can put you at risk of the depression coming back.

Some people erroneously believe that if they take low doses of their antidepressant or skip doses of their medicine, they will prevent becoming tolerant to its effects and will more easily be able to come off the medicine in the future. This may be true with certain medications such as sleeping pills, anti-anxiety medicines, or pain killers, but there is no evidence that this works with antidepressants. In fact, skipping or taking too little medicine likely puts you more at risk to relapse or develop tolerance. On the other hand, there is no evidence that taking more of an antidepressant than you need will prevent relapse. The right amount is the dose that it takes to get well and no more.

Some research suggests that taking antidepressants targeting two or more neurotransmitters puts you at less risk for developing tolerance. In other chronic health conditions, such as high blood pressure or diabetes, doctors frequently prescribe two or more medicines that have different mechanisms of actions to prevent the body from adapting to the medicine's effects. Unfortunately, this approach in depression does not work for everyone, and the evidence for this is not conclusive.

Determining whether your depression is coming back—or if you are developing tolerance to your antidepressant—is not always so clearcut. There are many possible explanations for why you may not be doing as well now as you had been. Each reason may require a different intervention to get you feeling well again. Working with your doctor or mental healthcare provider, and a little detective work, may give you some clues as to the most effective strategy to getting your depression back under control.

Chapter Eleven

Special Circumstances

Pregnancy, Moving and Traveling Overseas, Surgery and Inability to Afford Medications

Chris' Story Continues

Chris couldn't believe the news. He knew his company was having financial trouble, but had no idea how bad things were. When he learned he would be part of a massive layoff for his division, he called the human resource department to ask about continuing with the company's health insurance plan. He learned that his severance package would not give him enough money to allow him to stay on his current health plan.

He made an appointment to talk with his doctors about how he could afford to continue treatment and stay on his medicine.

"I just found out I'm losing my job and I'm losing my insurance. I won't be able to pay for the medicine. What can I do? I can't believe I've stayed so upbeat given the situation, but I don't want to come off the medicine now. It's going to be hard enough just trying to find a new job and making ends meet."

While taking antidepressants, special situations will inevitably come up that make you question whether you can continue taking your medication. This chapter tackles some of these situations, including what to do if you are on an antidepressant and are:

- Pregnant or trying to conceive.
- Unable to afford your medications.
- Buying medicine online.
- Traveling or relocating outside the country.
- Undergoing surgical or medical procedures.

Finding reliable sources to help guide you through any of these situations can be challenging.

Your doctor may be reluctant to give you specific suggestions about what to do or even where you should go for more information because there are no hard-and-fast medical guidelines for dealing with these circumstances. For example, many doctors are reluctant to advise their patients about taking antidepressants during pregnancy. Even though the data suggests few known risks, there is no guarantee that problems will not occur. Most doctors want expecting parents to be comfortable with their decision without coercion from others. Your doctor will share with you what she does know about possible harmful effects of antidepressants on a pregnancy, but, with a few exceptions in which the risks of coming off antidepressants clearly outweigh risks to the fetus, she will most likely leave the choice in your hands.

Similarly, your doctor may not advise you on how to safely and responsibly travel overseas with medication or buy medicines online. Each country has specific laws about importing and exporting prescription medication. Internet pharmacies are growing in popularity and can be economical and efficient ways of purchasing medicine. However, getting your medicine online can also be hazardous. There are medical risks and ever-changing legal aspects associated with these situations. Your doctor may not want to be held responsible if you encounter any problems.

You can make a responsible decision regarding any of these expected and unexpected situations if you have up-to-date and reliable resources. This chapter provides you the most recent information on these issues as well as resources you can reference in the future to keep current on any new developments.

"...I'm losing my insurance. I won't be able to afford the medicine. What can I do?"

Antidepressants can be costly, particularly brand-name medications. Even with insurance, co-payments for medicine add up after a while, especially if you take several different medicines. If you lose your insurance, or experience financial problems, you may be unable to afford to stay on your medication without some assistance. Fortunately, there are many avenues available to help you continue getting treatment, but they may require a little work on your end.

If you are on an expensive, brand-name medicine, you should ask your doctor if you can switch to a generic antidepressant. Your doctor may have started you on a brand-name medication because he felt you were most likely to respond to and tolerate that particular drug. However, once you have been stable for a while, you may be able to change to a generic medicine and continue doing well. Doctors are sometimes reluctant to use certain generic medicines because of occasional inconsistencies in reliability among different generic manufacturers. Additionally, you may have already tried many of the antidepressants available in generic formulations without success.

Generic medicines are usually less expensive than brand-name medicine, but they are not necessarily inexpensive. The price for a generic can vary widely depending on how long it has been available in a non-branded formulation and how many competing versions are manufactured. Some pharmacies offer special generic drug discounts or buying clubs you can join to reduce your cost. Ask your pharmacist about buying in three-month quantities or pre-packaged stock bottles that may be less expensive. Many people don't realize that medication prices can differ between different pharmacies. Call around to get the best deal. Some large discount shopping clubs that also have pharmacies do not require you to pay a membership fee if you are only purchasing medication from them.

You may be eligible for one of the many pharmaceutical company patient assistance programs available. Most drug companies provide free medicine to tens of thousands of people with financial problems each year. Each pharmaceutical company has different income requirements to qualify, and those requirements can change on a regular basis. Applications for these programs, and information on whether you qualify, are available on the drug company's Web site or through a telephone number your doctor's office should be able to provide. If your medicine is available in a generic formulation, that medication may not be offered through the drug company's program.

They all require your doctor to fill out part of the application and a prescription, so you need to be under a doctor's care to be eligible. Sometimes you receive a card to give to the pharmacist when you bring in your prescription, or the drug company mails the medicine to you or your doctor's office. Some programs help you with the process. Information on such resources is available at www.rxassist.org, www.phrma.org, and www.needymeds.org. These sites are particularly helpful if you wish to receive assistance for many different medicines. In addition, pharmaceutical companies frequently offer free trial coupons or discount co-pay cards if you use insurance. Check with your doctor's office or the pharmaceutical company Web site to see if there are any such programs available. Many of the discount cards have no minimum income requirements.

Another cost-saving approach is pill splitting. Many medications are scored and easy to break along the line on the pill. Often a higher dose of a medicine is the same cost or only slightly higher than a lower dose. In many cases, there is an equal distribution of medicine in each half of the pill but this is not always true. If you pay cash for your medicine, you can ask your doctor whether he can write you a prescription for a higher dose than you take and whether you can safely cut the pill to reduce your overall cost. However, if you use insurance, you cannot have your doctor give you more medication than you are to take. This is considered insurance fraud.

Medicines that are not scored should not be cut because there is most likely an unequal distribution of medicine in each half. Also, if the medicine is an extended or controlled release, cutting the pill will alter the absorption of the medicine which, for some medications, could be dangerous. See Appendix G "Dosing Formulations and Discontinuation Characteristics of the Most Common Antidepressants" and Appendix H "Table Dosing Formulations and Discontinuation Characteristics of the Less Common Antidepressants" for which medications are scored. Appendix I "Common Antidepressants that can Generally be Safely Cut" lists which medications can be safely cut.

If you will be getting new insurance soon or your financial problems are temporary, you can ask your doctor whether he can provide samples for a short period of time. Samples are available to help people start antidepressants and determine which one works best for them. You should not expect that your doctor can provide samples for long periods of time. Recently, pharmaceutical companies have greatly reduced the quantity of samples they give to doctors' offices. Some medical facilities and other healthcare institutions have stopped accepting samples from pharmaceutical companies because of concerns it encourages doctors to prescribe more of those products to their patients.

Recently, there has been growing interest in purchasing medicine online or from other countries, where they are often less expensive. Many people living in the United States purchase medications from Canada by personally crossing the border or by ordering from online pharmacies. For U.S. citizens, importing medications from other countries is illegal but the U.S. government has not been prosecuting people if they purchase less than three months' worth for personal use. There is a strong political push to change these rules to allow personal importation of medication across borders. If you are a U.S. citizen, you should check with the United States Customs Department or Department of Homeland Security (www.cbp.gov) for the latest regulations in this area.

In the United States, you can, and most likely will, be prosecuted for bringing in medications that are not approved by the FDA (even if prescribed by a foreign physician) or any medicine obtained through a fraudulent prescription. You can bring in medication for personal use if it was prescribed by a foreign doctor and is a medication available in the US. More up-to-date information on bringing medications in and out of the country is available at the department of homeland security Web site (www.cbp.gov/xp/cgov/travel/clearing/restricted).

If you decide to buy medicines online, you should conduct a thorough background check on the pharmacy and verify that it is state-licensed. In the United States, you can check the National Association of Boards of Pharmacy Web site, www.nabp.net, which lists licensed online pharmacies and has an accreditation process called the Verified Internet Pharmacy Practice Sites Seal, (VIPPS Seal). The Web site www.vipps.info assures that a site is licensed to sell online and complies with state and federal rules. It also lists known, fraudulent sites.

Be Careful With Online Pharmacies

The BBC reported in 2007 that a review of 3,160 online pharmacies showed only four had a Verified Internet Pharmacy Practice Site accreditation, although many falsely claimed they had, and more than half did not secure customer data.

Illegitimate online pharmacies may sell counterfeit or expired medicines. They may use contaminated ingredients or store and label their medications incorrectly. Without proper oversight by a reputable pharmacist, you could be taking a medicine that has dangerous interactions with other medicines you are on. Illegitimate online pharmacies may not respect your personal information. Never purchase medicine through a spam email you received. The vast majority of these emails are not from licensed, legitimate pharmacies.

If you buy online, make sure that the pharmacy:

- Has a live person and licensed pharmacist you can talk with.
- Requires a prescription from a physician who has personally examined you.
- Has a phone number and physical address.

Jane's Story Continues

Jane was busting with excitement when she opened the registered letter from the international physics association inviting her to attend a six-month teaching program at several universities in Asia and Europe. This was a once-in-a-lifetime opportunity and a personal goal she had for many years.

Despite nearly a year of feeling well, she knew that she did not want to stop taking her antidepressant now.

She thought, "What if I stopped the medicine and my depression returned while I was out of the country. How would I get help? Will I be able to get my antidepressant in other countries? Am I allowed to take antidepressants with me while traveling?"

"Will I be able to get my antidepressant in other countries? Am I allowed to take antidepressants with me while traveling?"

Don't fall into the trap of thinking that you won't need your medication in exotic places or on vacation. You can ruin your trip by having discontinuation symptoms or a depression relapse. Whether you travel overseas for a brief or extended visit, you need to take certain precautions to make sure you can continue your medication. This includes:

- Keeping all your medicines in their original containers with easily readable labels. The pills must be identifiable, so don't pre-pack them in a daily pill box. Not all medication names are the same in different countries, so make sure the generic name is on the bottle as well.
- Carrying a copy of your prescription with the brand and generic name of your medicine as well as the doctor's name and office contact information.
- Having a note from your doctor on the office letterhead with the name of each medicine you are on. This is particularly important for controlled medicines such as stimulants, anti-anxiety, pain, and sleep medicines.

Check with the embassy or consulate of any country you visit to determine whether you are allowed to travel with that medicine. The Centers for Disease Control's Web site has information about traveling with medicine and staying healthy in other countries at www.cdc.gov/travel. Antidepressants are generally not problematic, but any controlled medication you may take along with your antidepressant could be prohibited.

Most commonly used antidepressants are available in nearly every country, though they may go by a different name. You should check with a pharmacist or doctor to make sure that you are getting the right medication. In less well-developed countries, many medicines may only be available in the larger metropolitan areas. You are able to bring non-habit-forming medicines like antidepressants into most countries with proper paperwork, but you may be limited in the quantity you can import for personal use.

If traveling or living in another country for an extended time, you will most likely need to see a local healthcare practitioner who can prescribe and monitor your medication and provide assistance should you develop any side effects or recurrence of symptoms. Some countries do not require a physician's prescription to obtain medication from a pharmacy. A licensed physician will make sure that you take the correct medicine and obtain it from a legitimate pharmacy. Some storefront pharmacies that do not require a doctor's prescription may sell counterfeit or improperly handled medicines. These may not work and could be dangerous.

L ucy and her husband finally decided that if they wanted to have children, now was the time. Lucy was in a good place. Her career, health, and marriage felt solid. She reluctantly gave the antidepressants some credit for this. For the first time in her adult life, she felt she could handle the physical and emotional burden of raising a family. Her only anxiety came when she recalled how hard her sister struggled after giving birth to her first baby. While she felt concerned about taking an anti-depressant while pregnant, she felt even more nervous about being depressed and pregnant.

Lucy met with her doctor. "I want to get pregnant and I know I want to come off the medicine when I do. But who knows how long it may take? What are the risks to the baby and me if I get pregnant while taking an antidepressant? What if I have to get back on medicine? Will it be safe to breastfeed if I take antidepressants? Can antidepressants affect my fertility?"

"What are the risks to the baby and me if I get pregnant while taking an antidepressant? Will it be safe to breast feed if I take antidepressants?"

Ideally, you should avoid any medication while you're pregnant unless it's absolutely necessary. Clinical studies are not performed on pregnant women to determine whether a medicine poses any safety risks to the mother and child. Despite the need for this information, these types of studies are considered unethical research by today's standards and no one

Taking Antidepressants while Pregnant

A 2009 British Medical Journal reported that by 2003, 13 percent of women in the United States have taken an antidepressant while pregnant. This is doubled from 1999. This number is expected to continue to increase.

would likely participate in them anyway. What we do know about medicine safety in pregnancy is through animal studies and tracking mothers and their children who were intentionally or accidently exposed to medication during pregnancy.

There are large pregnancy registry databases in which patients can voluntarily enroll. They detail any adverse outcomes that they or their baby experienced while taking certain medicines. Through these databases, antidepressants have become one of the best-studied classes of medication for safety in pregnancy. The good news is that, with a few exceptions, antidepressants appear quite safe for the mother and child. However, there are some important factors to consider before deciding to start or continue an antidepressant while pregnant.

Choosing to take any medicine involves balancing the risks and benefits of treatment. When pregnant, you must also weigh the risk of untreated depression verses potential risks of the medication to you and your baby's health. The pharmaceutical company drug information is an inadequate resource for assessing a medicine's safety in pregnancy. Government regulatory agencies require that these companies take a very conservative approach in their labeling when it comes to this issue. Pregnancy safety rating systems (see Table 11-A "FDA Pregnancy Safety Rating System" on page 208) provide some guidance but these have significant limitations as well. Many Internet sites provide general information about antidepressant use in pregnancy but cannot address your specific needs.

Since it is more attention-grabbing, the media frequently reports problems that have occurred with antidepressants and pregnancy, rather than problem-free experiences. Your best resources are your obstetrician and the physician prescribing your antidepressant since they know your particular situation. If they do not have the expertise to advise you, they should be able to refer you to a specialist who specifically deals with managing depression and pregnancy.

If you are currently on an antidepressant and become pregnant, you and your doctor need to assess the likelihood that the depression would return if you were to stop the medication. In Chapter Fourteen, risk factors for recurrence of depression after stopping antidepressants are reviewed. Some of these include a history of repeated depression, residual symptoms, genetic predisposition, and stressful life events. A good response to treatment, few prior episodes, and healthy lifestyle choices will give you a greater chance of doing well off medicine. Pregnancy itself does not worsen or improve your chances of doing well off medicine.

Some women with long and difficult struggles with depression most of their life do well during pregnancy while others find that pregnancy triggers their depression. If you are not on an antidepressant and become depressed while pregnant, you may first want to try some of the proven psychotherapeutic approaches such as cognitive–behavioral therapy (CT) or interpersonal psychotherapy (ITP). These and others are discussed in Chapter Five. If you do have to take an antidepressant, choose one that has a long track record of safety in pregnancy.

All of the commonly prescribed antidepressants have the same safety rating (Category C), except for two: nortriptyline (Pamelor) and paroxetine (Paxil), which are Category D. Some limited data indicates that these two antidepressants may put the fetus at greater risk for congenital abnormalities but some researchers even question those findings. One study showed a 2 percent increase in heart defects in fetuses exposed to paroxetine verses 1 percent in unexposed fetuses, but all of these were exposed during early pregnancy when the risk is the highest. Another study of 6,000 mothers taking antidepressants during pregnancy showed no increase in congenital problems with any SSRI, except with paroxetine. In contrast, other studies show no increased risk with any antidepressant.

Of the other antidepressants, none has been shown to be safer during pregnancy than another, but doctors prefer to use medications that have had more pregnancy exposures. The older SSRIs, such as sertraline and fluoxetine, are preferred for use during pregnancy while the newer medicines, such as duloxetine (Cymbalta) and desvenlafaxine (Pristiq), are generally avoided since there is less experience with those. Fluoxetine

Pregnancy is Not an Antidepressant

A 2006 study conducted at Massachusetts General Hospital followed pregnant women who in the past had major depression. During their pregnancy, some of these women were not feeling depressed and stopped taking their antidepressant medicines. Others stayed on their antidepressant medicines while pregnant. The women who stopped their medicine were five times more likely to have a relapse of depression than those who stayed on their antidepressant, suggesting that pregnancy does not protect you from getting depressed as once thought.

(Prozac) is the best studied and most frequently used of the newer medicines. One study published in the Journal of Clinical Psychopharmacology in 2001 reviewed findings from more than 2,600 pregnant women and 4,000 children exposed to SSRIs and SNRIs, with fluoxetine being the most common, and found there were no safety issues. However, most doctors are comfortable using most any antidepressant if that is the one that has worked best for you and if your risk for depression relapse off medicine is high. See Table 11-B ("Antidepressant Reported Exposures in Pregnancy as of 2008" on page 208) for numbers of reported exposures to pregnant women to specific antidepressants.

One potential, unconfirmed complication that has received some attention is the increased risk to the newborn of developing persistent pulmonary hypertension (PPH)—a rare problem that prevents the baby from getting enough oxygen. Two studies showed slightly higher rates of PPH if the fetus was exposed to an antidepressant after 20 weeks of gestation, while several other studies showed no association at all.

Other identified risks with newborns exposed in utero to antidepressants include preterm labor, low birth rates, irritability, behavioral problems, and breathing difficulties. Fortunately, the incidence of all of these is fairly low. It is not clear whether any of these is caused by the antidepressant or occur as a result of the mother having depression. Some newborns whose mothers took antidepressants during the last few weeks of pregnancy may experience discontinuation symptoms (see Chapter Eight). This could account for some cases of behavior problems, sleeping difficulties, and irritability. Attributing these symptoms to discontinuation is difficult because most newborns exhibit all of these in normal circumstances. Discontinuation, as with adults, will resolve within one to two weeks.

Few studies followed exposed children for prolonged periods after birth. One study published in the *American Journal of Psychiatry* in 2002 and funded by a grant from Novartis and the Canadian Institutes for Health Research (CIHR) looked at children for up to 71 months after being exposed to fluoxetine or tricylics in utero and showed no detrimental effects on behavior, intelligence, or development.

If you are going to take antidepressants, there some other steps you can take to minimize risk to your baby:

If you are doing well on your current medicine, do not switch antidepressants while pregnant without consulting with a healthcare professional experienced in this area. There may be more risk in changing medicine than in staying on what you are on.

- Avoid additional medicines known to cause problems in pregnancy, such as anti-anxiety and sleeping medicines.
- Use the brand-name medication since generic formulations may contain untested additional ingredients.
- Avoid taking an antidepressant, if possible, in the first 12 and last 3 weeks of pregnancy.
- Take as low of a dose as you can to stay well.
- Consider using proven, non-medication depression treatments, with or without medicine, such as interpersonal or cognitive therapy.

Many women taking antidepressants who just gave birth would like the option of breastfeeding but have concerns about whether their baby will be exposed to the medicine through the breast milk. Several studies looked at concentrations of a number of antidepressants in breast milk. Citalopram (Celexa) and fluoxetine are detected in breast milk at concentrations around 10 to 12 percent of the mother's dose. Small amounts of paroxetine and sertraline were seen in the breast milk of mothers taking those medicines, but the levels were believed to be clinically insignificant. The literature shows some reports of breastfed children, whose mothers took antidepressants, experiencing mild irritability and sleeping difficulties. In most circumstances, the babies exposed to trace amounts of antidepressants in the milk appeared to be unaffected. The highest concentration of medicine in the milk is six to eight hours after the mother takes the medicine. Some women choose not to breastfeed during that time to minimize their child's medication exposure. Some suggestions if you are going to breastfeed include:

- Using an antidepressant that has been shown to have little or no detectable levels in the milk, such as sertraline.
- Taking the lowest dose possible.
- Avoiding milk expressed six to eight hours after taking the medicine. Keep in mind that supplementation of breast milk can cause breast feeding difficulties in some children.
- Discontinuing breastfeeding if you notice behavioral changes in your child.

More current information is available at the National Institutes of Health Web site (http://womenshealth.gov/faq/depression-pregnancy.cfm). Massachusetts General Hospital has a women's mental-health site (www.womensmentalhealth.org) that provides more detailed and comprehensive information on the latest research findings in this area.

"Can antidepressants affect my fertility"?

Antidepressants do not appear to have a significant effect on a woman's ability to become pregnant. A small number of women experience changes in their menstrual cycle while on antidepressants which could possibly impact fertility. This may be related to the serotonin antidepressants that can affect the levels of the female reproductive hormone prolactin. Sexual side effects of antidepressants could also reduce your chances of getting pregnant. Since the greatest risk of congenital defects occur with exposure to medicine early in pregnancy, you should avoid antidepressants, if possible, when trying to get pregnant. Untreated depression, stress, and anxiety have all been shown to negatively impact fertility. Depression may affect levels of certain reproductive hormones and is associated with other behaviors that can prevent a successful pregnancy such as smoking and alcohol abuse.

Men also have concerns about whether their taking antidepressants will affect their fertility or put the baby at risk in some way. There are sexual side effects of antidepressants that can impact a man's ability to achieve an erection and ejaculation. Additionally, there is a small, but growing, body of evidence showing that antidepressants can cause some reversible genetic damage to sperm. In a few studies with a small number of subjects, there was a change in the genetic makeup of sperm in men on antidepressants. One study looked at the sperm of men taking paroxetine compared with sperm of men taking no antidepressant. Nearly 50 percent of men on paroxetine had genetic damage to their sperm, versus 10 percent of those on no medicine. When the antidepressant was stopped, all of the subject's sperm returned to normal. These changes could affect a couple's chances of getting pregnant but would not cause congenital problems in their children because these sperm are unable to fertilize the egg.

Other antidepressants, including sertraline, buproprion, and citalopram, have been associated with documented cases of sperm damage, as well. Not all antidepressants available today have been studied. Keep in mind that there are many other possible—and more common—triggers to genetic damage of sperm, such as alcohol, illicit drug use, a variety of chemicals, heat, and sexually transmitted diseases.

Frank learned his prostate was enlarged again and he planned to undergo another procedure to treat it. This time it would be performed in the hospital because of his doctor's concern about whether the stress of the procedure would affect his underlying heart problem. When he was admitted to the hospital the night before, the nurse didn't give him his antidepressant. Frank also did not get a few other medicines he regularly takes.

He called his regular doctor and asked, "Am I supposed to stop taking my antidepressant if I'm having surgery?"

"Am I supposed to stop my antidepressant if I'm having surgery?"

If you are having a medical procedure, your doctor may suggest you stop taking your antidepressant for a short period of time. You should always first check with the doctor treating your depression before doing so. The doctor performing the procedure may not be that familiar with antidepressants and the risks associated with abruptly discontinuing the medication. The two older classes of antidepressants, the tricyclics and MAOIs, can interact with certain types of anesthesia or other medicines used during a surgical procedure. MAOIs usually have to be stopped about two weeks before surgery to prevent any problems with anesthesia medicines. SSRIs and SNRIs are typically safer to take with the majority of anesthesia medicines and during most surgeries. Be sure to let your surgeon and anesthesiologist know what antidepressant you are taking, and the dose, well before surgery so they can check up on possible drug interactions.

Some surgeons have concerns about the possible risk of increased bleeding (serotonin changes can affect clotting) in people taking SSRIs and SNRIs. They may ask their patients to stop the medicine as a precautionary measure. The evidence that these antidepressants have a significant impact on surgical outcomes is very limited. While there are a few reports of people having increased bleeding during surgery while on serotonin antidepressants, other studies demonstrate no such increased risk. One small study in 2009 looked at outcomes from plastic surgeries and found that taking herbal supplements or antidepressants puts you at more risk for complications. Possible reasons could be drug interactions, increased bleeding, or the effect of depression itself on surgical outcomes.

Increased bleeding with serotonin antidepressants occurs in only a small number of people taking antidepressants. There does not seem to be a way to predict if you are more likely to be affected. We do know that people who have a history of bleeding problems or take aspirin and other certain anti-inflammatory medicines like ibuprofen (Motrin) or naproxyn (Naprosyn) may be at greater risk. The blood tests that are used to determine whether someone has a bleeding problem do not reveal whether an antidepressant could contribute to bleeding in that person.

Make sure that the doctor prescribing your antidepressant talks with the doctor who will be performing the medical procedure. Together, they can best assess the risk of stopping your antidepressant versus the risk of staying on the medicine during surgery and recovery. If you have had trouble coming off antidepressants previously, have a history of severe, recurrent depression, or are early in treatment, you should most likely stay on the antidepressant. If you have a history of bleeding problems during surgery or are predisposed to anesthesia reactions, it may be safer to stop the antidepressant, at least until you have successfully recovered from the procedure.

If you stay in the hospital overnight, make sure the hospital has your medication in stock and that your doctor has written for it correctly. Some hospitals do not carry all antidepressants, particularly the newer agents, in their pharmacies. You should be allowed to take your own medicine if you give it to the nursing staff in the originally prescribed bottle with the correct labeling of the drug name, dose, and amount to take.

One group of surgical procedures growing in popularity includes gastric bypass, lap band, and other procedures for treatment of obesity. These surgeries present some challenges to anyone on antidepressants because they can affect absorption and blood levels of antidepressants both immediately after and in the long term. Many surgeons instruct their patients to crush their pills or switch to liquid formulations if possible to help with absorption. Antidepressants in sustained or extended release formulations can be changed to immediate release formulations, if available.

Unfortunately, some people do not tolerate immediate-release medications as well. Buproprion and velafaxine are two common examples that seem to cause more side effects with immediate release preparations in many people. Internet support groups for those who have had successful weight-loss surgery give varying reports of problems with their antidepressant post surgery. Many people successfully stay on their medicines in their current formulation while others notice less effectiveness

Table 11-A

FDA Pregnancy Safety Rating System

- **Category A:** There are no risks to the fetus with this medicine. No psychiatric medicines are in this category.
- **Category B:** There are no known risks in humans but there have been risks observed in animal studies.
- **Category C:** There are known risks in animals or no evidence of risks in humans but it has not been studied
- **Category D:** There is evidence of risk in humans.
- **Category X:** You cannot use these medicines in pregnancy.

unless they switch to a more easily absorbed formulation. A number of people are able to reduce or even stop their antidepressant once they lose weight from the surgery and begin to feel physically better.

Other situations may arise while you're taking antidepressants that have not been addressed here. If your doctor can't answer your questions to your satisfaction, she should be able to refer you to someone or someplace to get the information you need. If you use the Internet, books, or journal articles as references, make sure they contain the most recent information available and that they are objective and evidence-based resources. You should feel reassured that, with the use of antidepressants being so commonplace, many other people have probably encountered, and successfully overcome the same issues you face.

Table 11-B

Antidepressant Reported Exposures in Pregnancy as of 2008*

- **Fluoxetine (Prozac):** 2,500
- **Buproprion (Wellbutrin):** 1,200 (1st trimester, no malformations)
- **Nefazodone (Serzone):** 89
- **Trazodone (Desyrel):** 58
- **Mirtazapine (Remeron):** 104
- **Citalopram (Celexa):** 375
- **Venlafaxine (Effexor):** 150

*There are many more exposures but these are the ones reported to official registries.

Chapter Twelve

How to Decide When to Stop Taking Your Antidepressant

Lucy decided that she was doing well and no longer needed to be on an antidepressant. Also, because she was trying to get pregnant, this seemed to be a good time to stop the medication. Most of the people she knew on antidepressants had been taking them for years. Whenever she asked her doctor how long she should be on the medicine, he would not commit to a time. She never intended to be on them for long.

During her therapy session, she asked Elaine, the therapist, "You know, I want to be off the antidepressant, but I don't want to get depressed again. How long does someone have to take antidepressants? I can't get a straight answer from my doctor."

Most people hope to come off antidepressants at some point, but they need guidance to do so safely and responsibly. No one wants to have to take a medication for any health condition if they can avoid it. Medicines can be costly, produce side effects or safety concerns, and are inconvenient to take at times. Antidepressants are no exception. In fact, many people are even more reluctant to take an antidepressant than they are other drugs because of the stigma surrounding depression and having to use medicine to help control it. Some people are ambivalent about needing a medicine "to be happy" and fear antidepressants will change their personality. Doctors have observed that patients are more willing to start an antidepressant if they have some assurance that they will be able to eventually come off them. Unfortunately, no one can reliably tell you how long you need to stay on your medicine because of the many factors that determine the likelihood of staying well when you stop.

The length of time someone needs to stay on medication can vary widely from person to person. If you take an antibiotic for an infection, you may be told you can stop after 10 to 14 days. There is no such set time course for antidepressant therapy. There are, however, some general guidelines about length of treatment that will help you most successfully manage your depression and prevent a relapse once you stop taking your antidepressant. Having a realistic expectation of how long you should stay on your medicine, and understanding under what circumstances you may be able to stop, can help you eventually become medication-free, if possible.

Depression, like some medical conditions, can be an acute problem that requires brief medication intervention. If you develop poison ivy, you may take a short course of steroids and experience complete relief of symptoms without the need for ongoing treatment. Similarly, some people have a single episode of depression that responds to the typical 9 to 12 months of antidepressant treatment and do well when the medicine is stopped. Other medical illnesses are chronic conditions that can be stable for long periods of time with the occasional flare-up under certain circumstances. Asthma, for example, can be well controlled with a preventative inhaler but may occasionally require more aggressive intervention during an exacerbation. You may have to take additional medicines or inhalers until you can breathe clearly again. Depression, too, can be a chronic condition that is stable with one regimen of medicine (or non-medication treatment) but may require additional medicines or a change in dose if symptoms return or worsen.

Finally, chronic, persistent health conditions need more than just preventative therapy. Examples include insulin for diabetes or heart medicines for ongoing cardiac disease. In some cases of chronic depression, people with persistent depressive symptoms (though symptoms

Depression can be a Chronic Condition for Some

A 2008 study from Holma, et al looked at the outcome of 270 depressed patients in a community setting over five years: 55 percent spent most of their time in full remission after an initial episode, 10 percent were depressed most of the time, and nearly 35 percent had some symptoms most, but not all, of the time.

may vary over time from mild to severe) find they need to stay on a full regimen of medication all the time to manage their symptoms and prevent their condition from worsening. It is difficult early in the course of treatment to know whether your depression will be an acute problem that responds to short-term treatment without the need for maintenance medicine or a chronic condition that requires a more extended course of medicine.

This chapter begins with the process of examining your individual circumstances and determining whether it is realistic to consider reducing or stopping your antidepressant. I will review:

- What the research tells us about length of antidepressant treatment.
- The right reasons for stopping medication.
- The wrong reasons for stopping medication.
- How to determine whether you should try reducing or coming off medicine now.

"How long does someone have to take antidepressants?"

The generally recommended length of time on an antidepressant for a single episode of depression is about 9 to 12 months. If you have had three or more episodes of depression, you may be told to expect to stay on medication anywhere from "a few years" to "indefinitely." A year of taking an antidepressant is acceptable to most people but the notion of many years to a possible life sentence on these medicines is not welcome news. The truth is that these numbers come from large-scale, and grossly inadequate, research studies that evaluate the statistical likelihood of one group as a whole relapsing into depression after discontinuing medicine versus another group's likelihood of relapse if they stay on medicine. This type of research does not account for special circumstances or variations in any one person's particular situation. While the findings from these studies can give us some guidelines to follow, there is no reason to believe that these numbers apply specifically to you or that you cannot beat the odds with a little work.

To interpret the findings from these long-term studies, you need to understand the difference between relapse and recurrence, as well as acute versus continuation versus maintenance treatment. Often the terms *relapse* and *recurrence* are used interchangeably when people talk about depression, but, in research terminology, they mean different things. Relapse is when your current depressive episode being treated returns, whereas recurrence means a new episode has developed. Researchers say relapse occurs when a depression comes back within 9 to 12 months and recurrence is when depression emerges after that time. This implies that if you are successfully treated for 9 to 12 months for a single episode of depression, then there is no longer a need to continue the medication. If you have a chronic depression (it never completely goes away) or recurrent depression (goes away but comes back after treatment), then you may need either ongoing medication or some type of preventative antidepressant therapy.

The first 8 to 12 weeks of treatment is called the *acute phase*. Most antidepressant trials demonstrating that the medicine is safe and effective are acute studies. Treatment that continues for another six months is called the *continuation phase*, which assesses the effectiveness of the medicine in preventing a relapse once you have been successfully treated in the acute phase. In a continuation-phase study, those doing well on an antidepressant are randomized to either staying on the medicine or being switched to a placebo (neither the patient nor the researcher knows who stays on the medicine and who is taken off—only the people coordinating the study know). Typically, those staying on medicine have a better chance of staying well than those who switched to placebo. *Maintenance phase* studies are conducted for longer than one year and are intended to evaluate whether staying on the medicine prevents a recurrence, or new episode, of depression. Unfortunately, maintenance studies are rarely done, so we have limited information to tell us the best way to take medicine to prevent future episodes.

Studying long-term treatment of depression is very difficult, and this accounts for the lack of solid research in this area and the unsatisfying answers that these studies provide. Most of the research was conducted before many of the newer diagnostic criteria, assessment tools, and medications were available. This type of research is time consuming for doctors and the study participants, since they require frequent visits over the course of several years. Also, the people who agree to be involved in these studies may not reflect the typical individual who goes to their doctor for treatment. Often, these studies are conducted in academic facilities such as teaching hospitals, which may treat a different population than those seeing a general physician or psychiatrist in the community.

Furthermore, there is no way to control for all the variables in someone's life that may affect their success in staying well on or off medication. Researchers conducting these types of studies often try their best not to include people with significant medical problems, additional psychiatric conditions, or those likely not to take their medication reliably—all of which can affect the ability to evaluate the effectiveness of the medicine. However, when you restrict the study population to that degree, you have to wonder how applicable the findings are to a "real world" group of people.

The studies also do not often take into account life events or behaviors that can increase or decrease the chances of success when stopping medicine. What if:

- You still have the same life stressors that put you into depression after the 12 months of treatment?
- You are about to lose your job or marriage?
- You are still using alcohol to excess?

These and other obstacles put you at significant risk for doing poorly after going off medicine, even though you completed the 12 months of treatment.

Another limitation is the expense of long-term studies. One may need several hundred participants to obtain useful information. Too few study subjects can prevent researchers from detecting differences between two groups or cause them to detect a difference that does not really exist because there were some unusual circumstances that occurred in a handful of subjects in one of the groups. Including enough subjects in these studies increases the accuracy of the results. Consequently, these studies can cost several millions of dollars to conduct. Most studies are funded by pharmaceutical companies, which have little incentive to pay for research that would tell us when to stop taking an antidepressant.

There are some continuation studies on many of the newer antidepressants and a handful of maintenance studies that compare the benefits of staying on medicine to switching to a placebo. Few studies look out more than one to two years, and there are few that compare how effective different antidepressants are at preventing depression recurrence.

An additional challenge with this type of research is that there is no scientifically accurate measurement tool to detect whether depression is fully treated. If you have cancer, doctors can use an imaging scan or biopsy to detect if the tumor is gone. Rating scales or questionnaires used in antidepressant studies assess whether some symptoms may still be present, but they cannot determine whether any chemical changes in the brain resulting from depression have resolved. They also provide little information regarding the likelihood of your depression returning if you stop your medicine.

We also have no definitive way of determining whether you are experiencing a new episode or a flare-up of your last episode. The 9- to 12-month recommended treatment course is based on study results proving that the likelihood of depression coming back is greater if you stop medicine within the first six months than if you take it for at least a year. However, this is not enough evidence to prove that if depression comes back after 9 to 12 months, it is a new episode and not a return of the previously treated depression. This makes many researchers question whether the recommendation of 9 to 12 months of treatment is valid.

Depression studies typically enroll people with many different subtypes of depression. Therefore, the results may not be applicable to you if you have a different depression type than those in the study. We know that all depressions are not the same but scientists are unable to distinguish between these types reliably except by their symptoms. This is probably an inadequate method for differentiating between depression types. Most likely, of those people who experience similar depression symptoms, some may dramatically respond to treatment and easily stop their medicine after a short time, while others do not do as well and relapse quickly whenever they stop. They may have a different genetic predisposition to depression or chemical alterations in their brain, but symptomatically their depression looks the same.

Despite these many limitations, there are some consistent findings from these studies that identify certain high risk factors for recurring depression. These include:

- A high number of prior depressions.
- Less time spent doing well.
- A severe prior depression.
- First episode of depression occurring earlier than 17 years old and after 65 years old.
- A history of melancholic or psychotic depressions (see Chapter Two).
- Depression that has a big impact on your day-to-day life.

These findings also suggest that if you treat your depression early and aggressively (and make sure you stay well for a long period of time before stopping the medicine), you may be able to improve your chances of staying well when off medicine. If you recall, this is the same recommendation first discussed in Chapter Three based on research demonstrating the physical changes depression can create in the brain.

Does Staying on Medicine Keep You Well?

A 2000 study by Thase et al. looked at preventing future episodes of depression in 128 patients whose depression responded to an older tricyclic, imipramine, and interpersonal psychotherapy (ITP). After successful treatment, imipramine and ITP were continued in 20 percent of the subjects, imipramine was used alone in 20 percent, 40 percent received ITP alone, and 20 percent got placebo. Nearly 80 percent of subjects on the medication were stable after three years, whereas 85 percent on placebo had a recurrence. Doing ITP with medicine did not improve the outcome of those on medicine but using ITP alone had an effect somewhere in between medicine and placebo. *In summary: In a group of medication responders, continuing medication prevented recurrence. Adding one form of therapy, ITP, did not offer much if you were on medication but did help if you came off medication.*

What Happens when you Stop Medicine Three Years Later?

Those who were stable on medicine for three years were then randomized to stay on medicine or switch to placebo. Despite three years of doing well on medicine, those who switched to placebo had higher rates of recurrence than those who stayed on medicine. This makes some researchers wonder whether taking medicine long-term really offers any advantage when you try to stop them later.

Can you Lower your Dose Later On and Stay Well?

In another part of the same study, the 20 people who did poorly when coming off the medicine were put back on the medicine and recovered. Then, one half of them had their dose lowered in half once stable, while the dose for the other half stayed the same. The group with half the dose did half as well. This suggests that the dose that got you well may need to be the dose that keeps you well.

Most doctors instruct their patients that long periods of stability reverse the brain changes that may occur with depression, and such stable periods also translate into improved home life, relationships, and school or work performance. This means less overall stress, which will help reduce the chances of depression recurring. However, despite this commonly held belief, there is some evidence that contradicts the notion that the longer you take a medicine, the greater the likelihood of success coming off.

Chris' Story Continues

"I'm really not sure the medicine is doing much anymore," Chris said to his friend Carl. "I felt optimistic for a while and thought I was better, but now I'm not so sure. I know I'm under a lot of stress with losing my job and all but I don't think I should be feeling this bad. I think I'll stop the medicine. What's the point if it's not helping?"

Carl answered, "It seems like you go through this all the time and then when you stop, you feel even worse."

"I guess so. My doctor said if I stop my antidepressant, it should be for the right reason. What's the right reason? I don't mind taking the medicine if I know it's working."

"My doctor said if I stop my antidepressant, it should be for the right reason. What's the right reason?"

With some exceptions, a good reason to discontinue medication should fall into one of three categories:

- You no longer need the antidepressant to stay well.
- The side effects or risks of the medication outweigh any benefits you receive.
- The medicine never really helped you get better.

Too often, people believe they have a good reason to stop their medicine and decide to do so on their own without consulting their doctor. Others may notify their doctor to tell him or her that they are going to discontinue their medication and ask for instructions on how to do so, without eliciting the doctor's opinion on whether stopping is a good idea. In order to make the safest and most responsible decision (and to maximize your chances of success), you and your healthcare provider should decide together after reviewing your history, progress with treatment, and current circumstances.

The best reason for stopping your antidepressant is that you no longer need it. We have already discussed the recommendation of 9 to 12 months for a first depression episode. Stopping sooner greatly increases the likelihood that your depression will return. Those with more chronic depression, strong family history of mood disorders, poor physical health, significant stress, or a history of multiple depressions in the past will most likely require longer treatment. Poor lifestyle choices, including an unhealthy diet, little physical activity, inadequate sleep, and illicit drug or excessive alcohol use can also prolong the need for staying on antidepressants longer.

Unfortunately, no scientifically reliable test can tell you or your doctor that you no longer need to take antidepressants. If you have done well for an extended period on the medication and your current life circumstances favor a good outcome off the medicine, the only thing left to do is to slowly taper off the medicine and see how you do. The problem with the "stop the medicine and see what happens" method is that your depression may come back. The reemergence of depression symptoms can negatively impact your work, school, home life, physical health, and relationships. However, in this situation, getting back on the medicine early enough is usually sufficient to get you back to feeling well again.

What are your Chances of Having another Depression?

One of the most quoted research findings in the psychiatric literature about depression recurrence is that the risk of another episode of depression after your first is 50 percent, the risk after a second is 75 percent, and the risk after a third is 90 percent. This data comes from a fairly small sample size in a long-term maintenance study conducted in the 1980s, before many of the newer medications and diagnostic criteria were available. The population studied may differ considerably from you and current treatments could dramatically reduce your risk.

However, doctors have noticed that, in a small number of their patients, taking the antidepressant again does not help, and their depression worsens. This may be more likely to occur if you wait too long to restart the medicine. This has led researchers to wonder whether coming off the medicine can make some people resistant to it. There is not much evidence to back this theory up, though. In most cases, if you stop the medicine under your doctor's supervision and watch carefully for signs of recurrent depression, you can intervene early enough to ensure that getting back on the medicine will help.

If you experience unmanageable side effects, or you and your doctor believe that the medicine poses risks that outweigh the benefits, then the most responsible decision would be to discontinue the antidepressant. For example, you may decide not to take the risk of being on antidepressants while pregnant. Or, you may need to take a certain drug that interacts adversely with antidepressants. Serotonin antidepressants, for example, can negatively impact the effectiveness of the breast cancer medicine Tamoxifen. Fortunately, there are so many antidepressant options available that most people can find a medicine they can tolerate (see Chapter Nine) or that has no other significant risks associated with it. If you are one of the few who simply cannot take antidepressants, you may have to turn to one or more of the many proven, non-medication options available to manage your depression (see Chapter Five).

Another good reason to discontinue your antidepressant is that the medicine has not helped you. A few people do not improve with medication

Does Staying on the Antidepressant Longer Help You Come Off Later?

A 2003 study by Geddes et al. showed in a review of 31 studies of up to three years length with over 4410 patients treated with the newer SSRIs that 41 percent of the medicine responders had a recurrence when switched to placebo verses 18 percent who had recurrence when staying on medicine. Those who relapsed were more likely to do so within the first 12 months rather than subsequent months. The study also showed that the greater period of time on an antidepressant offered no additional protection against recurrence when you stopped. It may be just as safe and effective to stop the medicine after one year as to try stopping after three years if you are doing well.

(up to 30 to 45 percent in some clinical studies). In cases of true depression, this is unusual. Typically, when medicines do not appear to work there are either other factors at play (such as substance abuse, medication non-compliance, personality disorder, or a significant stressor) or a misdiagnosis. If you have not done well after multiple, aggressive medication trials, you should consider one of the many alternative treatments for treatment-resistant depression discussed in Chapter Six.

One more scenario that falls into this category is when you get better at the same time that you started an antidepressant, but not necessarily because of the direct effects of the medicine. You could have had a placebo response. Depression medication studies are often designed by giving half of the people the real medicine and half a dummy (or placebo) pill. Neither the researcher nor the study subject knows if they are getting the real or fake pill since they look the same. The purpose of doing it this way is to eliminate the chance of people being influenced to believe they are getting better because they are taking something and it also ensures the researcher cannot manipulate the results either knowingly or unknowingly. In the typical depression study, nearly 30 to 45 percent of people do just as well with the fake pill as with the real medicine (which usually works in 50 to 65 percent of study subjects). And these people that know they have a chance of getting a dummy pill because the consent form said so, which they read before agreeing to take part in the study. When a doctor gives you a prescription for a real medication in her office, it is conceivable that the placebo response could be higher because you believe you are getting something that's already proven to work.

A placebo response does not mean you are not doing anything to treat your depression and are just convincing yourself to feel better. The simple act of "doing something" or talking to your doctor about your problems could have a therapeutic benefit. When you start taking an antidepressant, you are more likely to monitor yourself for depression symptoms so you can track how you are doing with the medicine. Being more aware of these symptoms can encourage you to be more proactive in managing them. This includes eating better, improving your sleep patterns, or making more of an effort to get out and increase your activity level. You may have started some non-medication interventions such as psychotherapy at the same time as the medicine. If circumstances and factors other than taking the medicine are more responsible for your improved moods than the medicine itself, you should be able to stop the antidepressant and continue to do well. Just make sure that you continue with any non-medication interventions or lifestyle changes that may be helping.

ll **I** appreciate everything you've done for me," Frank told his doctor. "My wife thinks the happy pill you've put me on has helped things at home. I'm not that sure it's really done anything good but I don't think it hurts me either. But I take so many pills. I just don't want to be on an antidepressant anymore. What do I need to do to come off?"

Dr. Gregory responded, "I understand your frustration with taking all those medications. It's not the first time you've mentioned it. Of course, it is your decision but I don't think stopping the antidepressant because you take a lot of medicines is a good reason. It's a different story if it's not helping or you want to see how you would do off of it. Are you experiencing side effects or other problems from the medicine?"

"I just don't want to be on antidepressants anymore. What do I need to do to come off?"

Now that I have reviewed the right reasons, let's examine fifteen of the more common wrong reasons for stopping your antidepressant. A wrong reason may be a legitimate concern for you but there could be better ways to address the issue rather than stopping the medicine and risking a depression recurrence. You may be continuing to have some of the same concerns you had when first starting antidepressants. Others concerns may have developed over time on the medication.

Wrong Reason 1: The medicine isn't helping me (when it really is).

If you still experience some depressive symptoms, you may not believe the medicine is helping, even though you are better. Some people experience mood changes under severe stress, such as problems at work or school, a recent loss, or trauma and expect the medicine to prevent them from feeling poorly. Remember that the medicine is not intended to blunt your emotions, and, if something difficult happens in your life, you should still react emotionally to it despite taking an antidepressant.

Others may not want to accept that they need medicine, so they deny to themselves and others that they have benefited from it. Or, they have done well for a while and forget how their depression affected them before taking antidepressants. Some people will stop taking the antidepressant, believing that they are no better with it, and then are surprised when the depression returns, and they quickly "remember" how badly they felt before taking the medicine.

If your medicine truly is not working as it should, or has stopped being effective, you should talk with your doctor about adjusting the dose, augmenting, or switching medication as reviewed in Chapters Six and Ten. Sometimes, when depression returns while you're still on an antidepressant, you can become pessimistic about treatment altogether and give up hope of improvement with any medication. Depression itself can influence your judgment and optimism about medicine. This is all the more reason to trust your healthcare practitioner's suggestions and reassess your current medicine treatment. Stopping medicine completely in this situation will most likely only make you feel worse.

Wrong Reason 2: The medicine is giving me too many side effects.

Side effects may be a good reason to adjust or switch your medication, but they're not necessarily a reason to stop taking antidepressants altogether. There are exceptions in a small subset of people who simply do not seem to be able to tolerate any antidepressant. With so many new options available today (both medication and non-medication) to treat depression, there may be other types of medicine or therapies that could help. Often, non-antidepressant medications, such as mood stabilizers or certain anti-anxiety medications can be of benefit. Review Chapters Five and Nine for ways of managing both immediate and long-term side effects and non-medication treatments.

Wrong Reason 3: Getting my medication is a hassle.

Going to see a doctor regularly and getting to a pharmacy for your medicine can be a major inconvenience. However, the inconvenience of going through another depressive episode is much greater. Not only can depression negatively impact your day-to-day functioning but you could also end up going to see doctors more frequently in an attempt to get better. If you take antidepressants, you should be seen routinely by a doctor to make sure you are doing well and to monitor for side effects. Once stable, you may be able to stretch out visits to every three to six months. In some situations, your doctor may even be willing to go longer.

You can reduce the financial burden of the medicine by:

- Price shopping (pharmacies charge different prices).
- Using less-expensive generic medicine.
- Applying for pharmaceutical patient assistance.
- Using community health centers where doctors' visits and medicine may be provided at minimal or no cost if you qualify.

See Chapter Eleven for more details on ways to obtain medicine if you are having financial problems.

Wrong Reason 4: I don't want to have to depend on medicine to feel normal.

While doctors commonly hear this complaint from their patients, you would not stop your diabetes or high blood pressure medicine because you don't want to depend on medicine for normal blood sugars or blood pressure readings. Some people mistakenly believe that a dependency develops with antidepressants such as with certain habit-forming medications. See Chapter Eight for more on this subject. There is no more physical dependence that develops with antidepressants than with other medications such as a thyroid medicine or cholesterol-lowering agent. While there can be some temporary discontinuation symptoms when you stop an antidepressant, this is far different from developing a dependency on the medicine to be happy or feel normal. Some people may develop a psychological dependence on the antidepressants, meaning that even when they no longer need them, they fear stopping because they worry their depression may return. You can overcome psychological dependence by working with your doctor or counselor to help you slowly withdraw from the medicine.

Wrong Reason 5: Family or friends tell me I shouldn't take antidepressants. People judge me for having depression and taking medicine.

This obstacle to taking antidepressants is unique from most other classes of medicines. You don't usually hear negative comments about taking blood pressure or asthma medicines, but may get a few raised eyebrows when you tell people you take an antidepressant. While there is still a pervasive stigma and much misunderstanding around mental-health problems and treatment, you should not allow the ignorance of others to affect your personal health and happiness. If you feel pressured by those who do not understand your condition and how you benefit from treatment, you can work at educating them, or you can choose to tune them out. If someone really cares about you and your health, they will take the time to learn more about what you are going through. There are plenty of reliable resources you can provide for them, including this book. If they are not willing to educate themselves, then you have to wonder to what extent they are really concerned and whether you should value their opinion. In the end, you are the one who will suffer any consequences of stopping your medicine and having your depression return.

Wrong Reason 6: I don't want taking antidepressants to affect my career.

Fortunately, most employers are not allowed to ask about your medical history and, with depression treatment being so commonplace and more accepted, this has become less of an issue. However, in certain careers, taking antidepressants can be problematic. This includes the defense industry, transportation jobs, and the military. If you have been successfully treated and believe you can continue to do well off of medication, then you may want to stop your antidepressant to make yourself eligible for certain career opportunities. You should give yourself enough time off the medicine before applying or taking such a job to make sure you will stay well off medicine. If you stop your antidepressant prematurely, you could put yourself, and your career, at risk. Generally, those industries that restrict hiring someone with depression or on antidepressant treatment do so either because the jobs are very demanding or because they tend to be inflexible with regards to mental-health problems. You may want to consider whether that job environment is conducive to maintaining your physical and emotional health. Your health should be your number one priority.

Wrong Reason 7: I am getting into a relationship and don't want my significant other to know.

If you are starting a relationship, you may feel self-conscious about telling the other person that you are on antidepressant or, for that matter, that you have a problem with depression. Not everyone is open minded and understanding about what having depression and being on antidepressants means. You can usually tell how someone will react by discussing the issue in more general terms to see what their attitude is on the subject. If you find the person to be receptive and knowledgeable, it should not be an issue. However, if they seem judgmental on the matter, you should try to educate them about depression and its treatment (see Wrong Reason 5). Healthy relationships are based on honesty and a willingness to accept the other person for all their attributes and flaws. You should not have to hide an important aspect of your life from someone you care about or who cares about you. Furthermore, if your depression returns off medicine when you go off the medicine, those symptoms could be more detrimental to your relationship.

Wrong Reason 8: I am concerned about the long-term risks to my health from taking antidepressants.

As discussed in Chapter Nine, any medication can pose risks but, as a class, antidepressants are comparatively safe. We are not aware of any long-term dangers associated with antidepressants and the few rare problems you may hear about are not always definitely linked to the medicine. If there were serious long-term concerns about antidepressants, we would have established a clear causality by now, given that we have over more than 50 years of patient experience and millions of people exposed to these medicines for extended periods of time. What we do know is that untreated depression has profound consequences on one's health. Being followed regularly by a healthcare professional who is knowledgeable about depression treatment is the best method for protecting you from any problems that may they occur.

Wrong Reason 9: Taking antidepressants may affect my eligibility for insurance.

Taking antidepressants can affect some people's eligibility for affordable life, health, disability, and long-term care insurance. This is frustrating if you are in otherwise excellent physical health and have no other conditions that would cause you to be a high insurance risk. Typically, insurance companies look at the actuarial cost of covering people on antidepressants as a whole and not necessarily at your individual circumstances and risk. While some insurance companies work under a compassionate business model and provide a valuable community service, others are more profit focused.

You should not deny yourself the care you need because of concerns that it will affect your insurability. Fortunately, inevitable political changes will no longer allow denial of insurance for these types of pre-existing conditions. Additionally, insurance companies are recognizing that many otherwise healthy people take antidepressants and they don't want to unnecessarily deny themselves a huge pool of potential business. If you stop taking your antidepressant and your depression returns, this could lead to greater problems that could affect your insurability such as ending up taking more medicine or experiencing worsening depression that impacts your work or physical health or, in severe cases, leads to hospitalization.

Find yourself a good insurance agent who has a close relationship with the companies whose policies she sells. Sometimes an agent can advocate for you personally by providing more information about your individual situation. Make sure you check with multiple companies on cost and eligibility, since many of them follow different guidelines. Don't accept the rejection or high premium of one or two insurance companies, since chances are that another company will come through for you at a reasonable rate. If you have to pay a higher premium, do it. Many people have chronic health issues that cause an increased premium. Don't let an insurance company, or its higher cost, decide how you will feel on a daily basis.

Wrong Reason 10: When I'm on antidepressants, it's not me.

Some people believe that antidepressants affect them in an artificial or unnatural way and, consequently, think they are not "themselves" on medication. Feeling emotionally numb or developing antidepressant apathy syndrome (see Chapter Nine) is not the intended effect of the medicine. If that occurs, it is a side effect. Antidepressants are designed to treat depression, not simply mask the symptoms. Sadness, despair, or tension may be natural responses to stress, but depression is not. Depression takes away who you really are, and when an antidepressant works properly, it helps restore you to your true self. Using antidepressants is no more artificial or unnatural than taking a medicine to lower your blood sugar, blood pressure, or cholesterol. Ideally, you could manage any of those medical conditions with lifestyle changes such as diet and exercise, but, unfortunately that doesn't always work. Sometimes medicine is necessary.

Depression is common in creative individuals who, on occasion, report that their artistic talents are suppressed when they take antidepressants. Sometimes the emotional intensity that comes with depression can be an unhealthy, but creative, source of inspiration. If medication treats the depression, you could lose that creative spark. In some people, the medicine itself dampens their creative energy. If this is the case, you need to learn other ways to tap into your abilities. Over time, untreated depression can impact not only your productivity but also other important aspects of your life.

Some people are so accustomed to being depressed that they fear the change that may come, or the demands that will be required of them, when they no longer have depression. They may be worried about rejoining the workforce after being out of work or re-engaging in social relationships. Exploring the source of this concern, and overcoming the fear of getting well, is best addressed with a trained mental-health counselor.

Wrong Reason 11: I take too many medicines.

While we are fortunate to live in an age when we have medical treatments that can manage and prevent a number of disabling health conditions, many people become frustrated when they find themselves on multiple medications for prevention and treatment of various health problems. Taking multiple medications can be costly and burdensome. You should make sure you are not being too quickly prescribed medication for something that can be treated with alternative means. Those who are frustrated with taking multiple medicines often view antidepressants to be "optional," and often discontinue taking those first. However, depression is as serious, and potentially disabling, as most other health conditions. You should periodically have all the doctors prescribing your medications review what you take and make sure each drug is absolutely necessary. Occasionally, doctors may be reluctant to discontinue a medicine if you are doing well, or continue a medication prescribed by another physician without considering whether you could do without it. Also, you can ask whether one medicine could replace two or more medicines you take or whether you can consolidate the times you take the medicines to minimize your inconvenience.

Wrong Reason 12: I want to treat my depression without medicine.

Setting a goal of overcoming depression without medicine is admirable and, if you are able, you should certainly try. Chapter Five reviews non-medication options. However, too often people feel guilty or inadequate if they are unable to do so. They can feel like they failed at something they should be able to control, which only fuels the depression. However, many forms of depression can only be managed with the addition of medication, despite whatever effort you put in.

If you are determined to treat your depression without medicine, the most responsible approach is to integrate non-medication strategies with your antidepressant and then slowly work on tapering the medicine. Too often people will abruptly stop their antidepressant in their enthusiasm for a more natural approach. They may be unable to follow through with their non-medication treatment strategy or find it inadequate to control their symptoms. Depression can impact your motivation, energy level, and concentration. If your depression returns, you might find these symptoms make it harder to comply with the demands of your treatment program. Also, be careful not to get seduced by heavily advertised or expensive, unproven treatments that promise you a quick fix without medicine.

Wrong Reason 13: The things that made me depressed are no longer there. I don't think I need the medicine anymore.

Often, when someone experiences an overwhelming amount of stress in his life, it can trigger a depressive episode. Stressors can include problems with school, work, health, relationships, or trauma. If the problems that may have set off the depression resolve, you may believe you no longer need the medicine. However, simply resolving the stress in your life will not necessarily make your depression disappear once it has occurred. This is particularly true if you are genetically predisposed to mood problems or have a history of depression in the past. Imagine if you injured your knee while skiing. Even if you stop skiing, the knee does not restore to full health by itself. Similarly, once depression has set in, whatever the triggers, you most likely need to treat it while doing your best to resolve those issues that may have contributed.

Wrong Reason 14: I don't have depression. I think something else is making me feel this way.

You may read or hear about medical problems that can mimic depression. If you believe there is a medical cause that better explains your depressive symptoms, get a second or third medical opinion from a responsible medical expert before stopping your medicine. You may rethink your diagnosis after becoming inspired by a self-help book, motivational speaker, or religious leader. Making lifestyle alterations that improve your motivation and outlook, or making additions to your spiritual life, can be positive changes that may, over time, allow you to fully recover from depression and eventually stop taking antidepressants successfully. If you believe a motivational, spiritual, or religious issue is triggering your depression, you should work to correct those problems before stopping your medicine.

Too often people get overly enthusiastic and abruptly stop their medicine because they believe they have found a better alternative to manage their depression. Take the time to make the changes in your life that you believe will help, and then, with your doctor's consent, you can slowly try to come off your medicine. With patience, you have a greater likelihood of success.

Wrong Reason 15: I heard I shouldn't drink and take antidepressants.

You may read or hear from your doctor that you should not drink alcohol while taking antidepressants. Some people stop their antidepressant because they want to continue using alcohol (or illicit drugs), and they believe that by doing so they are making a responsible decision. While there are dangers to using alcohol or drugs with antidepressants, there are far more dangers with alcohol or drug abuse with depression. Ideally, you should not abuse alcohol or drugs while on antidepressants, but some doctors have been known to tell their patients they would rather they continue on the medicine despite the destructive behavior than stop the medicine and continue the abuse. The risk of drinking alcohol with antidepressants is that you can become more sensitive to the intoxicating effects or increase your risk of liver damage. Mixing certain types of alcohol or drugs with certain medications such as MAOIs can be life-threatening.

If you are considering discontinuing your antidepressant because of alcohol or drug use, you should be open with your physician so he can best direct you on the most appropriate course of action. Keep in mind that alcohol or drug abuse can dramatically impair your ability to respond to antidepressants and recover from depression. Those with substance abuse problems often blame the depression for their drug or alcohol use. Even if the depression came first, the substance abuse usually needs to be treated as a separate issue. This can include Alcoholics Anonymous (AA), counseling, substance rehabilitation programs, or taking medications that reduce the urges to use. Managing the depression alone will most likely not be enough.

Jane had the date marked off on her calendar. She had started taking the antidepressant exactly one year ago. She vividly recalled her doctor telling her to expect to be on the medicine for about a year before deciding whether to stop. Jane felt that the last year was one of the better periods of time in her life. Her moods had leveled even though she still experienced occasional down times. But these bad spells never lasted more than a weekend, and she always returned to her usual self within a few days. She had just returned home from an exciting six months abroad. Her time away so inspired her that she began to consider a major career change, as well as look forward to a life off the antidepressant.

"So doc, it's been a year on the medicine, and you said I probably wouldn't need it anymore after that," Jane said during her recent doctor's visit.

"Yes, you've done well. But the one-year mark is no guarantee of staying well off the medicine," replied the doctor. "If you think the time is right and are willing to take a chance of your depression coming back, we could try. My only concern is the stress you may have in making a career change."

"I certainly don't want the depression to come back," Jane said. "How do I know when it's the right time for me to stop?"

"How do I know when it's the right time for me to stop?"

Since there is no diagnostic test or proven system for determining when you will be able to successfully stop taking your antidepressant, the safest method is to assess the factors that favor your doing well and those that may work against you. These include the following:

- Have you been on the medicine for at least a year and done well during that time? The likelihood of a depression relapse (or recurrence) decreases after 9 to 12 months following a depression response.
- Are you still having some residual symptoms of depression? The more ongoing symptoms you have, the greater the chance of another depressive episode.
- Have you recently tried unsuccessfully to come off the medicine? If you gradually reduced your medicine and still had depression symptoms return within the last three to six months, you may need to wait a little longer before trying again. If you stopped the medicine abruptly, your depression symptoms may have recurred because of the sudden dose decrease, or they may have been discontinuation symptoms. In that case, you may be able to try again, but go more slowly.
- Have you had multiple episodes of depressions in the past, or do you have a strong family history of mood problems? These could indicate a strong biological predisposition to depression and a possible need for ongoing medication maintenance therapy.
- Is your physical health good, and are you taking care of yourself? Medical problems, chronic pain, poor sleep habits, little physical activity, and poor dietary habits can all work against doing well off antidepressants.
- Are you using excessive amounts of alcohol or illicit drugs? Substance abuse will work against you when trying to come off medication.
- How is your current stress level? Timing can be everything when it comes to stopping your medication. Problems in areas such as work, school, home, health, relationships, and finances can affect your ability to stay well. If the conditions are not ideal, you should consider waiting until those issues resolve.

I have developed the START (Successfully Tapering Antidepressants Rating Test) to help you evaluate your chances of success stopping the medicine at this time. See Appendix F "Tapering Antidepressants Rating Test (START)." The test is not a scientifically validated tool, but rather a questionnaire designed to give you a means of assessing your personal risk factors in a more objective manner. Using this test, as well as the input from a knowledgeable healthcare professional who is familiar with you and your history, can provide a good foundation to assist you in deciding whether the time is right to stop your medication.

You now have the tools to help you decide whether to stay on your antidepressant, lower the dose, or come off of it completely. If you are going to reduce the dose or stop taking the medicine, the final two chapters will help you plan out (with your doctor) the most responsible way to do so. If you have decided to stay on the medication for now, you can refer to any of the sections of the book to address concerns or problems you may be having with your antidepressant. You will maximize your chances of successfully coming off the medication if you make sure the timing is right and you have a plan in place to help improve your physical and emotional well being.

Chapter Thirteen

How to Safely Taper Off Your Antidepressant

If you have decided to try to reduce—or completely stop—your antidepressant, you and your doctor need to agree on a safe and effective medication taper schedule. Many people who have tried unsuccessfully to come off their medication may have failed because they reduced their medication dose too aggressively or did not allow enough time between each dose change. Unfortunately, like a number of aspects of antidepressant treatment, there is little useful research available to help guide you in this area. The direction your doctor steers you in is most likely based on her clinical experience in helping other patients stop their medicine. In other words, you and your doctor are on your own to decide how to reduce the dose and over what period of time to do so. Most doctors have found that everyone responds differently when reducing their medicine. Some people are able to taper their medication rapidly without problems, while others may need a more gradual schedule.

This chapter discusses some consistent observations doctors have made when trying to reduce their patients' medications. I review the available doses of each of the more commonly prescribed antidepressants on the market today that can be used in a medication taper schedule and give each medicine a discontinuation difficulty rating. Other topics covered here include:

- How to determine the rate and dose of your taper.
- Managing difficulties and relapse with your taper schedule.
- Challenges in coming off multiple psychiatric medications.
- Coming off one antidepressant to switch to another.

The advice presented in this chapter is not intended to substitute for your doctor's recommendations on how you should best proceed with coming off your antidepressant. The information in this chapter is intended only to inform you about obstacles you may encounter when stopping your medication and to provide you some options to discuss with your doctor to help you through the process.

Lucy decided it was time to stop taking her antidepressant, but she had some concerns.

"You remember how much trouble I had when I missed a few doses," she told her doctor. "I felt terrible. You explained how that was from coming off so quickly. How do I stop taking my medication? I don't want to go through that again."

"As long as you aren't planning on getting pregnant right away, you should take your time in tapering off the antidepressant," he replied. "Let's go down by half a pill and see how you do. I'll see you back in four weeks," he replied.

"Four weeks!" Lucy exclaimed. "It's going to take a long time to get off the medicine at that rate."

"If you're doing well, we can speed it up. It's just a start to see how easy or hard it's going to be for you."

"How do I stop taking my medication?"

There is no reliable, proven method to stop taking antidepressants that consistently works for everyone. While there are published guidelines for initiating antidepressant therapy, neither the FDA, other government agencies, medical professional organizations such as the American Psychiatric Association, or pharmaceutical companies publish guidelines for coming off your medication. The only consensus found from the medical community is to reduce your medicine slowly.

There are a few suggested methods in print and online, but they have not been validated under research conditions. Most of them are promoted by individuals or organizations that are opposed to antidepressant use or have an agenda to promote natural alternatives to medications. They tend to focus on the dangers of antidepressants and exaggerate the difficulties you are likely to expect when trying to stop taking them. They hope to generate enough fear that you make every effort to get off your medicine and never go on it again. And, in some cases, they hope you will purchase the alternative treatments they promote.

The recommendations outlined here are based on the limited scientific data available, as well as my personal experience in treating thousands of patients with depression and helping many of them eventually reduce and stop taking their medication. Most mainstream psychiatric physicians use similar methods for getting their patients off antidepressants with some minor variations. This is one of those areas in which the art of medicine plays a greater role than the science.

The two variables in your medication taper schedule are the degree of dose reductions and the period of time between dose reductions. Chapter Twelve examines "right" and "wrong" reasons for stopping your antidepressant. Ideally, you are coming off the antidepressant because you are doing well and have completed the necessary course of treatment. If so, you should have the luxury of being able to reduce your medication gradually over an extended period of time. This allows your body to adjust to the changes in dosing and any discontinuation problems you may experience. If depressive symptoms return, you will be able to respond quickly before they become too pronounced.

However, you may be in a position in which you have to come off your antidepressant more rapidly. Perhaps you aren't doing well and need to switch to an alternative medication, are having side effects that outweigh the benefits, or have concerns about risks such as taking antidepressants while pregnant. Coming off the medicine quickly in any of these situations could lead to significant discontinuation symptoms (see Chapter Eight) and a greater chance of worsening depression. If you decide to stop your medicine too fast for one of the many "wrong reasons" people choose to come off antidepressants, such as frustration with having to take medicine, cost, or because of lack of support from friends or family, you are less likely to be successful and could sabotage your entire treatment.

In most acute and continuation-phase antidepressant drugs studies (see Chapter Twelve), participants are tapered off their antidepressant over one to two weeks. The British National Formulary recommends tapering over four weeks if you have been on antidepressants more than two months. These rates of discontinuation are too fast for many people. There are a number of review articles about antidepressant discontinuation that suggest more gradual dose changes, such as 1/4-dose reductions every four to six weeks or, in some cases, even more gradual reductions. Since there seems to be no additional risk to a slow taper, why not err on the side of caution and use a more conservative approach? Since four to six weeks is often the required time to notice an improvement with a dose increase, then four to six weeks with each dose decrease may allow sufficient time to see if your depression worsens. That amount of time should also be more than adequate to reduce the risk of discontinuation symptoms or adjust to any if they occur.

The amount by which you should reduce the dose each time varies widely among the different antidepressants and from person to person. Typically, your doctor decides how much to reduce your dose based on how difficult she believes it will be for you to come off that particular medicine, the total amount of medicine you are currently taking, the length of time on the medicine, and, probably most importantly, the available doses of your antidepressant. Using only the available dose formulations limits you from making more gradual changes, if needed. In fact, some doctors have been known to reduce their patient's dose by as little as 10 to 20 percent at a time. However, this can be logistically impossible for certain medications. Antidepressants that are available in liquid formulations or have multiple doses of scored tablets make these minor dose adjustments easier. Fortunately, few people are that sensitive to minor dose changes and most do well tapering their medicine with the available formulations. Appendix G "Dosing Formulations and Discontinuation Characteristics of the Most Common Antidepressants" and Appendix H "Table Dosing Formulations and Discontinuation Characteristics of the Less Common Antidepressants" list the most commonly prescribed antidepressants by their available formulations as well as whether they are delayed release, extended release, or scored tablets.

Medications available in a liquid formulation offer the most flexibility during dose reductions. Unfortunately, they are often more expensive and typically are not available in a generic form. Pill splitting is another means of making more gradual dose changes, but this is not as reliable and not always safe. You should always check with your doctor and pharmacist to see whether you can cut your antidepressant, even if it is scored. Other suggestions regarding pill splitting include:

- Use a pill cutter rather than a knife. Pill cutters are inexpensive and available at most pharmacies. They are designed to ensure more even distribution of the medicine.
- Avoid cutting pills into thirds, quarters, or even smaller fragments. Multiple breaks in the tablet make it difficult to control the amount of medicine you are taking.

- Ask your doctor or pharmacist whether you can cut the pills in advance. Some medicines lose effectiveness when their interiors are exposed to air for more than a day or two.

Appendix I "Common Antidepressants that can Generally be Safely Cut" lists which of the more popular antidepressants are most likely safe to be cut.

As a rule, delayed- or extended-release medications cannot be safely cut. Some tablets are designed to slowly release into the body or are enteric coated to prevent absorption or breakdown in the stomach. By cutting either controlled- or delayed-release or enteric-coated medicines, you can affect the amount of medicine that gets into your system. This can be dangerous. Venlafaxine XR (Effexor XR) is an extended-release drug (and difficult to come off of for many people), but it is in a capsule formulation that can be opened. Some doctors allow their patients to open the capsule and mix the medication with applesauce. Dose reductions can be made by eating a certain portion of the applesauce.

Some pharmacies that are trained to "compound" medications are able to make doses of certain medications not commercially available. This can be costly and is not usually covered by insurance. Another less expensive option for reducing the dose is to take the medicine every other or even third day. This is only safe with antidepressants with longer half lives, such as fluoxetine (Prozac), or those with a lower risk of discontinuation symptoms as with desvenlafaxine (Pristiq). Consult your doctor about whether this is safe to do with the medication you're taking.

Table 13-A "Sample Taper Schedules for Commonly Prescribed Antidepressants" (on page 240) gives examples of medication taper schedules for several of the most popular antidepressants. These are not meant to be specific recommendations for you to follow, but rather to demonstrate how your doctor may instruct you to decrease your dose. As a general rule, going from your current antidepressant dose to a middle range is often easier than going from a middle dose to a low dose or off the medicine completely. This means that you may be able to make more aggressive dose reductions at the higher doses, but will have to make more gradual decreases at the lower doses.

" I did what you said about the medicine," Frank told his doctor. "I think I could have just stopped it without a problem. But I went down real slow. I did well until I got to the last dose. What should I do now? Does this mean I have to go back up on this stuff?"

Dr. Gregory answered, "Not necessarily. When you say you aren't doing as well on this dose, we first have to figure out what you mean by that. If your old symptoms are showing up again, we may need to get you back on a little higher dose than you're on now. There could be other reasons you're not doing well, which means we might not increase the medicine. Tell me exactly what you have noticed."

"I was doing well with coming off the medicine until I got to the last dose. What should I do now?"

If you start having trouble during your medication taper, there may be some solutions to help you along that do not necessarily require you to go back on the full dose of your antidepressant. Most difficulties with medication tapers are due to:

- Giving yourself too little time between dose reductions.
- Making too big of a dose drop with each change.
- Not adjusting your medication taper if you are having problems.
- Confusing discontinuation with depression recurrence.

Having a positive attitude and being flexible during this process are essential to a good outcome.

The Internet is chock full of stories documenting the challenges some people have had as they try to come off their antidepressants. Rest assured that most people, if the timing is right, do not have such severe difficulties stopping their medicine when they do so carefully and under their doctor's guidance. You don't hear those stories as much because few people bother to report a good experience, and it doesn't make for interesting reading. Too often, antidepressant tapers are unsuccessful because the depression is not fully treated or the person requires ongoing maintenance or preventative therapy. You may want to stop the medicine, but your brain and body are not ready.

Along with those stories are countless solutions that may have worked for one person but may not necessarily be helpful to you. In order to make a good decision about handling problems coming off medicine, you have to know what is going on. You could be having a depression recurrence or discontinuation syndrome. It is not always easy to tell them apart since they can look so similar. Some of the more physical symptoms such as electric shocks, dizziness, flu-like symptoms, or stomach distress are likely to be from discontinuation. Mood changes such as irritability, mood swings, anxiety, or depression are more difficult to distinguish. If you are experiencing discontinuation and it is manageable, you may want to stay with the present dose and see if you feel better. If the symptoms do not improve after three to four weeks, or if they worsen, you are probably experiencing recurring depression. In that case, going back up on the last dose you felt well on should help.

There are other ways to manage discontinuation if it continues to be an obstacle to your getting off antidepressants. As discussed in Chapter Eight, you may be able to switch to a serotonin antidepressant with a longer half life, such as fluoxetine (Prozac). This can mitigate the withdrawal symptoms and be easier to taper. The risk is that fluoxetine may not work well for your depression, or it may cause other side effects. Fluoxetine has a five-week half-life, and discontinuation may still occur but be delayed for several weeks after the dose is decreased. Some people have benefited from a low dose of over-the-counter diphenhydramine (Benadryl) 25 to 50 mg. There are no known herbal remedies or non-medication techniques that help with discontinuation.

If you are experiencing an increase in depression symptoms and have not reduced your dose very much, you are not likely to do well with your medication taper at this time. If you have reduced your medicine by 50 percent or more before noticing problems, you may be able to get back on a slightly higher dose and do well. Most doctors recommend going back on the last dose that last worked for you. Or you could try a middle dose, if available. For example, if you went from 40 mg of escitalopram (Lexapro) to 20 mg and experienced some depression symptoms, ask your doctor if you could try 30 mg. There is no 30-mg pill, but you could take 1½ 20-mg pills.

Jane thought about what her doctor had said. She was making a lot of changes in her life, and maybe stopping antidepressants wasn't such a good idea right now. Though she was doing well, she felt like the antidepressant somewhat numbed her emotionally. She hoped she could try a medicine that wasn't "as strong."

"I have a close relative who had a similar feeling with this medicine," Jane told her doctor. "She changed to a different antidepressant and felt more like herself. What do you think? How do I stop my antidepressant if I am going to switch to another one?"

Her doctor responded, "Now is as good a time as any to try something different if you are still having that side effect. We can always go back if it doesn't work as well for you. Let's slowly reduce the dose and then go up slowly on the new medicine at the same time."

"How do I stop my antidepressant if I am going to switch to another one?"

If you are switching antidepressants, you can usually taper your medication more rapidly than if you were stopping medicine altogether. You may want to change medication because you aren't doing well, have side effects, or want a less costly medication. When switching medicine, the risk of depression recurrence is less of a concern, and discontinuation symptoms are not as problematic if the new medicine has a similar mechanism of action.

If you are experiencing side effects or your medicine is not helping as it should, your doctor may taper the medicine quickly (over one to four weeks) to try you on something else. If you are having more severe side effects and switching medicine, she may stop your medicine abruptly or taper it off within a few days. Many doctors switch patients from one antidepressant to another by cross-tapering. This means slowly reducing the dosage on one as you increase the dosage on another. Although different methods of switching antidepressants have not been extensively studied, years of shared clinical experience among doctors has suggested that the practice of cross tapering seems to be the least disruptive and most effective.

Table 13-A

Sample Taper Schedules for Commonly Prescribed Antidepressants

Only your doctor can determine whether it is safe for you to reduce or stop taking your antidepressant and suggest the most appropriate method to reduce your medicine. These sample schedules are only meant to demonstrate examples of how doctors instruct certain patients to reduce their medicine in a specific clinical situation. Work with your doctor to determine your own taper schedule.

Note: The taper schedule examples use four weeks for each dose reduction, but your doctor may instruct you to go faster (such as 1 to 2 weeks) or slower (such as 6 to 12 weeks).

Effexor XR (Venflaxine)

Dose	300 mg or more	225 mg*	150 mg	75 mg	37.5 mg
Week	4	8	12	16	20

*If someone begins to have discontinuation symptoms at 225 mg or less, they can reduce their dose by 37.5 mg at each interval. Some compounding pharmacists can make even lower doses available. You may ask your doctor whether you can open the capsule and mix the contents in applesauce or other food and reduce the dose by taking 1/3, 1/2, or 3/4 of the mixture.

Paxil/Paxil CR (Paroxetine)

Paxil Dose	60 mg or more	40 mg*	30 mg	20 mg	10 mg
Paxil CR Dose	62.5 mg or more	50 mg**	37.5 mg	25 mg	12.5 mg
Week	4	8	12	16	20

*If someone begins to have discontinuation symptoms on Paxil 40 mg or less, they can reduce their dose by 5 mg (1/2 of 10 mg) or switch to liquid.
**Paxil CR tablets cannot be cut. Your doctor may be able to switch you to Paxil tablets or liquid for smaller dose decreases.

Lexapro (Escitalopram)

Dose	20 mg or more	15 mg*	10 mg	5 mg
Week	4	8	12	16

*If someone begins to have discontinuation symptoms on 15 mg or less, they can reduce their dose more gradually by switching to liquid.

Celexa (Citalopram)

Dose	40 mg or more	30 mg*	20 mg	10 mg
Week	4	8	12	16

*If someone begins to have discontinuation symptoms on 30 mg or less, they can reduce their dose more gradually by switching to liquid.

Zoloft (Sertraline)

Dose	200 mg or more	150 mg*	100 mg	75 mg	50 mg	25 mg
Week	4	8	12	16	20	24

*If someone begins to have discontinuation symptoms on 150 mg or less, they can reduce their dose more gradually by switching to liquid.

Prozac (Fluoxetine)

Dose	60 mg or more	40 mg*	30 mg**	20 mg	10 mg**
Week	4	8	12	16	20

*If someone begins to have discontinuation symptoms on 40 mg or less, they can reduce their dose more gradually by switching to liquid.
**Because of fluoxetine's long half-life of the medicine, you can get the equivalent of 30 mg by alternating between 40 mg one day with 20 mg the next day. To get the equivalent of 10 mg, you can take 20 mg every other day.

Cymbalta (Duloxetine)

Dose	90 mg or more	60 mg	30 mg*
Week	4	8	12

*There is a 20-mg dose available. Cymbalta should not be cut because of the delayed-release formulation.

Wellbutrin (Buproprion)

Dose	300 mg or more	200 mg*	150 mg	100 mg**
Week	4	8	12	16

*200 mg not available in XL (150, 300 mg only). Wellbutrin, in any formulation, should not be cut.

**75 mg available in IR formulation only.

Pristiq (Desvenlafaxine)

Only available in 50- and 100-mg formulation. Because of the delayed-release capsule, the medicine should not be cut. The risk of discontinuation symptoms is low with Pristiq. Some doctors will suggest reducing the dose by taking 50 mg every other or every third day.

The challenge with the cross-taper method is reducing the old medicine slowly enough to prevent discontinuation or worsening depression but not so slowly that you end up with drug interactions from taking too much of either. Most antidepressants can be safely cross-tapered, but there are a few exceptions. Always check first with your doctor or pharmacist whether it is safe to take both together, even for a short time. Mixing MAOIs with other antidepressants can be dangerous and must be avoided. There should be at least a two-week gap before starting one after the other (fluoxetine requires five to six weeks before starting an MAOI). Some antidepressants can affect the blood levels of other antidepressants. For example, paroxetine (Paxil) and fluoxetine (Prozac) can increase the levels of several tricyclic antidepressants. High levels of tricyclics can be dangerous, so you need to be extra cautious if using these medicines together or cross-tapering from one to another. If you want a medicine out of your body completely before starting another, remember that most antidepressants are washed out of your system within five to seven days. Fluoxetine (Prozac) is the exception, at five weeks.

Cross tapering does not always protect you from having discontinuation symptoms, particularly when switching antidepressants from different classes (refer to the lists of antidepressant classes in Chapter Three). For example, changing from paroxetine (Paxil) to venlafaxine (Effexor) may go smoothly because they impact many of the same neurotransmitters. However, cross-tapering from paroxetine to bupro-prion (Wellbutrin) could be more challenging because they have completely different effects in the brain. If you are cross-tapering from one serotonin antidepressant to another, your pharmacist may warn you that taking two serotonin medicines at the same time can precipitate serotonin syndrome (see Chapter Seven). While this can occur if you are highly sensitive to increases in serotonin, or if you are on unusually high doses of serotonin medications, the typical doses used in most cross tapers are not likely to cause problems.

Chris' Story Continues

Chris decided to try to come off of all his antide-pressant medicines and see how he would do. His doctor disagreed with his decision and felt that he should gradually change to a different medicine rather than make such abrupt changes. But Chris had already made up his mind.

"You know, I'm still on the first antidepressant you put me on and that other medicine you added at night that was supposed to help my moods and sleep," he told his doctor. "Since I'm taking two medicines for depression, do I stop taking them both at the same time?" Chris asked.

"I'd rather you didn't. If you experience a problem, I wouldn't know whether stopping one or both medicines caused you trouble. Let's try to come off the newer medicine first. It's probably not helping you as much as the first medicine but you may have trouble sleeping without it. Let's just go slowly and watch for any changes," said the doctor.

"Since I'm taking two medicines for my depression, do I come off them both at the same time?"

Doctors commonly use two or more medicines to help treat depression, which can present some unique challenges when trying to come off of them. Do you try to stop both medications at the same time? Do you stop one completely before starting to reduce the other? Do you alternate reducing one and then the other? The answer is: Whatever ends up working best for you. There are advantages and disadvantages to whichever approach you try.

The first step is to identify the "foundational" antidepressant. This is the primary medication that the additional agents are augmenting. Not everyone has a foundational antidepressant; in other words, each medicine may play an equally important role. Ideally, you should come off of the add-on medicine completely to see how you might do on the foundational medicine alone. The downside is that the medicine you stop may be more helpful than the foundational medicine you stay on, particularly if that add-on medicine is also an antidepressant. The add-on medicine may also be helping with some residual symptoms. A sedating medicine could help your sleep, or an activating medicine keeps you more active. Some people find they do better reducing their foundational medicine dose while keeping the add-on medicine unchanged. Some people end up reducing the dosage of both medicines they take for depression but need some of each to stay well.

Some common add-on medicines have significant risks or side effects that are more pronounced than their foundational antidepressant. Examples are atypical antipsychotic/mood stabilizers that can affect weight, blood sugar, or cholesterol. Lithium, also a mood stabilizer, can cause kidney or thyroid problems. Stimulants can be habit forming and lead to anger or irritability. In these cases, your doctor may preferentially want to discontinue those medicines first. Most non-antidepressant add-on medicines can be tapered rapidly and are not associated with the same discontinuation symptoms seen with antidepressants. Table 13-B "Common Add-On Medications and Recommended Doses that Should be Tapered" (on page 245) lists many common add-on medications and their doses that may require a taper. Stopping a sedating medicine can cause rebound insomnia, while stopping an activating medicine such as a stimulant can cause rebound sleepiness or fatigue. Rebound is usually temporary and means that your body is used to the effect of a certain drug and has to readjust when that medicine is abruptly stopped.

Your doctor may choose to reduce each medicine a little at a time or stop one completely before coming off the other, depending on the impact he thinks each may have on you. With either approach, the same recommendation when coming off of one antidepressant applies: Go slowly and give yourself enough time to assess whether you are doing well before making any more adjustments. Don't get frustrated

Table 13-B

Common Add-On Medications and Recommended Doses that Should be Tapered [1]

Medication and Taper Dose

- **Buspirone (Buspar):** 30 mg and higher
- **Lithium (Lithobid, Eskalith):** 600 mg and higher
- **Aripiprazole (Abilify):** 7.5 mg and higher*
- **Quetiapine (Seroquel):** 100 mg and higher
- **Quetiapine XR (Seroquel XR):** 150 mg and higher**
- **Olanzapine (Zyprexa):** 7.5 mg and higher***
- **Risperdone (Risperdal):** 2 mg and higher
- **Ziprasidone (Geodon):** 120 mg and higher
- **Lamotrigine (Lamictal):** 100 mg and higher
- **Methyphenidate (Ritalin):** No taper necessary
- **Dextroamphetamine (Dexedrine):** No taper necessary
- **Mixed amphetamine salts (Adderall):** No taper necessary
- **Pindolol (Visken):** No taper necessary
- **Thyroid (Cytomel, Synthroid, Armour thyroid):** No taper necessary
- **Ropinirole (Requip):** No taper necessary
- **Pramipexole (Mirapex):** No taper necessary
- **Modanfinil (Provigil):** No taper necessary
- **Armodafinil (Nuvigil):** No taper necessary

*Aripipazole is FDA approved for partial responders to antidepressants
**Quetiapine XR (Seroquel XR) is FDA approved for adjunctive add-on treatment to antidepressants in adults with Major Depressive Disorder
***Olanzapine is FDA approved for treatment-resistant depression when used in conjunction with fluoxetine (Prozac)
[1]These dose taper suggestions are the author's opinion. There are no FDA-recommended dose tapers for these medications.

if you are unable to come off of one, or all, of the medicines you are taking. There is always another opportunity later on, and you will have learned something in the process that may improve your chances of success at that time.

Your main goal should be to become depression-free, not medication-free. If you experience difficulties when reducing your medicine, you should not feel defeated or believe that you will never be able to stop taking your antidepressant in the future. Even doing well on a lower dose may help reduce any side effects you could be having and position you better to reduce the medicine more easily next time. However, you do not want to stay on a lower dose if you actually need to take more to feel well. You could end up having to take more medicine later on if you under-treat your depression now. There is no evidence that taking less medicine is better for you and, in some ways, it could be the "worst of both worlds"—you are still on medication and you're feeling poorly at the same time.

Chapter Fourteen

Life after Antidepressants

and Staying Medication-Free

The road to recovery from depression does not suddenly end when you stop taking antidepressants. You may feel well soon after stopping your medication, but there is a high risk of experiencing another episode of depression in the next 3 to 12 months. Researchers have shown that past episodes of depression increase the likelihood of future episodes, but many additional factors can increase or decrease your risk. Because of this, anyone who has had depression and been on antidepressants should take proactive steps to prevent another episode.

Often, making small lifestyle modifications, such as reducing your stress level, taking care of yourself physically, engaging in meaningful work, hobbies, or social activities can go a long way in nurturing your emotional health. Many types of psychotherapies can help keep you mentally well and have been shown to prevent depression relapses and recurrences. Making lifestyle changes or engaging in psychotherapy cannot guarantee that you won't have another episode of depression, however. You may go through a difficult life event and find yourself needing another course of antidepressant treatment. Or, you could get depressed out of the blue without any apparent trigger. This might indicate that you may need a longer course of antidepressant next time or possibly ongoing maintenance medication. Still, these steps are worth taking.

This chapter is dedicated to helping you make adjustments to improve your quality of life after stopping antidepressants and, hopefully, to help prevent another depression. The chapter covers:

- What to expect after coming off your medication.
- Dealing with family and friends after stopping antidepressants.

- Steps you can take to prevent future depressive episodes.
- When to go back on antidepressants.
- Staying informed on new developments in depression treatment.

After conferring with his doctor, Chris came off his medicines. When he finally stopped them all, he couldn't believe how good he felt. He had more energy, thought more clearly, and felt more motivated than he had when he took medication. He felt optimistic about staying off antidepressants.

"How have you been doing since coming off your medicine?" his doctor asked.

"It was a little rough in the beginning. I came off them faster than you suggested and haven't taken any medicine for a week now. Am I supposed to feel different after stopping my antidepressant? I feel surprisingly better than ever. Could the medicine have been making me feel worse?"

"You may feel better because you aren't having the side effects from the medicine but are still getting some good effects. Let's see what happens over the next few weeks. But let me know immediately if you notice any sudden changes for the worse."

"Am I supposed to feel different after stopping my antidepressant?"

Assuming you completed the necessary treatment course with your antidepressant and gradually came off the medication under your doctor's supervision, you should not feel any different after stopping your medication, with the exception of possible temporary discontinuation symptoms or rebound depression (see Chapter Thirteen). Discontinuation or depression symptoms that do not improve after several weeks, or that seem to worsen over time, may indicate that you are not ready to completely stop your medication. You may need to go back on a partial or full dose of the medicine that got you well and try again at another time.

Some people go through a "honeymoon phase" when they accidentally (or intentionally) miss a few doses during their course of antidepressant treatment. This has also been observed during carefully supervised medication tapers. This honeymoon phase is characterized by feeling as well—or even better—than you did when you were on the medicine. When this occurs, you may mistakenly believe that you no longer need the medicine and, in fact, would be better off without it. If you decide to stay off the medicine, you can experience your depression coming back quickly and, sometimes, with more severity.

The honeymoon phase is not mentioned often in the medical literature and has not been formally studied by clinical researchers. But doctors and therapists see the honeymoon phase in many of their patients who miss their medicine. They also see their patients end up back on medicine soon after the honeymoon phase disappears. Some doctors speculate that their patients feel temporarily better because any side effects they were experiencing from their medication go away fairly soon after the medicine is stopped, while the medication's good effects linger, at least for a short while. Remember that most side effects develop soon after starting antidepressants, and the mood-enhancing properties take several weeks to appear. The reverse may occur when stopping the medicine; the good effects may take longer to disappear than the side effects do. Apathy, flattening of mood, or cognitive dulling are antidepressant side effects that can mask the full benefits of your medication. When these resolve, you could find yourself thinking more clearly and feeling better. If you do well after missing or stopping your medication, do not assume you must be going through a honeymoon phase, but do watch closely for any sudden worsening in moods. Doctors often recommend that their patients not wait too long to go back on their medication if they start having problems again.

You may also feel better soon after coming off your antidepressant simply because you feel hopeful that you have overcome depression and no longer need to take medication. Or, you could have stopped your antidepressant at the same time that you started a new intervention such as psychotherapy, exercise, diet, yoga, meditation, or a spiritual/religious program. You could be making positive changes in your relationships, living situation, or work. Often these changes bring on a certain degree of optimism that could contribute to your success in coming off antidepressants. However, you could find your depression returning if any of these activities fails to live up to your expectations or if you are highly predisposed to depression recurrence.

Don't be immediately concerned if you begin to notice minor symptoms that you, or people close to you, think may be a sign of returning depression. In some cases, antidepressants can dampen your emotional reactivity to stressful life events. If you have a tendency to become temperamental, anxious, irritable, or easily bothered by conflict, antidepressants could mask these reactions. Now that you are no longer on medicine, these emotional responses could come back, and you need to learn new or different ways of managing them. Going back on antidepressants in these situations may not be necessary unless you find these symptoms escalating, starting to affect your ability to function, or negatively impacting others.

Frank's Story Continues

"You know, I don't think I'm doing too bad since I've stopped the medicine, but my wife and kids are always saying something about it to me. Whenever I get upset, they say it's because I stopped the antidepressant. How do I deal with my family when they tell me I should get back on medicine?" Frank asked his doctor.

"It depends on whether you're getting upset because you still need to be on the medication or if you have good reasons to react that way. You think everything is fine, and you might be right. If I remember correctly, you didn't think anything was wrong before getting on medicine," he responded.

"Yeah, but if something pisses me off, shouldn't I get be able to get upset? They want me to be calm all the time, but that's not me."

"They may be nervous that you'll go back to how you were before getting on medicine. There are some things you can do to reduce their anxiety."

"How do I deal with my family when they tell me I should get back on medicine?"

When you experience depression, repercussions often extend out to family, friends, and co-workers. Don't be surprised if you start to get unsolicited suggestions or concerned comments from those close to you when they learn you no longer take an antidepressant. You may or may not agree with what they have to say. You could find your decision to come off medication supported by some and strongly discouraged by others.

Even if your family and friends are knowledgeable about mental-health problems and treatments, they may not be very objective in their opinions. While their input can be helpful, your doctor or therapist is in a better position to advise you about specific treatment options. Ultimately, you have to decide how to handle their feedback and act in what you feel is in your best interest, not act because of coercion by your family or friends. If you want feedback from those close to you, your doctor or therapist will most likely welcome their contribution. Some people may give information to your doctor that could be unreliable, such as reporting that you are not functioning well or are having mood swings when, in fact, you are not. They may be giving information about you that is irrelevant to your doctor, such as an argument you may be having with each other. In these situations, your doctor may find herself caught in the middle of a family dispute or other conflict that could be unrelated to depression and be disruptive to your treatment.

In most cases, friends or family members mean well when they share their concerns with you about your coming off your antidepressant. However, they may not always communicate these concerns in a helpful or empathic manner. Unfortunately, not everyone has people close to them who are well meaning. Someone may harbor anger or resentment at you for something you did to them when you were depressed. They could use your problems with depression in the past to justify a malicious action on their part or as a means of control in a relationship. Or, they could just be concerned that, without medication, your depression could come back and have a negative impact on their lives. In any of these scenarios, someone may overreact to your emotional responses or behaviors and question whether you should still be off medication.

When someone suffers from depression, they may not always be able to tell whether their emotional response to a difficult situation is normal and appropriate. While taking an antidepressant, you may have heard derogatory comments such as, "Did you take your medicine today?" whenever you got upset. Now that you are off the medication and doing well, you still may feel that certain people attribute any mood disturbance or bothersome behavior to your having quit the antidepressant and see it as an indication that your depression has come back. This can become frustrating if you feel justified in being angry or frustrated by something going on in your life. You may feel that someone is invalidating your emotions because of your past problems with depression. In some cases, family or friends may be astutely observing a change in you that suggests worsening depression. In other causes, your reactions may be completely appropriate.

The best way to get unsupportive family or friends on your side is to talk to them about their specific concerns with your being off medication. You may be tempted to tell them to "mind their own business" (and sometimes this may be the best option), but this usually creates more frustration and aggravation for you in the long run. There are far more effective ways to alleviate their concerns, including:

- Let them know you take your decision to come off medicine seriously. You are watching yourself carefully and agree to get help if things worsen. Be specific about how you are monitoring yourself, such as with a mood diary or periodic check-in visits with a healthcare professional.
- Keep them up to date with your preventative measures, such as counseling, exercise, diet, or other interventions.
- Periodically ask for their feedback on how they think things are going, before they offer it.
- Educate them early on about how your depression manifests itself so they will not misinterpret normal emotional responses to stress or conflict as a sign of something more ominous.

You should also set limits early on regarding with whom they can discuss your condition, what information you are comfortable having them share, and the best way for them to communicate their concerns. Some suggestions include:

- If you decide to allow family or friends to communicate with your doctor or therapist, choose one representative to do so. This gives your healthcare practitioner one reliable source and prevents him from having to sort through redundant or conflicting information.
- If someone has concerns about how you are doing, ask for specific examples.
- Make sure that any changes they see are in the present and not examples of mood or behavior problems that occurred prior to treatment.
- Re-enforce that it is not their role to determine your treatment, including whether or not to go back on medicine. Their feedback should only be used as information to help you and your doctors (or counselor) make the right treatment decision.

Initially when Lucy stopped her medicine, she seemed to be doing well. She kept seeing her therapist, Elaine, on a regular basis, but had not gone back to her yoga or exercise routine in several months. Work kept her busy, and she felt good anyway. Because she wanted to get pregnant, she stopped taking her herbal supplements like her doctors recommended. Recently though, she told Elaine that she started noticing a few changes.

"How will I know if I need to get back on the medicine?" Lucy asked Elaine. "Why are you asking that question now?"

"I've started sleeping a little more and have had a few late food binges. It's nothing like I had before I started medicine. I think it's because I've been working so much lately and am trying to get pregnant. Is there anything I can do to prevent the depression from coming back?"

"Maybe it's just stress-related, but you don't want to get worse," said Elaine. "Maybe you need to set some limits at work and get back into your yoga and exercise. If you take action now, you may be able to avoid getting back on meds."

"How do I know if I need to go back on medication?"

For some people, the decision to go back on medicine is simple and straightforward. You may be able to readily identify your depression symptoms and know at what point you need to start taking medicine again. For others, the signs of depression can be more subtle or present differently from prior episodes. If your symptoms from past depressions were lack of energy, motivation, and insomnia, you may not realize that recent feelings of irritability, anxiety, and sleeping too much could suggest you are slipping into another episode. You may attribute minor depression to stressors in your life, and overlook them. If you can address these symptoms early enough with a lifestyle change or other non-medication intervention, you may be able to avoid having to get back on an antidepressant.

Another potential complication in identifying and overcoming depression symptoms early is when someone refuses to see the obvious signs because they don't want to admit their depression has returned. The psychological terminology for this is *denial*. There are plenty of reasons why you could be in denial, including:

- Your previous episode was painful or difficult to overcome.
- You expected that you would never have to take medication again.
- Having another depression makes you feel inadequate.
- Someone makes you feel guilty or responsible for your depression.

Some people, particularly those less intuitively aware of their emotional states, could benefit from a structured method to keep track of their progress off medication. Keeping a mood diary or chart is one useful, convenient tool you can use. Multiple sample charts are available online, or you can create one that best fits your needs. You can decide how frequently to make entries and which specific symptoms you will track. You may want to make daily, weekly, or biweekly entries. Determine the symptoms that most affect you when you get depressed. Examples include lack of motivation or interest, irritability, anger, or anxiety. Use a simple scoring system, such as one through five or ten. Try to keep track of some objective, measurable symptoms, such as hours of sleep or appetite changes. Make sure to record both good and bad periods. Some people who monitor their moods tend to record only problem episodes, which does not accurately reflect your overall progress. See a sample mood chart in Appendix J "Sample Mood Diary." Other types of mood charts can be downloaded from www.psychiatry24x7.com, www.moodreporter.com (which also makes an easy-to-use cell phone application), and a number of pharmaceutical Web sites that also provide patient resources.

You should also consider following up with a mental-healthcare professional on a periodic basis. Many people stop seeing their doctor or counselor once they feel good. You won't need to go often, but occasional well checks are useful because you can get a more objective assessment of how you are doing, and you may uncover subtle symptoms you did not recognize. A good therapist can help you identify what is, and what is not, normal. If the symptoms suggest worsening depression, a therapist can recommend specific non-medication interventions that could prevent you from having to go back on medication. They may also detect any increase in self-medicating behaviors you could be using to mask depression symptoms such as:

- Increase in alcohol or illicit (and prescription) drug use.
- Compulsive spending.
- Gambling.
- Sexual indiscretions.

These may be things you have done in the past when depressed to lift your moods temporarily, or they could be new behaviors you recently adopted. They can indicate problems you were not aware of.

If your symptoms escalate to the point that your day-to-day function is affected and other non-medication interventions don't help, you may have no option but to go back on medicine. Don't wait too long for this, since your depression can be harder to treat the longer you wait. You should not feel like you failed or that you have let yourself or others down. This particular depression episode may be something you are unable to control without medicine. You can always work toward coming off the antidepressant again another time.

"Is there anything I can do to make sure the depression doesn't come back?"

Risk factors for having another episode of depression include family history of mood disorders, severity and number of past episodes, and age of depression onset. Unfortunately, there is nothing you can do to change those. You cannot control your genetic predisposition to depression and have no way to alter your number of past depressive episodes. However, you can affect other risk factors, such as stressful life events and active substance abuse, through lifestyle changes.

You can undertake other preventative measures as well. Two types of psychotherapies have been shown in well-controlled studies to reduce the risk of depression recurrence: CT and ITP. This does not mean that other psychotherapies would not also work. They simply have not been as extensively studied in preventing depression recurrences as CT and ITP. In fact, many therapists successfully use a variety of other therapies, including psychodynamic, group, and dialectical behavioral therapy to keep their clients well after stopping antidepressants. CT and ITP have an advantage in clinical research because they are more structured therapies and can be easily standardized to ensure that everyone in the study receives the same quality of therapy.

Many other non-medication interventions have been shown to help treat depression, such as exercise, diet, and natural supplements (see

Chapter Five). However, little data exists to prove that any of these prevent future episodes in the absence of taking maintenance medication. You are not likely to find these types of studies because such research is difficult and expensive to undertake. Pharmaceutical companies, a major source of research funding, are reluctant to support such studies when there are no medications involved. Doctors frequently recommend these non-medication interventions to their patients anyway, assuming that if they can help treat depression, they probably have some long-term prevention benefits as well.

Exercise is well studied and known to help treat depression, but little is known about whether it can prevent future episodes. Even if it does help, no one knows specifically how frequently or intensely you would have to exercise to get benefits. Many doctors treating depression do believe that staying physically active helps keep depression away. Most people with a history of depression who exercise will agree. This observation is so common that it cannot be ignored. Either something about exercise itself prevents depression, or the people who are willing to exercise are for some reason less likely to get another episode of depression. In other words, exercise may be associated with a good long-term outcome but it is not necessarily the *cause* of the good outcome.

How Effective is Psychotherapy at Preventing Depression Recurrence?

A 2009 study by Frank et al. showed that monthly "maintenance" ITP helped prevent depression recurrence in women and was just as effective as ITP given two or four times a month. These results suggest that there are proven preventive benefits to ITP that may not require the frequency of visits needed to get well in the first place. Those who did best with maintenance ITP were the women whose depression had initially improved with ITP alone, without medication. Those who needed an antidepressant to get well had the best outcome if they stayed on medicine *and* underwent ITP. However, another ITP study in a group of people over 70 years of age showed no benefit in preventing depression recurrence. These two findings suggests that ITP may work better in preventing certain types of depression (one that doesn't require medication treatment initially) and less helpful with others (depression in those over age 70 or those who require initial medication treatment).

The same is probably true for engaging in other healthy activities, such as good eating habits, sleeping well, and reducing your stress level. Although scientists have yet to prove that any of these improve your chances of staying well, doctors repeatedly recommend making these changes to their patients. Again, no one knows for sure whether the people who actually follow through with their doctor's recommendation are the ones who may be healthier to begin with and less likely to get depressed, or if the activities actually change something in the brain and body. Certainly there are significant overall health benefits to making these changes, and they are not harmful or particularly expensive. So why not do anything possible to improve your health, feel better mentally and physically, and possibly improve your chances of staying depression-free?

The role of herbal remedies in depression prevention is another matter. While the evidence is quite strong that some of these products can have antidepressants effects, (particularly in mild to moderate depression or as augmentation agents), there is no substantial proof that any of these products prevent future episodes of depression. Unlike exercise, sleep, or diet changes, many of these natural products can come with risks and can be costly. It is hard to justify recommending them for their preventative effect, but you may choose to integrate them into your daily routine anyway. This is a personal decision.

The natural supplements that are the most likely to help with the fewest risks are omega-3 fatty acid and vitamin B complex (including folate). Doctors do not know whether the dosing for any of these products is lower for depression prevention than it is for acute depression treatment. Make sure you fully understand the risks of such products and their possible interactions with any of your other medicines. As with acute depression treatment, you should find out the typically effective dose (which may differ from the label) and purchase a high-quality product. Since they are not regulated to the same degree as medications, they may contain less than advertised active product or have contaminated additives. Dosing recommendations and resources for finding good products are discussed in Chapter Five.

The Four Pillars Model is a useful tool to guide you in integrating healthy lifestyle choices into your daily routine (see Figure 7). The model is premised on finding balance in four important pillars in your life: Physical, Mental/Emotional, Spiritual/Meaning, and Social. Everyone can benefit from fulfilling a void in any one of these areas. You may have a greater or lesser need in one or more specific pillars. Some people can satisfy a

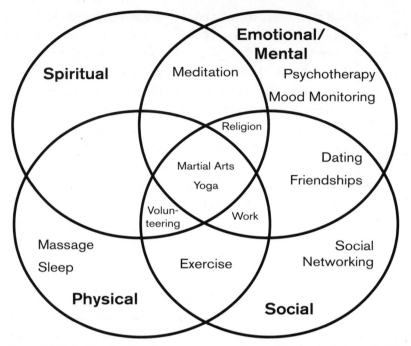

Figure 7. This illustration is a representation of how certain activities help reinforce specific pillars in one's life. Some activities can fill a void in several pillars, such as exercise, which is physical, but, if done with others, can fill a social void as well.

void in more than one pillar with one activity. For example, one person may take up running on a treadmill for exercise, fulfilling just the physical pillar, while another person may join a cycling group, which provides both physical and social stimulation. Volunteering can fill a Spiritual/Meaning void as well as Social and Physical (if it is a strenuous activity). Identify which pillars in your life need more time and energy. Satisfying your Spiritual/Meaning and Social pillar may be more important to you than the Physical or Emotional ones. Everyone is different and probably requires some level of activity in each pillar, though the degrees may differ.

Jane's Story Continues

Jane had tried a few different antidepressant medicines, but each of them had some bothersome side effect. None of the side effects was particularly uncomfortable, but they were bad enough that she decided to go off the medication completely and see if she would still feel good.

"How have you been since stopping the medicine?" her doctor asked.

"I noticed some anxiety here and there and had to take some over-the-counter sleeping pills a few times. I hadn't done that in a while. Maybe I'm just nervous about being off the medicine and am being overly watchful."

"I think it's better to be careful," said her doctor. " You don't want to ignore a possible problem."

"Is there anything new I can try if I do have to go back on medicine? I keep seeing these ads on TV for new antidepressants. What's the best way to learn about new treatments?"

"Is there anything new I can try if I do have to go back on medicine?"

There are always new discoveries being made about depression and innovative treatments that may better help manage your symptoms or prevent future episodes. With new technologies to better identify specific physical changes in the brain that go along with depression, scientists are constantly uncovering new targets for future medications. Ideally, these medications work faster, more effectively, and have far fewer risks and side effects. Most new medication research for the last several decades has focused on altering serotonin, norepinephrine, and dopamine. These medications have proven to be effective but still can take too long to start working, do not help everyone, and can have uncomfortable side effects.

Sometimes in medical research, scientists hit a wall in innovation and there is little progress for a while until a new discovery is made. Serotonin reuptake inhibitors and the subsequent antidepressants were a significant advance in the treatment of depression compared to the tricyclics and MOAIs. However, there has not been a similar innovative leap in antidepressant medication since then. That could soon change. Pharmaceutical companies are investigating new medications for depression that target cortisol and other stress hormones, brain-nourishing proteins such as BDNF (see Chapter Three), and other neurotransmitters, including glutamate. They are studying drugs that work on different 5-HT, NE, and DA receptors than currently available antidepressants do.

The biggest roadblock to some of these already discovered compounds coming to market is that they either do not work much better than placebo in clinical trials, or they have side effects that concern government approval agencies like the FDA. Some researchers argue that some of these medicines may work but do not beat placebo in clinical studies because of other factors such as poor study design, improper dosing, or enrolling subjects with milder forms of depression (see sidebar, "Placebos are No Dummies"). All of these can increase the risk of placebo response. Pharmaceutical companies are only willing to gamble so much money before they decide to put a potential new medicine to rest.

When you hear about new medicines approved for depression, do not assume that new is better. Pharmaceutical companies often aggressively advertise new medicines with some marketing angle giving the impression that it is uniquely effective in a certain area. Except for the long disclaimers that usually accompany these advertisements, companies are good at leaving you with an impression that this medicine is something special. Only when real-world doctors use a medicine to treat real-world patients do the true benefits and risks become known. Doctors have been recently disappointed with many of the "me too" medicines that have come out to treat a variety of medical problems, including depression. In some cases, these new medicines are more expensive but work only a little differently from the older medications. Some drug companies tweak the chemical formulation of older medicines a bit, just enough to qualify it as a new medication or to extend a patent. They may offer some minor advantages, but not necessarily enough to justify the cost.

Researchers are creating better tools to help diagnose depression and other mood disorders. They are also developing ways to more accurately predict which medicine may be most helpful to you. In the near future, imaging machines that measure electrical, chemical, or physical changes in the brain may be able to determine whether you have depression and which particular medicine will be most effective. Genetic testing is another promising diagnostic tool. Many studies of new medications collect DNA samples from the participants so scientists will be able to determine whether there are genetic markers that can predict who is more likely to respond to the medicine. There is already a genetic test (cytochrome p450) that can detect whether you are among a group of people who metabolize certain medicines differently through the liver. If you have a tendency to experience side effects or simply don't respond to typical doses of some antidepressants, your doctor can order this blood test (and now available as a mouth-swab) through most clinical laboratories. This test helps guide doctors on whether a medicine may need to be dosed higher or lower than usual.

New medications that have not completed the government approval process are usually only available by participating in a clinical trial. Some may be available in another country, but there are laws against importing these medicines. There are some risks associated with participating in clinical trials because the medication has usually only been tried in a small number of people. You could be placed in a placebo group in which you unknowingly may not even get the medicine. However, some medications are far along the development track or have been used successfully in other countries, so there is much more safety data available. Also, some

Should You Participate in a Clinical Trial?

Before deciding to participate in a clinical trial, make sure you do your homework about the study and the researcher. Studies have to be approved by an institutional review board (IRB), which could be a local agency at your hospital or a national board that makes sure the study is generally safe and being conducted in an ethical manner. You will also get a consent form that reviews how the study is conducted, how many people have taken the study medicine, what problems they may have had, and your alternatives for approved treatments. Make sure the investigator is experienced in the field and has been doing research for some time. Do not feel coerced into participating, and avoid research sites that over-promise results. You can always quit a study for any reason in the middle of it, and it should not affect your healthcare in any way later on.

Phase 1 and Phase 2 studies carry more risk because they are earlier in the development phase. Phase 3 and Phase 4 studies are conducted on medicines that have been more extensively used or are already available for other indications. Some people participate in a study because they do not have access to healthcare or for money (some studies pay a modest amount for participation). There are other ways to access treatment (these are discussed in Chapter Eleven). A better reason for participating in a study is to make a contribution to science and the development of new treatment options. Remember that every new treatment available today had to have someone volunteer in a study to prove it was safe and worked.

studies will eventually put you on the new medicine even if you get the placebo initially. One reliable source of information on new treatments and studies is through the National Library of Medicine (www.nlm.nih.gov). More information on clinical trials in your area is available at www.nimh.nih.gov/health/trials/index.shtml, www.center watch.com/clinical-trials/listings, and www.searchclinicaltrials.org.

The best way to avoid having to go back on antidepressants is to identify and address life stressors and depression symptoms early on. Little scientific data exists on the best way to stay well once off medication, but doctors and therapists with years of experience suggest there are things you can do. Hopefully, over time, researchers will be able to prove that lifestyle changes and different types of psychotherapies will help prevent depression from coming back. There is also hope of new medications that may not only treat acute depression, but may also protect against future episodes. If you do need to get back on medicine, you should do so before your symptoms worsen to the point that you end up having to take a higher dose of medicine for a longer time. Although you may have hoped to stay off your medication for good, your main goal should be to stay well, whether or not you need medication to do so.

Two years later...

Lucy did what her therapist suggested and got back into her yoga and exercise. She also cut her hours at work. She started feeling better and, within a few months, got pregnant. While she felt good throughout the pregnancy, she noticed some old signs of depression soon after the baby was born. She breast fed for two months and then decided to go back on an antidepressant. She improved, stopped taking the medication three months later, and is still doing well. She takes her baby with her to yoga class every week.

Chris ended up back on medicine soon after his brief period of doing well without it. He eventually took part in a clinical trial of a new medication. At first it seemed to help, but by the end he was not much better than he had been on his old medicine. After much encouragement from his doctor, he found a good therapist he could relate to and began to explore some areas in his life where he felt his depression kept him stuck. He started going out more and joined a local service club. At the same time, he ended up taking two antidepressants that he had taken before and a newer medicine for bipolar disorder that supposedly "boosted" the other medicines. He started to feel well and, more importantly, looked forward to each day. He swore it was the medicine combination that was responsible for his recovery, but his doctor wasn't so convinced, given the additional steps he had taken to improve.

Frank called his doctor's office a few months after stopping his medicine, asking for a refill on his antidepressant. His doctor called him back and asked, "Has something changed?" Frank insisted that he felt fine but his wife had pestered him so much to go back on the antidepressant that he thought it would be worth it if it kept her off his back. He still comes in to see the doctor every three months to check his blood pressure and cholesterol, and every time he makes sure he tells him, "Don't forget my happy pill!"

Jane hasn't taken any more antidepressants, but continues to read everything she can about depression and new drugs in development. She wants to be prepared just in case she has a recurrence, plus she finds the whole area intellectually stimulating. Unlike the physics that she teaches, the science of mental-health seems "curiously unscientific." She keeps a regular mood diary on her computer and, even though it has had a few dips here and there, she has done well overall. She continues traveling and teaching overseas and has never felt more content with her professional and personal life. Whenever the subject of depression or antidepressants comes around, she is open about her past experiences and says unequivocally that, if she needed, she would go back on medication again.

Everybody's story is different, and everyone will have a different ending. Unlike many medical conditions, there is no right way, or one way, to best overcome depression. A number of medication and non-medication interventions exist to treat depression. Some people will do better with one type of treatment than another. We do know that antidepressant medications are not for everyone, but they are certainly necessary for some. Hopefully, *Taking Antidepressants* has given you a solid foundation to understand what depression is, how medications work, and how to find and take the antidepressant that can best help you. Whatever your feelings about antidepressants after reading this book, the most important thing to remember is that depression is a serious but treatable condition that, with the right attitude and effort, can be overcome.

Antidepressants for Children and Adolescents

The number of children and adolescents diagnosed with depression and treated with antidepressants has risen consistently over the last several decades. From 1997 to 2005, the percent of the United States population under 17 years of age taking antidepressants rose from 1.4 to 2.5 percent. Some mental-health advocates applaud the recognition and treatment of depression in this population and believe that addressing mood symptoms early prevents more serious problems later on. Others argue that child and adolescent depression is over-diagnosed and that antidepressants are too quickly prescribed.

The medical community also has concerns about the safety of antidepressants in those under 25 years of age. However, everyone agrees that too little is understood about identifying and managing depression in this population, and more research is needed to help guide doctors, parents, and patients. This special section guides you through some of what is known about childhood and teenage depression and answers the following questions:

- How can you recognize and diagnose depression in a child or adolescent?
- What treatment options are available?
- Are antidepressants safe in children?
- Where can you get good care and reliable information?

Recognizing and Diagnosing Childhood Depression

Nearly 2.5 percent of children and 8.3 percent of teenagers in the United States are thought to suffer from clinical depression. Researchers once believed that children, particularly the very young, were unable to experience true depression because they lacked the necessary emotional maturity. This has proven not to be the case. Developmental psychology studies over the last several decades have demonstrated that children are far more emotionally developed, even at very young ages, than originally thought. In fact, research has shown that there are symptom and behavior patterns consistent with depression in those as young as three years old.

Some of the symptoms of depression in children are similar to those of adults. However, some notable differences make it challenging to accurately identify depression in children. Unlike adults, who may be more aware of their moods and often report feelings such as sadness or anger, young children tend to act out when depressed. You may see more aggressive behavior or frequent physical complaints in a depressed child. Other common symptoms depressed children experience more than adults include:

- Severe fatigue.
- Anhedonia—an inability to experience pleasure.
- Feelings of guilt.
- Focus and cognition problems.

The DSM-IV manual (see Chapter Two) uses the same symptom criteria for depression in children and adults. Only irritability or anger is mentioned in the DSM as a unique symptom that may help identify depression in children. Pre-pubescent boys and girls have equal rates of depression. Teenage girls are twice as likely to become depressed as teenage boys.

The American Academy of Child and Adolescent Psychiatry (www.aacap.org) lists the following symptoms as other possible warning signs of depression in children:

- Frequent sadness, tearfulness, crying.
- Decreased interest in activities or inability to enjoy previously favorite activities.
- Hopelessness.
- Persistent boredom and low energy.
- Social isolation, poor communication.
- Low self esteem and guilt.
- Extreme sensitivity to rejection or failure.
- Increased irritability, anger, or hostility.
- Difficulty with relationships.
- Frequent complaints of physical illnesses such as headaches and stomachaches.

- Frequent absences from school or poor performance in school.
- Poor concentration.
- A major change in eating and/or sleeping patterns.
- Talk of, or efforts to, run away from home.
- Thoughts, or expressions, of suicide or self-destructive behavior.

Depression in children often co-occurs with other psychiatric problems, such as attention deficit hyperactivity disorder (ADHD), anxiety disorders, and oppositional defiant disorder. These conditions share many of the same symptoms, making it difficult to know whether a symptom is from depression or some other condition. Adolescents with depression also have high rates of substance abuse. They may be using alcohol and drugs to self-medicate depression, or their depressive symptoms can result from the substance abuse. An accurate diagnosis is important since it will dictate the primary focus of treatment.

Bipolar disorder (manic-depression) can present with similar symptoms as depression in children and adolescents. Bipolar disorder in children may look different from bipolar disorder in adults. Mood disorder experts continue to debate which symptoms are most predictive of bipolar disorder in this age group. Irritability, anger outbursts, sleeping difficulties, and mood swings are typical childhood bipolar symptoms but are also seen in other psychiatric conditions in this age group. As with adults, a strong family history of bipolar disorder and hyperactivity or nervous energy with an antidepressant is suggestive of a bipolar diagnosis. An accurate diagnosis is important because the treatment for bipolar disorder often involves mood stabilizers. Antidepressants should be avoided, if possible, in bipolar children.

Because of the complexities of childhood mood disorders, only someone with specialized training and extensive experience in this area should diagnose mental-health problems in this population. This means a board-certified child and adolescent psychiatrist, psychologist, master's-level

Depression in Children Usually Does Not Occur Alone

One in five depressed children and adolescents suffer only from depression, while four of five have other psychiatric problems as well. Studies estimate that 10 to 40 percent of children with attention deficit hyperactivity disorder (ADHD) also have depression.

counselor with additional training in treating children, or a pediatrician or child neurologist with special expertise in behavioral disorders. A diagnostic assessment usually includes interviewing the child and the parents (or guardians) separately and together (which allows the clinician to observe their interactions). Because parents or guardians may have trouble being objective about their child's behaviors and symptoms, the doctor or counselor may want additional information from the school, guidance counselors, school therapists, and anyone else who spends time with the child, including other family members. Psychological and neuropsychological testing is often helpful in revealing symptoms the child may not otherwise share, as well as any learning or cognitive problems that could be causing problems. Art or play therapy in kids who have trouble talking about how they feel can also provide useful information in an assessment.

Using Antidepressants and Other Treatments for Childhood Depression

Most mental-health practitioners prefer to avoid medications in children. A number of psychotherapy interventions have been proven to work in childhood depression, including CT and ITP. When family issues negatively affect a child, family therapy is helpful as well. All of these therapies involve a commitment of time, mental energy, and money. For therapy to be useful, the family and the child must be willing to actively participate.

Antidepressants become a consideration when psychotherapies do not seem to be working or the symptoms become so severe that the child is:

- Causing significant disruption at home or school.
- Not eating.
- Having psychotic symptoms.
- At risk for self harm.

A large NIMH study (not funded by pharmaceutical companies) called Treatment of Adolescents with Depression Study, or TADS, looked at cognitive therapy and antidepressants in teenage depression. The response rates with antidepressants (Prozac) and cognitive therapy together were the highest at 71 percent, followed by Prozac alone at 61 percent, cognitive therapy alone at 43 percent, and placebo at 35 percent. In this population, it appears that medicine and therapy together was the best treatment.

There are limited studies of antidepressants in children and adolescents. Many of these trials have failed to show that antidepressants were more effective than placebo. In fact, the results have not been collectively as good as adult antidepressant studies, which have their fair share of failed studies as well. One explanation for these failed studies is the difficulty in accurately diagnosing depression in children. Some of the participants in these studies may have other problems causing their symptoms or co-occurring conditions (even though researchers try to restrict those people from participating). Also, the types of children (and their parents) who are willing to enroll in clinical studies may not reflect real-world patients. Both the child and the parents must be willing to be part of an experiment, which many families are reluctant to do. Finally, there could be something about the immature brains of this age group that makes them less responsive to antidepressants.

Some antidepressants have been proven to be safe and effective in this population. Fluoxetine (Prozac) is approved for ages eight years and up. Escitalopram (Lexapro) is approved for ages 12 and up. Clomipramine (Anafranil), sertraline (Zoloft), and fluvoxamine (Luvox) are psychiatric medicines approved for depression and obsessive-compulsive disorder (OCD) in adults and for OCD in children. Even though they are not approved for childhood depression, doctors may preferentially use these medicines for depression in children because they have an indication for a condition in this age group.

Doctors still use antidepressants approved only for adult depression if the child-approved medications have failed or if the doctor believes a non-child-approved antidepressant would be effective or safer than the child-approved antidepressants. Some of the augmentation strategies discussed in Chapter Six are also used in children who partially respond to antidepressants alone. Doctors prefer to use augmentation agents that are approved in other conditions for children or that have a long track record of being safe in younger people

How Safe are Antidepressants
for Children and Adolescents?

Despite the positive results from TADS and other antidepressant trials, antidepressants are still not usually first-line treatments for children for several reasons. As already discussed earlier in this section, depression is hard to accurately diagnose in this age group. If antidepressants are prescribed for children who have been incorrectly diagnosed, the medication will be ineffective and can, in some cases, worsen their condition. For example, antidepressants in a bipolar child can trigger disruptive symptoms such as irritability, anger, and mania. Researchers have speculated that some adverse reactions to antidepressants in children and adolescents may be due to an underlying, unrecognized bipolar disorder.

Common antidepressant side effects seen in adults (see Chapters Seven through Nine) are also seen in children, such as sedation, activation, weight gain, weight loss, gastrointestinal problems, sleeping problems, cognitive dulling, and apathy. In addition, one concerning finding with antidepressant treatment in those under 25 years of age is a small, but statistically significant increased risk of suicidal ideation. Because of the potentially serious outcome of this side effect, the FDA has issued a public warning about this risk. The warning is not to avoid antidepressant use altogether in those under 25 years of age, but rather to "monitor appropriately and observe closely for clinical worsening, suicidality, or unusual changes in behavior."

Suicidal thoughts are common in children and adolescents with depression. It is estimated that 40 to 80 percent of those 17 years of age and younger with depression have suicidal thoughts, and up to 35 percent of adolescents with those thoughts act on them. Nearly 2,000 teenagers die of suicide a year in the United States alone. Completed suicides in this age group are rare but devastating to family and friends, and the effects ripple throughout the entire community.

Children and adolescents should be educated about suicide and what to do should they have those thoughts. Family, friends, and healthcare practitioners must take any such thoughts seriously. Children must understand that they need to tell an adult they trust when they have these thoughts and that they will not be punished or get into trouble as a result. They should have a "go to" person if suicidal thoughts occur. There is no truth to the commonly held belief that if someone talks about suicide, they will not do it. However, many children and adults who do attempt suicide do not share with anyone that they had these thoughts. The

Teenage Girls at Greater Risk for Suicide

The Center for Disease Control (CDC) reports that 12 percent of teenage girls and 5 percent of teenage boys with depression attempt suicide.

American Foundation for Suicide Prevention (www.afsp.org) lists the following risk factors for suicide:

- Family history of substance abuse or mental illness.
- Access to weapons.
- Impulsivity.
- Family history of violence or suicide.
- Exposure to others who have committed suicide.
- Physical or sexual abuse.

The FDA warning about antidepressants being associated with suicidal thoughts and behaviors in those 25 years of age and younger created a stir in the medical community. The warning was based on combining all the data from 23 studies of nine different antidepressants in children and adolescents. There was a 4 percent increased risk of suicidal thoughts with medication and 2 percent in those on placebo. The limitations of these findings are reviewed in Chapter Seven. Not all the studies used a measurement tool specifically assessing the suicidal thought, which has made some researchers question whether the child actually was suicidal as reported. Of the 17 studies that did use a measurement tool, there was no difference (and actually a slight decrease) in suicidal thoughts in those on real medication verses placebo. In the TADS study, the number of depressed teenagers with suicidal thoughts dropped from 30 percent before treatment to 10 percent after treatment three months later.

How to Access Good Care for Children with Depression

Finding the right mental healthcare for children and teenagers can be difficult, since diagnosis and treatment of this population requires specialized training. There is a general shortage of child psychiatrists, particularly in less populated areas. Many parents first turn to their pediatrician or family doctor for help. Some of these physicians take a

More Antidepressants, Less Teen Suicide

A 2003 study in the Archives of General Psychiatry showed that for every 1 percent increase in antidepressant prescriptions there was an associated 0.2-per-100,000 reduction in teenage suicide.

FDA Warning: Good or Bad?

In a 2009 study by Libby et al. in the Archives of General Psychiatry, the rates of depression diagnosis in children from 1999 to 2004 rose from 3.3 to 5.2 per 100,000. From 2004 to 2007 the rates dropped to 3.5 per 100,000. Some attribute this to the 2004 FDA warning that made physicians reluctant to diagnose and treat childhood depression.

There was a spike (up 18 percent) in teenage suicides in 2004 after the FDA warning. This was the first increase in 12 years. The rate decreased in 2005 and 2006 but remained above the 2003 level.

Many doctors feel that the warning has done more harm than good because some parents or guardians may decide not to put their children on antidepressants even though the child could benefit from them. On the other hand, it does make patients, families, and doctors more vigilant about watching for possible problems with medications. The risk to not treating or undergoing inadequate treatment is that untreated depression can lead to poor academic performance, school drop out, substance abuse, eating disorders, teenage pregnancy, future depressive episodes, and suicide.

special interest in mental-health problems in children. They may have a good deal of experience or additional training in this area. But most have neither the time nor expertise to accurately diagnose and treat mental-health problems in this age group. Pediatricians are often comfortable diagnosing (or at least knowing where to send children for proper diagnosis of) ADHD. There is a tendency to attribute children's behavior problems to ADHD when a mood disorder may be a more accurate diagnosis.

Many insurance plans do not reimburse doctors or therapists appropriately for the necessary extra time required to do a thorough comprehensive assessment of a child. As a result, many mental healthcare practitioners who work with children do not accept insurance. In your area, you may need to go out of network of your insurance to see a qualified healthcare practitioner. Your best source for good clinicians in your area is from other healthcare practitioners who know your particular situation. Also, local psychiatric hospitals, medical schools, or other training schools for psychologists or master's-level therapists can often direct you to well-qualified people. You can go to the state professional associations for names of qualified psychiatrists, psychologists, master's level therapists, and other practitioners (see Resources on page 295). Web sites that review doctors or therapists in your community are often unreliable because disgruntled people are more likely to submit reviews than those with good things to say. It is also difficult to know the source of positive reviews. Be careful when searching for information about antidepressants in children. There is a great deal of misinformation and sensationalism. Reputable Web sites and books are listed in the Resources (on page 295).

Depression in children and adolescents is a real and serious problem, but there are many effective treatment options available. The key to success is early identification. Make sure that you have explored other treatment options before considering medications. Although our understanding of how and when to use antidepressants in children and adolescents is more limited than in adults, medications are a viable and, at times, necessary treatment. Anyone under 25 years of age on an antidepressant should be monitored carefully by an experienced healthcare practitioner.

Past Medication History Form

This form provides a useful format to document your past medication history so your doctor can make a more informed decision about the best medication treatment for you. A similar form is available free online at www.pastmeds.com.

Medication Name				
Dates Taken				
Results*				
Side Effect and Rate: **Mild, Moderate, Severe** (Circle if stopped medicine because of it)				
Maximum Dose				
Why Stopped**				

Number of Times Tried				
Other Medicines Used With***				
Would You Take Again?				
Doctor Prescribing				
Other				

*Results. Examples include 1. Worked; 2. Worked but stopped working; 3. Partially helped; 4. Did not help.

**Why stopped. Examples include 1. Side effects; 2. Didn't need it anymore; 3. Insurance/Couldn't afford it; 4. No doctor; 5. Not sure.

***Other medicines. This should include other psychiatric medicines that may have been used to help with symptoms including other antidepressants, anti-anxiety, or sleeping medicines.

Mood Disorder Questionnaire

This scale is a self-rated tool to determine the probability of a bipolar diagnosis. It is a screening tool only and is insufficient for a diagnosis done without a comprehensive assessment by a healthcare professional. The test is scored only positive or negative.

Answer each question as best you can. Upon completing this form, print your completed form and take it to your healthcare practitioner.

1. Has there ever been a period of time when you were not your usual self (and while not using drugs or alcohol)?..❑ Yes ❑ No

You felt so good or so hyper that other people thought you were not your normal self, or you were so hyper that you got into trouble? ....❑ Yes ❑ No

You were so irritable that you shouted at people or started fights or arguments?...........................❑ Yes ❑ No

You felt much more self-confident than usual? ....❑ Yes ❑ No

You got much less sleep than usual and found you didn't really miss it? ....❑ Yes ❑ No

You were much more talkative or spoke faster than usual? .....❑ Yes ❑ No

Thoughts raced through your head or you couldn't slow your mind down?.......................................❑ Yes ❑ No

You were so easily distracted by things around you that you had trouble concentrating or staying on track? ......❑ Yes ❑ No

You had much more energy than usual?..........................❑ Yes ❑ No

You were much more active or did many more things than usual? ....❑ Yes ❑ No

You were much more social or outgoing than usual; for example, you telephoned friends in the middle of the night? ....❑ Yes ❑ No

You were much more interested in sex than usual?.............❑ Yes ❑ No

You did things that were unusual for you or that other
people might have thought were excessive, foolish,
or risky? ....❑ Yes ❑ No

You were spending money that got you or
your family into trouble?...❑ Yes ❑ No

2. If you checked YES to more than one of the above,
have several of these ever happened during at least a
four-day period of time?..❑ Yes ❑ No

3. How much of a problem did any of these cause you, such as being
unable to work; having family, money, or legal troubles; getting into
arguments or fights?

_____ No Problem
_____ Minor Problem
_____ Moderate Problem
_____ Serious Problem

Scoring:
All three must be met for a positive score

Question 1 : Score at least 7 of 13 Yes Responses

and

Question 2 : Yes

and

Question 3: Moderate or Severe Response

Reference: Hirschfeld RM Am J Psychiatry. 2003 Jan;160(1):178-80. Department of Psychiatry and Behavioral Sciences, University of Texas Medical Branch, 1.302 Rebecca Sealy, 301 University Blvd., Galveston, TX 77555-0188, USA. rohirsch@utmb.edu

Patient Health Questionnaire (PHQ-9)

This is a quick screening tool for depression. It assesses for diagnosis as well as severity of symptoms.

This easy-to-use patient questionnaire is a self-administered version of the PRIME-MD diagnostic instrument for common mental disorders.[1] The PHQ-9 is the depression module, which scores each of the 9 DSM-IV criteria as "0" (not at all) to "3" (nearly every day). It has been validated for use in Primary Care.[2]

Answers

Not at All = 0 Point
Several Days = 1 Point
More Than Half the Days = 2 Points
Nearly Every Day = 3 Points

Over the last 2 weeks, how often have you been bothered by any of the following problems?

1. Little interest or pleasure in doing things? _____
2. Feeling down, depressed, or hopeless? _____
3. Trouble falling or staying asleep, or sleeping too much? _____
4. Feeling tired or having little energy? _____
5. Poor appetite or overeating? _____
6. Feeling bad about yourself, or that you are a failure or have let yourself or your family down? _____
7. Trouble concentrating on things, such as reading the newspaper or watching television? _____
8. Moving or speaking so slowly that other people could have noticed? Or the opposite—being so fidgety or restless that you have been moving around a lot more than usual?_____
9. Thoughts that you would be better off dead, or of hurting yourself in some way?_____

Total Score:_____/27

Depression Severity

0-4 = None
5-9 = Mild
10-14 = Moderate
15-19 = Moderately severe
20-27 = Severe

[2] Validity has been assessed against an independent structured mental health professional (MHP) interview. PHQ-9 score ≥10 had a sensitivity of 88% and a specificity of 88% for major depression.

Source: PHQ9 Copyright ©Pfizer. Reprinted with permission, courtesy of Pfizer Limited. PRIME-MD® is a trademark of Pfizer.

Starting Dosing Characteristics of Most-Common Antidepressants

Generic Name	Brand Name	Best Time of Day*	Available Formula-tions**	Typical Starting Dose***	Dosing Range†
Amitriptyline	Elavil	Bedtime	Tablets-NS	10-25 mg	50-300 mg
Buproprion	Wellbutrin IR	Morning and noon (Twice day dosing)	Tablets-NS	75 mg	150-400 mg
Buproprion Sustained Release	Wellbutrin SR	Morning and noon (Twice day dosing)	Extended-release	100-150 mg	150-400 mg
Buproprion Extended Release	Wellbutrin XL	Morning	Extended-release	150 mg	150-450 mg
Citalopram	Celexa	Bedtime	1. Tablets: 10 mg-NS; 20, 40 mg-S 2. Liquid	10-20 mg	20-60 mg

Generic Name	Brand Name	Best Time of Day*	Available Formulations**	Typical Starting Dose***	Dosing Range†
Desvenlafaxine	Pristiq	Morning	Extended-release	Some start 50 mg every other day	50-100 mg
Duloxetine	Cymbalta	Morning	Delayed-release Capsule	20-30 mg	60-120 mg
Escitalopram	Lexapro	Morning or evening	1. Tablets: 5 mg-NS; 10, 20 mg-S 2. Liquid	5-10 mg	10-20 mg
Fluoxetine	Prozac	Morning	1. Capsules-NS 2. Liquid 3. Tablets: 10, 20mg-S	10-20 mg	20-80 mg
Fluvoxamine	Luvox	Bedtime	Tablets: 50, 100 mg-S, 25 mg-NS	25-50 mg	50-300 mg
Fluvoxamine Controlled Release	Luvox CR	Bedtime	Extended-release Capsules	100 mg	100-300 mg
Mirtazapine	Remeron	Bedtime	Tablets: 15, 30 mg-S; 45mg-NS. Dissolving Tablet	15 mg	15-45 mg
Nefazodone	Serzone	Bedtime	Tablets: 100, 150 mg-S	50-100 mg	200-600 mg
Nortryptline	Pamelor	Bedtime	1. Capsules 2. Liquid	10-25 mg	50-150 mg
Paroxetine	Paxil	Bedtime	1. Tablet-S 2. Liquid	10-20 mg	20-60 mg
Paroxetine Controlled Release	Paxil CR	Bedtime	Extended-release Tablet	12.5-25 mg	25-62.5 mg
Sertraline	Zoloft	Morning	1. Tablets-S 2. Liquid	25-50 mg	50-200 mg††
Venlafaxine	Effexor IR	Morning and noon (Twice day dosing)	Tablets-S	25-37.5 mg	75-225 mg
Venlafaxine Extended-release	Effexor XR	Morning	Extended-release Capsules—can be opened	37.5- 75 mg	75-225 mg

*Author's recommendation for best time of day to start. Some people will find a medicine they start at night too energizing and will prefer to switch to taking in the morning. Others will find an energizing medicine sedating and may choose to change to taking it at bedtime.

**S = Scored, NS = Not Scored; Extended- and delayed-release cannot be split or opened, with the exception of velafaxine XR.

***These are not the manufacturer's recommended starting doses. This is recommended starting dose range if you want to go more slowly in the beginning.

†Many prescribers use higher-than-typical doses under some circumstances.

††Higher doses are used with other disorders.

Commonly Prescribed Antidepressants by Side-Effect Risk*

Generic Name	Brand Name	Weight Gain Risk	Sexual Side Effect Risk	Sedation (S), Energizing (E), or Neutral (N)
Amitriptyline	Elavil	High	Medium	S
Buproprion	Wellbutrin IR	Low	Low	E
Buproprion Sustained Release	Wellbutrin SR	Low	Low	E
Buproprion Extended Release	Wellbutrin XL	Low	Low	E
Citalopram	Celexa	Low-Medium	Medium	S
Desvenlafaxine	Pristiq	Low-Medium	Medium	E
Duloxetine	Cymbalta	Low-Medium	Medium	E
Escitalopram	Lexapro	Low-Medium	Medium	N
Fluoxetine	Prozac	Low-Medium	Medium	E
Fluvoxamine	Luvox	Low-Medium	Medium	S
Fluvoxamine Controlled Release	Luvox CR	Low-Medium	Medium	S
Mirtazapine	Remeron	High	Low	S
Nefazodone	Serzone	Medium	Low	S
Nortryptline	Pamelor	Medium-High	Medium	S
Paroxetine	Paxil	High	High	S
Paroxetine Controlled Release	Paxil CR	High	High	S
Sertraline	Zoloft	Medium	Medium	E
Venlafaxine	Effexor IR	Medium	Medium	E
Venlafaxine Extended Release	Effexor XR	Medium	Medium	E

*These are general risks but any one person's experience can differ considerably with any given medication.

Successfully Tapering Antidepressants Rating Test (START)

This is a self-test to help you assess your likelihood of successfully coming off your antidepressant. **This is not a scientifically validated tool** to measure your odds, but it can give you a general sense of whether this is the right time to stop your medication. This test incorporates many of the major risk factors for depression that researchers have determined can increase your chances of a recurrence.

There is no foolproof method for determining your ability to stay well without medication. A high score does not mean you will be unable to stop, and a low score does not guarantee success. You should review your ratings with your physician, or a mental health professional, and decide together on the best course of action for you.

Add up your points as you answer the following questions:

1. How often have you experienced depression?

_____ I have had only one episode of depression, or I rarely experience depression. (0 points)
_____ I have struggled with occasional episodes of depression on and off for many years but generally do well between episodes. (2 points)
_____ I have episodes of depression fairly frequently, and I often experience milder depression between episodes. (4 points)
_____ I have severe episodes of depression almost all of the time. (6 points)

2. How many individual, significant episodes of depression have you had in your life?

_____ One (0 points)
_____ Two (2 points)
_____ Three or more (6 points)

3. For how long have you been on your current dose of medication and feeling fairly stable?

_____ Two years or more (0 points)
_____ One to two years (2 points)
_____ Six months to a year (4 points)
_____ Less than six months (6 points)

4. How well is the medicine working?

_____ Great! I have never felt better. (0 points)
_____ Pretty well. I still have symptoms of depression, but I'm feeling better. (2 points)
_____ Fair. I could be doing much better. (4 points)
_____ Poor. I haven't gotten that much better. (6 points)

5. How would you rate your current stress level?

_____ Low (0 points)
_____ Medium (2 points)
_____ Significant (4 points)
_____ The most I've ever had (6 points)

6. Have you tried to stop medication in the last six months?

_____ I haven't tried, or I did try for a short while without having any problems. (0 points)
_____ I tried, but went back on because I thought my depression was starting to come back. (2 points)
_____ I did stop, and the depression came back, but it wasn't as bad as it was when I first started taking medication. (4 points)
_____ I did stop, and my depression came back worse than ever. (6 points)

7. Which best describes your alcohol or illicit drug use?

_____ Fewer than two glasses of alcohol (wine, beer, or liquor) a week. (0 points)
_____ Four or fewer glasses of alcohol at a time, four or fewer days of alcohol use a week, or less than one use of marijuana a month. (2 points)

_____ Four or more alcoholic drinks almost every day, marijuana use more than once a month, and any other illicit drug use at least once within the last three months. (6 points)

_____ Daily excessive alcohol use or regular weekly drug abuse. (8 points)

8. How would you rate your physical health?

_____ Great! I am in very good shape and I am physically active. (0 points)

_____ Fair. I am not in great shape and I have a few controlled medical problems, but I am somewhat physically active. (2 points)

_____ Not good. I am in poor shape, I am fairly sedentary, and I have several medical problems that affect my functioning. (4 points)

_____ Terrible. I am not physically active and I have many poorly managed medical problems. (6 points)

9. How would you rate your diet?

_____ Excellent! I eat a very healthy diet. (0 points)

_____ Fair. I try to watch what I eat, but I don't always follow a healthy diet. (2 points)

_____ Poor. I eat a very unhealthy diet, including a lot of junk food. (4 points)

10. What best describes how you feel during this time of year (the time of year at which you are thinking of stopping medication?

_____ My moods are not affected by the seasons or the time of year. This time of year is usually good for me. (0 points)

_____ I sometimes struggle with depression during this time of year. (2 points)

_____ I usually have some depression during this time of year. (4 points)

11. Rate your experience with the following symptoms over the last month:

_____ Sleep: Normal (0 points), Average (1 point), Poor (2 points)

_____ Interest/Activity Level: Normal (0 points), Somewhat less than normal (1 point), Very low (2 points)

_____ Self-esteem: Good (0 points), A little low (1 point), Poor (2 points)

_____ Energy: High (0 points), Lower than normal (1 point), Very low (2 points)

_____ Concentration: Normal for me (0 points), Less than normal (1 point), Hard to function (2 points)

_____ Appetite: Normal (0 points), A little low/a little high (1 point), Very low/very high (2 points)

_____ Agitation: None (0 points), Moderate (1 point), Very much (2 points)

_____ Suicidal thoughts: Never (0 points), Occasionally (2 points), All of the time (4 points)

Add up your scores.

0 to 18 points: You have highest probability of doing well off your medication. You will want to focus on Chapters Twelve to Fourteen. These chapters discuss the process of stopping medication, developing a responsible medication taper strategy, and watching for early signs of problems off medicine.

19 to 36 points: You are in the upper range of probability of doing well off your medication. You should review your personal reasons for wanting to come off medication discussed in Chapter Twelve to make sure this is the best time. Then, if you are still feeling positive about your decision, proceed to Chapters Thirteen to Fourteen. You may want to review any sections of the book that address your concerns about antidepressants if you decide to stay on them a little longer.

37 to 56 points: You fall into a lower probability category of doing well off medication, but that does not mean you are unable to reduce or completely stop your antidepressant. You will need to be more cautious and make a commitment to non-medication strategies to help ensure your success. You should review Chapters One through Five and Twelve to educate yourself about depression, antidepressants, and what the research tells us about the required treatment duration. Make sure you are stopping for the right reasons, and get input from your doctor and others who know and care about you.

57 to 76 points: You are in the lowest probability category and have many factors working against your likelihood of doing well off medication. There may be good reasons for you to stop taking your antidepressant at this time anyway, but you should discuss these with your doctor or any other health care professional familiar with your current situation and history. Chapters One to Three will help you develop a better understanding of depression and how medications work. You may want to review sections of the book that address any concerns you may have about antidepressants such as Chapter Seven on safety issues and Chapter Nine on side effects. If you can stick with your medication for a little longer, you may have a greater chance of success later on.

Dosing Formulations and Discontinuation Characteristics of Most-Common Antidepressants

Generic Name	Brand Name	Discontinue Difficulty Rating	Formulations	Available Dosing	Dosing Range
Amitriptyline	Elavil	**	Tablets-NS	10, 25, 50, 75, 100, 150 mg	50-300 mg
Buproprion	Wellbutrin IR	*	Tablet	75, 100 mg	150-400 mg
Buproprion Sustained-release	Wellbutrin SR	*	Extended-release	100, 150, 200 mg	150-400 mg
Buproprion Extended-release	Wellbutrin XL	*	Extended-release	150, 300 mg	150-450 mg
Citalopram	Celexa	**	1. Tablet: 10 mg-NS 2. Liquid	20, 40 mg-S 10, 20, 40 mg	20-60 mg
Desvenlafaxine	Pristiq	**	Extended-release	50, 100 mg	50-100 mg
Duloxetine	Cymbalta	**	Delayed-release Capsule	20, 30, 60 mg	60-120 mg
Escitalopram	Lexapro	**	1. Tablet: 5 mg-NS 2. Liquid	10, 20 mg-S 5, 10, 20 mg	10-20 mg
Fluoxetine	Prozac	*	1. Capsule-NS 2. Liquid 3. Tablet 10, 20mg S	10, 20, 40 mg	20-80 mg
Fluvoxamine	Luvox	**	Tablets: 50, 100 mg-S 25 mg-NS	25, 50, 100 mg	50-300 mg
Fluvoxamine Controlled-release	Luvox CR	**	Extended-release Capsule	100, 150 mg	100-300 mg
Mirtazapine	Remeron	**	Tablets: 15, 30 mg-S; 45 mg-NS Dissolving Tablets: 15, 30, 45 mg	15, 30, 45 mg	15-45 mg
Nefazodone	Serzone	**	Tablets: 100, 150 mg-S 200, 250 mg	50, 100, 150,	200-600 mg
Nortryptline	Pamelor	**	1. Capsule 2. Liquid	10, 25, 50, 75 mg	50-150 mg

Generic Name	Brand Name	Discontinue Difficulty Rating	Formulations	Available Dosing	Dosing Range
Paroxetine	Paxil	***	1. Tablet-S 2. Liquid	10, 20, 30, 40 mg	20-60 mg
Paroxetine Controlled-release	Paxil CR	***	Extended-release Tablet	12.5, 25, 37.5 mg	25-62.5 mg†
Sertraline	Zoloft	**	1. Tablet-S 2. Liquid	25, 50, 100 mg	50-200 mg
Venlafaxine	Effexor IR	***	Tablet-S 75-225 mg	25, 37.5, 75, 100 mg	
Venlafaxine Extended-release	Effexor XR	***	Extended-release Capsule—can be opened	37.5, 75, 150 mg	75-225 mg

*Least discontinuation S = Scored
**Moderate discontinuation NS = Not Scored
***Highest discontinuation †For depression use. Higher doses are used to treat other conditions.

Appendix H

Dosing Formulations and Discontinuation Characteristics of Less-Common Antidepressants

Generic Name	Brand Name	Discontinue Difficulty Rating	Formulations	Available Dosing	Dosing Range
Amoxapine	Asendin	**	Tablet-S	25, 50, 100, 150 mg	100-300 mg
Bupropion Hyrdobromide	Aplenzin	*	Extended-release Tablet	174, 348, 522 mg	174-522 mg
Clomipramine	Anafranil	***	Capsule	25, 50, 75 mg	25-250 mg
Desipramine	Norpramin	**	Tablet-NS	10, 25, 50, 75,	100-300 mg
Doxapine	Sinequan	**	1. Capsule 2. Liquid	100, 150 mg 10, 25, 50, 75, 100, 150 mg	25-300 mg
Fluoxetine Weekly	Prozac Weekly	*	Capsule	90 mg	90 mg a week

Generic Name	Brand Name	Discontinue Difficulty Rating	Formulations	Available Dosing	Dosing Range
Imipramine	Tofranil	**	Tablet-NS	10, 25, 50 mg	100-300 mg
Imipramine Pamoate	Tofranil PM	**	Capsule	75, 100, 125, 150 mg	100-300 mg
Isocarboxacid	Marplan	***	Tablet-S	10 mg	10-60 mg
Maprotyline	Ludiomil	**	Tablet-S	25, 50, 75 mg	25-150 mg
Paroxetine Mesylate	Pexeva	***	Tablet-NS	10, 20, 30, 40 mg	20-60 mg
Phenelzine	Nardil	***	Tablet-NS	15 mg	15-90 mg
Protryptline	Vivactyl	**	Tablet-NS	5, 10 mg	15-60 mg
Selegiline Transdermal	EMSAM	**	Patch	6, 9, 12 mg	6-12 mg
Tranylcypromine 30-60 mg	Parnate		***	Tablet-NS	10 mg
Trazodone	Desyrel	**	Tablet-S	50, 100, 150, 300 mg	150-600 mg
Trimimpramine	Surmontil	**	Capsule	25, 50, 100 mg	50-300 mg
Venlafaxine Hydrochloride	Venlafaxine ER	***	Extended-release Tablet	37.5, 75, 150, 225 mg	75-225 mg

*Least discontinuation
**Moderate discontinuation
***Highest discontinuation

S = Scored
NS = Not Scored
†For depression use. Higher doses are used to treat other conditions.

Appendix I

Common Antidepressants that can be Safely Cut

- Escitalopram (Lexapro) 10, 20 mg
- Citalopram (Celexa) 20, 40 mg
- Fluoxetine (Prozac tablets) 10, 20 mg
- Sertraline (Zoloft) all doses
- Paroxetine (Paxil) all doses
- Fluvoxomine (Luvox) 50, 100 mg
- Mirtazapine (Remeron) 15, 30 mg
- Nefazodone (Serzone) 100, 150 mg
- Venlafaxine (Effexor IR) all doses
- Venlafaxine extended release (Effexor XR) Capsules can be opened and mixed in applesauce to reduce dose

Sample Mood Diary

Mark the the symptoms you are going to monitor with a simple rating system, such as 1 to 5 or 1 to 10 (with 1 being the worst and 5 or 10 the best).

Track both good and bad days. Make the frequency of ratings realistic, such as once a day, week, or every other week.

Day or Week (Circle one)	1	2	3	4	5	6	7
Depression							
Anxiety							
Irritable							
Appetite/Diet							
Energy/Motivation							
Sleep							
Stressors							

Abbreviations

5-HT: Serotonin

ADHD: Attention Deficit Hyperactivity Disorder

ADS: Antidepressant Discontinuation Syndrome

ALA: Alpha-linolenic acid

BDNF: Brain-derived neurotrophic factor

DA: Dopamine

DHA: docosahexaenoic acid

DSM: Diagnostic Statistical Manual

ECT: electroconvulsive therapy

EPA: eicosapentaenoic acid

FDA: Food and Drug Administration

GABA: gamma-aminobutyric acid

HAM-D: Hamilton Rating Scale for Depression

MADRS: Montgomery Asberg Depression Rating Scale

MAOI: monoamine amine oxidase inhibitors

NE: Norepinephrine

NIMH: National Institute of Mental Health

PhRMA: Pharmaceutical Research and Manufacturers of America

TADS: Treatment of Adolescents with Depression Study

SAD: Seasonal Affective Disorder

SNRI: serotonin norepinephrine re-uptake inhibitors

SSRI: selective serotonin re-uptake inhibitors

STAR-D: Sequenced Treatment Alternatives to Relieve Depression Study

TMS: Transcranial Magnetic Stimulation

Glossary

Acetylcholine: A neurotransmitter found in the central nervous system that helps regulate motor movement and memory.

Addiction: A mental-health condition in which someone repeatedly engages in a behavior despite its negative effects, such as continued use of a habit forming medicine or compulsive gambling.

Akathisia: An unpleasant syndrome in which the person is unable to sit still or remain motionless. It can be a side effect of a number of different medications including some antidepressants and antipsychotics.

Amino acids: Molecules with a specific chemical structure that make up proteins, which are critical for normal bodily function. Some of the 20 amino acids can be manufactured by the body but others must be brought in through one's diet.

Antidepressant discontinuation syndrome: A syndrome that occurs when the antidepressant dose is lowered too quickly or is abruptly stopped. Symptoms include dizziness, electrical shock–like feelings, irritability, and depression. Discontinuation symptoms can be uncomfortable but are not dangerous, and do eventually go away.

Antidepressant induced apathy: An antidepressant side effect in which the person experiences a lack of interest, concern, or enthusiasm.

Anxiety disorders: A group of mental-health disorders described in the DSM-IV-TR that includes such conditions as generalized anxiety disorder (GAD), panic disorder (PD), obsessive-compulsive disorder (OCD), post-traumatic stress disorder (PTSD), and simple phobias.

Apathy: An absence of emotion or enthusiasm.

Art therapy: A type of therapy that uses creativity and artistic expression to help express one's thoughts and feelings and to help manage stress, self esteem, conflict, and emotional problems.

Attention Deficit Hyperactivity Disorder (ADHD): A common mental-health condition that first appears in childhood but can continue into adulthood. It is characterized by inattention, distractibility, impulsivity, hyperactivity, and a number of other symptoms.

Behavior therapy: A type of therapy based on changing maladaptive behaviors with more appropriate ones. There is less focus on the unconscious or emotional causes of the behaviors.

Brain-Derived Neurotrophic Factor (BDNF): A protein found in the human body that helps neurons grow and develop. BDNF is found to be lower in chronic pain, stress, and depression and may account for brain changes in these states.

Cognitive dulling: A possible medication side effect characterized by slowed thinking and short-term memory loss.

Cognitive processing therapy (CPT): A type of cognitive therapy specially designed to help with post-traumatic stress disorder (PTSD) symptoms.

Cognitive therapy: A type of therapy developed in the 1960s that helps people change how they behave and feel by helping them identify maladaptive ways of thinking and behaving and giving them new ways to think and respond to emotional events.

Continuation: A term used in psychiatric research to describe the phase of antidepressant treatment that occurs six to nine months after acute treatment. There is a high likelihood of depression returning if antidepressants are stopped during the continuation phase.

Cortisol: A natural hormone produced in the adrenal gland that regulates many bodily functions including metabolism of sugar, fat and protein as well as the body's anti-inflammation response. It is released in larger amounts when the body is under stress.

Dexamethasone suppression test: A blood test used to diagnose disorders where the body produces high levels of cortisol. It was once a popular test to detect certain types of depression but fell out of favor because of its unreliability for this condition.

Diagnostic statistical manual: A manual published by the American Psychiatric Association that provides the diagnostic criteria for the currently recognized mental disorders. First published in 1952, there have been five revisions with the current version called DSM-IV-TR (Text Revision).

Dopamine: A neurotransmitter and hormone in the human body that affects many bodily functions including mood, energy, concentration, and motor movements. Disorders of dopamine function can cause a variety of health problems including Parkinson's disease, depression, and schizophrenia.

Endorphins: Chemicals produced in the brain that resemble narcotic pain medications. They are natural pain relievers and are released during excitement, pain, exercise, and sexual activity.

GABA: Aminobutyric acid, a neurotransmitter produced in the central nervous system that inhibits neurons firing. Medications that affect GABA have been known to reduce seizures, anxiety, and pain.

Generalized anxiety disorder: A mental-health disorder described in DSM-IV-TR in which a person has persistent fear and worry lasting at least 6 months over everyday things to the point that it affects one's ability to function.

Glutamate: An abundant neurotransmitter in the brain that regulates many neuronal functions including learning and memory.

Hamilton Rating Scale for Depression (HAM-D): A commonly used depression rating scale used in clinical research studies to measure the effectiveness of depression medicine versions that have as many as 29 questions.

Light therapy: A treatment for depression that involves exposure to bright, artificial light for a specific amount of time. It is an effective treatment for seasonal affective disorder.

Lipids: A group of organic molecules that includes fats and certain vitamins. They play an important role in the human body with energy storage, cell structure, and cellular signaling.

Maintenance: A term used in psychiatric research to describe the phase of antidepressant treatment that occurs after nine months of continuation phase therapy. People at high risk for recurrent depression often require maintenance phase to continue doing well.

Montgomery Asberg Depression Rating Scale (MADRS): A commonly used depression rating scale used in clinical research studies to measure the effectiveness of a depression treatment. The scale was developed in 1979 in Europe and has ten questions. Some researchers prefer this scale to the HAM-D.

Norepinephrine: A neurotransmitter and hormone in the human body that regulates mood, attention, and the body's cardiovascular system. It is activated during stress and causes an increase in blood pressure, heart rate, and heart function. Medications that target norepinephrine may improve mood, energy, and concentration.

Obsessive-Compulsive Disorder (OCD): A mental-health disorder described in DSM-IV-TR characterized by intrusive and upsetting thoughts, images, impulses, or ideas as well as repeated behaviors that attempt to suppress these thoughts through irrational or ritualistic actions such as excessive hand washing, counting, or organizing things in certain way, The obsessive thoughts and compulsive behaviors are associated with a great deal of anxiety and are time consuming.

Omega-3 fatty acid: An essential fatty acid that is found in high concetrations in fish and ceratin plant/nut oils. It is composed of DHA, EPA, and ALA each of which are shown to have certain health benefits. Omega-3 can help lower triglycerides, prevent abnormal heart rhythms and strokes, as well as protect against plaque build up in the blood vessels. There is also some benefit in depression and has anti-inflammatory effects.

Omega-6: A fatty acid necessary for normal body functioning and brain function. It also helps promote inflammation. A healthy diet includes a greater ratio of omega-3 to omega-6. Most western diets have an unhealthy overabundance of omega-6 to omega-3 consumption.

Oppositional defiant disorder: A disorder in children and adolescents described in the DSM-IV-TR has a pattern of disrespectful, hostile, uncooperative, and defiant behavior lasting more than six months and causing disruption in home or school activities.

Panic disorder: A mental-health disorder described in DSM-IV-TR in which someone develops sudden, unexpected attacks of intense fear and anxiety.

Play therapy: A type of therapy typically used with children in which play activities are used to help the person describe their experiences and express their thoughts and feelings.

Poop out: A commonly used term used to describe antidepressant tachyphylaxis in which the body adapts to the medication and it is no longer as effective. No one knows why poop-out occurs in some people on certain medications.

Post-Traumatic Stress Disorder (PTSD): A mental-health disorder described in DSM-IV-TR that develops from a severe trauma in one's life that leads to mood changes, anxiety, feeling as if you are re-experiencing the trauma, flashbacks of the event, nightmares, and avoiding situations that remind one of the trauma.

Proteins: Organic compounds made up by amino acids that have multiple, critical bodily functions such as helping with body structure, metabolism, immune response, and a number of cellular functions.

Psychoanalysis: A type of psychotherapy first developed by Sigmund Freud in which the person shares whatever thoughts come to mind as well as dreams and fantasies. From this information, the therapist helps the person understand unconscious conflict that may affect their emotions and behaviors. There are many different types of psychoanalysis that have developed over the years.

Psychotherapy: A treatment for managing mental-health problems and emotional difficulties through talking about your thoughts and feelings with a trained mental-health practitioner. There are many different psychotherapies based on different theories about the how psychological problems develop and are overcome.

Recurrence: A term used in psychiatric research to describe another depressive episode that occurs nine months or later after a treatment response.

Relapse: A term used in psychiatric research to describe a re-emergence of a depressive episode after six to nine months following a treatment response.

Remission: A term used in depression research to signify a near resolution of symptoms based on measurements with a recognized depression scale such as Hamilton Rating Scale for Depression (HAM-D) score 10 or less and Montgomery Asberg Depression Rating Scale (MADRS) score 7 or less.

Residual symptoms: A term used in psychiatric research to describe ongoing symptoms of depression that are not of sufficient quantity or intensity to meet criteria for a depressive episode.

Response: A term used in depression research to signify at least 50 percent improvement based on measurements with a recognized depression symptoms scale such as the Hamilton Rating Scale for Depression (HAM-D).

SAM-e: S-Adenosyl-L-Methionine is a naturally occurring substance that plays a role in cell maintenance and cell function. It is available as a nutritional supplement and believed to help with several health conditions, including osteoarthritis, depression, fibromyalgia, and some liver problems.

Seasonal affective disorder: A type of depression that develops in relationship to certain seasons, usually fall and winter months.

Serotonin 5-Hydroxytryptamine (5-HT): A neurotransmitter that plays an important role in the central nervous system and digestive tract. Many antidepressants work by affecting serotonin.

St. John's Wort: An herbal extract from the plant Hypericum perforatum shown to treat depression. It is more commonly used in Europe. The research suggests that it is more helpful with mild to moderate depression.

Supportive therapy: A commonly used, short-term psychotherapy in which the therapist uses many different techniques to help the person relieve symptoms or adapt better to conflict without focusing as much on changing one's character or exploring unconscious conflict.

Tolerance: A medical term that describes when a person becomes used to a medication they are taking so that more is needed for the same effect or a new medication is required. Some medications are more prone to tolerance than others such as pain or sleeping medications.

Transference: A psychological term describing a person's redirecting their feelings about someone in their life toward their therapist. Interpreting transference in therapy is a useful treatment tool.

Vagus nerve: A cranial nerve in the human body that runs from the brain, down the neck, and into the abdomen. The nerve plays a role in regulating moods through the release of certain neurotransmitters.

Vagus nerve stimulator: An implantable device that delivers small elelctrical stimulation to the vagus nerve. It is an approved treatment for treatment-resistant depression and seizures.

Resources

In addition to the following, more resources are available at www.takingantidepressants.com.

Post-Partum Depression

http://womenshealth.gov/faq/depression-pregnancy.cfm
A United States government–sponsored Web site through the Department of Health and Human Services providing information about women's mental-health issues and pregnancy.

www.fda.gov/ForConsumers/byAudience/ForWomen/default.htm
United States FDA government–sponsored Web site providing resources about taking specific medications during pregnancy.

www.womensmentalhealth.org
An informational Web site from Massachusetts General Hospital/Harvard Medical School on reproductive, psychiatric health topics.

Bennett, Shoshana and Indman, Pec. *Beyond the Blues: A Guide to Understanding and Treating Prenatal and Postpartum Depression.* Written by a psychologist who experienced post-partum depression. A guide through depression during and after pregnancy.

Kleiman, Karen and Raskin, Valerie. *This Isn't What I Expected: Overcoming Postpartum Depression.* An older, but still relevant, book written by a psychiatrist and social worker.

Shields, Brooke. *Down Came The Rain: My Journey Through Postpartum Depression.* A personal account by the well-known actress.

Patient Prescription Assistance and Internet Pharmacies

www.buysafedrugs.info
A PhRMA-sponsored Web site that provides information on buying medicine safely online and overseas.

www.medhelp.org
A privately funded, for-profit Web site providing health information and prescription assistance.

www.nabp.net
A Web site sponsored by NABP, the National Association of Boards of Pharmacy, that provides information on licensed, online pharmacies.

www.needymeds.org
Sponsored by a non-profit organization dedicated to helping people who access medication who cannot afford medicine or healthcare costs.

www.phrma.org
Sponsored by PhRMA, Pharmaceutical Research and Manufacturers of America, and provides information on new medicines, public policy issues, and prescription assistance.

www.rxassist.org
An Internet information resource center created by Volunteers in Health Care (VIH), a national resource center for safety net organizations, helping to provide medicines to individuals and communities during emergencies.

www.vipps.info
An NABP-run site (see page 197) that verifies legitimate online pharmacies.

Advocacy Groups

www.dbsalliance.org
The Depression and Bipolar Support Alliance (DBSA) is a non-profit, patient-directed, national organization providing information on depression and bipolar disorder as well as offers support groups and other services.

www.nami.org
National Alliance for the Mentally Ill, a grassroots, non-profit mental-health advocacy organization. The Web site provides information on local chapters, support groups, advocacy issues, and other services.

www.nmha.org
Mental Health America (MHA) is a non-profit organization dedicated to helping those with mental-health problems access information and care.

www.postpartum.net
Sponsored by Post-Partum Support International, a non-profit organization dedicated to helping those with pregnancy-related mood disorders.

Depression Information

www.healthyplace.com
A for-profit consumer healthcare information Web site.

www.ifred.org
A depression informational Web site supported by The International Foundation for Research and Education on Depression (iFred), a non-profit organization dedicated to helping research the causes of depression and to support those dealing with depression.

www.webmd.com
A popular, consumer-friendly, for-profit healthcare information Web site.

www.nimh.nih.gov
A Web site sponsored by the United States National Institute of Mental Health (NIMH), providing information on mental-health disorders, treatment, and current research.

Karp, David. *The Burden of Sympathy.* A book written by the families of those suffering from severe mental-health problems.

Kramer, Peter. *Listening to Prozac.* An older, but still relevant, book written in 1993 by a psychiatrist about the role of antidepressants in our society.

Medication Information

www.pdrhealth.com
A comprehensive Web site providing information on currently available medications from the publishers of *Physicians' Desk Reference.*

www.safemedication.com
An informational Web site about currently available medications maintained by the American Society of Health-System Pharmacists (ASHP).

Travel and Overseas Information

www.cbp.gov
A United States Customs and Border Protection Web site that provides information about obtaining medication overseas.

www.cdc.gov/travel
A Web site maintained by the United States Center for Disease Control (CDC) that provides information about travel and finding medical care overseas.

Child and Adolescent Information

www.bpkids.org
An information and support Web site from the Child and Adolescent Bipolar Foundation (CABF), a parent-led, not-for-profit organization of families raising children diagnosed with, or at risk for, pediatric bipolar disorder.

www.kidshealth.org
A non-profit Web site dedicated to children's health issues supported by the Nemours Center for Children's Health Media.

www.teendepression.org
A for-profit, but informative, site about depression in teenagers and resources for treatment.

Crisis and Suicide Support

www.afsp.org
The American Foundation for Suicide Prevention is a non-profit organization dedicated to providing information and resources about suicide.
National Suicide Prevention Lifeline: (800) 273-8255. A free suicide hotline, available 24/7, free and confidential.

Jamison, Kay. *Night Falls Fast.* Well-written book about suicide by psychiatrist/author who herself suffers from bipolar disorder and has made a suicide attempt.

Natural and Alternative Information

www.consumerlabs.com
A for-profit Web site that allows the consumer to verify quality of nutritional supplements. There is a fee involved.

www.nccam.nih.gov
A United States government–sponsored Web site by the National Center for Complementary and Alternative Medicine (NCCAM) that provides information about research on nutritional and alternative medical treatments.

www.psychletherapy.com
Information on integrating exercise into depression treatment.

Kabat-Zinn, Jon. *Full Catastrophic Living.* A best-selling book about using mindfulness to manage stress, pain, and illness.

Stoll, Andrew. *The Omega-3 Connection.* Book written by Harvard psychiatrist and researcher about the efficacy and safety of this popular natural supplement.

Accessing Care

www.aacap.org
An American Academy of Child and Adolescent psychiatrists Web site providing information on childhood depression and providers in your area.

www.amhca.org
Web site of the American Mental Health Counselors Association.

www.apa.org
Web site of the American Psychological Association. Although focused more on resources for psychologists, there is a "Find a Psychologist" section.

www.healthgrades.com
A for-profit Web site at which, for a fee, you can do a background check on any listed physician.

www.psych.org
Web site of the American Psychiatric Association. Main focus is resources for psychiatrists, but the site also lists state chapters that provide information on psychiatrists in your area.

www.socialworkers.org
Web site of the professional organization for social workers. There is a section on finding a social worker/counselor in your area.

www.psychologytoday.com
A for-profit Web site with mental-health information and a listing of mental-healthcare practitioners in your area. The listings are not screened, and providers pay to be listed.

www.psychsource.org
A non-profit organization providing information on mental-health resources in your area, such as hospitals, support groups, residential treatment centers, and more.

Mood Charts

www.moodreporter.com
A free Web site with a mood chart and link for a mobile phone application for mood monitoring.

www.psychiatry24x7.com
A Web site sponsored by Janssen Pharmaceuticals that provides a sample mood chart.

Personal Accounts of Depression

Casey, Nell. *Unholy Ghost.* Harper Perennial, 2002. A collection of essays from those suffering from depression.

Cronkite, Kathy. *On the Edge of Darkness: Conversations About Conquering Depression.* Delta. 1995.

Jamison, Kay Redfield. *Touched with Fire: Manic-Depressive Illness and the Artistic Temperament* Free Press, 1996.
A personal account from a psychiatrist/author about her struggles with bipolar disorder.

O'Brien, Sharon. *The Family Silver: A Memoir of Depression and Inheritance.* University Of Chicago Press, 2004.

Solomon, Andrew. *The Noonday Demon: An Atlas of Depression.* Scribner, 2002.

Styron, William. *Darkness Visible: A Memoir of Madness.* Modern Library, 2007.

Treatment Resistant Resources

www.neurostartms.com
Web site of Neuronetics, the manufacturer of NeurStar, the FDA approved Transcranial Magnetic Stimulation device.

www.vnstherapy.com
Web site of Cyberonics, the manufacturer of the Vagus Nerve Stimulator.

Donovan, Charles. *Out of the Black Hole: The Patient's Guide to Vagus Nerve Stimulation and Depression.* A personal account of someone successfully treated with Vagus Nerve Stimuation.

Fink, Max. *ELECTROSHOCK: Restoring the Mind.* Written by one of the world's most prominent ECT experts.

Clinical Research

www.centerwatch.com/clinical-trials/listings
A Web site sponsored by the for-profit organization Centerwatch that helps research sites, physicians, and pharmaceutical companies with research-related resources. Information is available on clinical trials in your area.

www.clinicalstudyresults.org
A Web site that provides results of clinical trials maintained by PhRMA.

www.nlm.nih.gov
National Institute of Health Web site has information on clinical trials in your area.

www.searchclinicaltrials.org
Web site maintained by the Center for Information and Study on Clinical Research Participation (CISCRP), a non-profit organization providing information about clinical research studies.

Index

in children and adolescents, 265-268
obtaining, 19-27
self, 27-29
tools, 38, 42-43, 59-60, 260
Diagnostic and Statistical Manual (DSM), 40-42, 44
Diet. *See* Food
Digestive system side effects, 98
Discontinuation syndrome (ADS)
addiction and, 152, 155-156
causes, 155
preventing (*see* Tapering)
risks of specific antidepressants, 161
symptoms, 157, 159, 160
Doctors of osteopathic medicine (Dos), 20, 21-22, 25
Dopamine (DA), 74, 189
Dosage
changing, 103-104, 187-188, 235-236
determining, 92-94
effectiveness and, 127
insurance payments and, 127
neurotransmitters targets and, 188
side effects and, 140
tapering and, 241
therapeutic window, 181-182
time of administration, 279-280
typical of common antidepressants, 279-280
Down regulation, 75, 84-85
Drug interactions, 149-150
Duloxtine, using off label, 93

E
Effectiveness of antidepressants
augmentation medications and, 130-133
compliance and, 126-127
dosage and, 127
FDA and, 102, 122
residual symptoms, 95, 123-129
response time, 84-85, 95-96, 121
tolerance, 181, 187-191
Electroconvulsive therapy (ECT), 134-135
Electroencephalograms (EEGs), 42-43
Emotional flatness as side effect, overcoming, 171-172
Employment, 101, 124, 223
Exercise, 120, 256-257

F
Fatigue as side effect, overcoming, 176-177
Feel-good neurotransmitter, 74, 189
Fertility, 205
Fibromyalgia, 176
Folic acid, 113
Food
to avoid with MAOIs, 141
to improve sexual functioning, 167
to treat depression, 113-117
weight gain and, 169-170
Food and Drug Administration (FDA)
approved augmentation medications, 133
efficacy of drugs and, 102, 122
label guidelines, 92-93
obtaining drug approval, 100
Four Pillars Model, 257-258

G
Generic medications
costs, 91, 100, 195
discontinuation syndrome and, 159
effectiveness, 91, 100, 185, 195
generic name, half-life, active metabolite and discontinuation risk of common, 161
Genetics, 48-49, 260
Glaucoma, narrow-angle, 148

H
Half-life table, 161
Hamilton Depression Scale (HAM-D), 123
Health conditions
effect of depression on, 79-81
effect on depression of, 28-29, 183-184
fatigue and, 176
questionnaire, 278-279
safety of antidepressants and, 147-148
sexual problems and, 164-165
sleep and, 173
weight gain and, 168
Health insurance
dosage and, 127
generic vs. brand-name medications and, 100, 159
loss of, 195-197
obtaining, 224-225
Healthcare professionals
able to prescribe medication, 20-23
medication compliance and, 126
not able to prescribe medication, 23-25
notifying about antidepressant changes, 97
notifying about side effects, 99
notifying when start antidepressants, 101
relationships with pharmaceutical industry, 31
types of, 20-25
Herbs. *See* Natural supplements
High blood pressure, 149
Hormone supplements, 190-191
Hypomania, symptoms, 54
Hyponatremia, 148

I
Inflammation, described, 63-64
Insomnia, 173-176
Insurance eligibility, 224-225
Internet pharmacies, 194, 197-198
Interpersonal psychotherapy (ITP), 108, 255, 256

L
Libido, improving, 163-167
Licensed counselors, 24
Life coaches, 25
Light therapy, 118
Limbic system, 65, 66, 76, 77
Liver problems, 149
Low blood pressure, 149

M
Magnesium, 115
Mania, symptoms, 54
Medical doctors (MDs), 20-22, 25
Medical issues and residual symptoms, 128
Medications, non-antidepressant
as cause of depression, 68-69, 128-129

Also Available from Sunrise River Press:

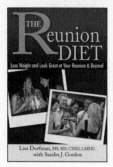

The Reunion Diet
Lose Weight and Look Great at Your Reunion and Beyond

by Lisa Dorfman with Sandra Gordon For millions of us, reunions offer a wake-up call and shore up weight-loss motivation. In *The Reunion Diet*, sports nutritionist Lisa Dorfman and health and nutrition writer Sandra J. Gordon show readers how to set specific weight-loss and other lifestyle goals and achieve them within the time allowed. At the core of the book is a diet plan calibrated by calorie levels according to how much time you have to lose weight before a reunion. Whether you've got 10, 20, 30 pounds or more to lose before your reunion, *The Reunion Diet* can help you look and feel great when mingling and reconnecting with those you may not have seen in decades. Softbound, 6 x 9 inches, 192 pages. **Item # SRP605**

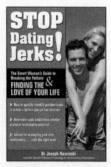

Stop Dating Jerks!
The Smart Woman's Guide to Breaking the Pattern and Finding the Love of Your Life

by Joseph Nowinski, PhD Are you ready to find true love, but afraid you'll make another painful mistake? Unlike the vast majority of dating books currently out there, this book is written by a psychologist who has spent years in clinical practice counseling men and couples. He understands male personality types and offers sound advice on how to identify a good man with whom a relationship is worth pursuing, and also how to tell if a man has a personality flaw that you should walk away from fast! Dr. Nowinski includes practical tests you can use to quickly spot characteristics in a man that have the potential to doom a relationship. Softbound, 6 x 9 inches, 176 pages. **Item # SRP604**

The Anti-Cancer Cookbook
How to Cut Your Risk with the Most Powerful, Cancer-Fighting Foods

by Dr. Julia Greer, MD, MPH Dr. Julia Greer explains what cancer is and how antioxidants work to prevent pre-cancerous mutations in your body's cells, and then describes which foods have been scientifically shown to help prevent which types of cancer. She then shares her collection of more than 220 scrumptious recipes for soups, sauces, main courses, vegetarian dishes, sandwiches, breads, desserts, and beverages, all loaded with nutritious ingredients chock-full of powerful antioxidants that may slash your risk of a broad range of cancer types. Softbound, 7.5 x 9 inches, 224 pages. **Item # SRP149**

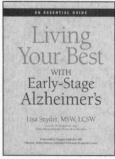

Living Your Best With Early-Stage Alzheimer's
An Essential Guide

by Lisa Snyder, MSW, LCSW Recent medical advances have made it possible to diagnose Alzheimer's when symptoms are only mild. New drugs are under investigation to help slow progression of the disease, and there is hope on the horizon for more effective treatments to keep the disease at bay. Today, when a person is diagnosed with Alzheimer's, they may have many years ahead with only mild symptoms. The result is that a growing number of people with early-stage Alzheimer's are seeking information about how to cope effectively with the disease. This book is a practical guide on effectively managing symptoms, finding meaningful activity, planning for the future, strategies for easier communication, participating in research and clinical trials, and much more. Numerous testimonials from people with Alzheimer's throughout the book give authenticity to the book content and provide practical suggestions as well as illuminating and insightful commentary. Softboubnd, 7 x 9 inches, 288 pages. **Item # SRP603**